Transforming Command

Transforming Command

THE PURSUIT OF MISSION COMMAND

IN THE U.S., BRITISH, AND ISRAELI ARMIES

Eitan Shamir

Stanford Security Studies
An Imprint of Stanford University Press
Stanford, California

Stanford University Press
Stanford, California

The material describing the U.S Army's adoption of Mission Command in Chapters 4, 8, 9, 10, 11, and 12 first appeared in the author's article "The Long and Winding Road: The US Army Managerial Approach to Command and the Adoption of Auftragstaktik (Mission Command)," in the *Journal of Strategic Studies* 33, no. 5 (Routledge), www. informaworld.com/fjss.

Printed in the United States of America on acid-free, archival-quality paper

Library of Congress Cataloging-in-Publication Data

Shamir, Eitan
    Transforming command : the pursuit of mission command in the U.S., British, and Israeli armies / Eitan Shamir.   ·
        p. cm.
    Includes bibliographical references and index.
    ISBN 978-0-8047-7202-0 (cloth : alk. paper) -
    ISBN 978-0-8047-7203-7 (pbk. : alk. paper)
    1. Command of troops–Case studies.   2. United States. Army.
3. Great Britain. Army.   4. Israel. Tseva haganah le-Yisra'el.   I. Title.
    UB210.S43 2011
    355.3'3041-dc22   2010030490

Typeset by Westchester Book Group in 10/14 Minion

In memory of my father, Haim Shamir
Professor of Modern European History
1929–2008

CONTENTS

ACKNOWLEDGMENTS

I WOULD LIKE to thank Dr. David Betz from King's College for his superb mentorship and his timely encouragement. I would also like to thank Dr. Robert T. Folley, who was the first to take on this study. My friend Lieutenant Colonel Dori Pinkas was the first to introduce me to the concept of mission command and its importance. For that I owe him a debt of gratitude. In addition, I would like to express my thanks to the Department of War Studies and the School of Social Science and Public Policy at King's College London, the University of London Central Research Fund, and the Anglo-Israeli Association for the research grants that enabled my research trips to the United States and Israel between 2005 and 2007.

Many people repeatedly provided help and direction throughout the research and writing of this study. Of those, I wish to single out the following. In the United Kingdom: Professors Brian Holden-Reid and Beatrice Heuser; Doctors Sergio Catignani and Stephen Bungay; General (Ret.) Sir Rupert Smith, Colonel (Ret.) David Benest, Lieutenant Colonel (Ret.) Dr. Jim Storr, and Commander (Ret.) Dr. David Slavin. In the United States: Doctors David E. Johnson, Adam Grissom, and the rest of the team at the RAND Arroyo Center; Dr. Douglas A. Macgregor and West Point's Lieutenant Colonel Dr. Isaiah Wilson. In Israel: Brigadier General (Ret.) Dr. Shimon Naveh, Colonel (Ret.) Moshe Shamir, and Major Uzi Ben-Shalom. Thank you all for your time, helpful comments and insights, hospitality, and generosity. I am indebted to Colonel (Ret.) Dr. Hanan Shai, a pioneer of mission command studies. His seminal work on the subject of mission command served as a foundation for many of the ideas in this book. Additionally I had the good fortune to benefit from the important input of Professor Martin van Creveld, Dr. Yossi Hochbaum, and Dr. Eado Hecht. Special thanks go to Dr. Dov Glazer for numerous helpful suggestions and remarks on the final draft.

I wish to thank Dr. Geoffrey H. R. Burn, the director and acquisitions editor at Stanford Security Studies, and his team at Stanford Press, Jessica Walsh and John Feneron, as well as Michael Haggett and Julie Palmer Hoffman with Westchester Book Services, for their dedication, professionalism and personal approach. Portions of this book are based on an article previously published in the *Journal of Strategic Studies*, I would like the journal's editors, Dr. Joe Maiolo and Dr. Thomas G. Mahnken for their kind permission to use this material. I have also greatly benefited from the assistance of Aviva Cwang, chief librarian of the IDF General Staff library, and Haya Shalom, the chief librarian of the IDF Staff and Command College library.

Unfortunately, a few months before I completed this work my dear father, Prof. Haim Shamir, passed away. He was a history professor at Tel Aviv University. Growing up I was always surrounded by books and conversations on history. His intellectual influence has guided me ever since and inspired me throughout this work. This book is dedicated to his memory.

Last but certainly not least, my deepest gratitude is reserved for my family: my wife, Carmela, and my children, Ella, Ido, and Yael. Without their support and optimism this study would have remained an unfulfilled dream.

FOREWORD

THE U.S. ARMY'S Capstone Concept for future operations emphasizes the need for military forces to adapt quickly in environments of uncertainty and complexity.[1] Central to that capability is the long-standing doctrine of mission command, defined as the conduct of military operations through decentralized execution based on mission orders. It is important that future military leaders and civilians who study or oversee military affairs understand both the theoretical basis for mission command and its application to contemporary and future armed conflict. *Transforming Command* is an ideal starting point for developing that understanding. Particularly valuable is Eitan Shamir's examination of how the doctrine and application of mission command evolved over time in different strategic and cultural contexts. Combat experiences since the beginning of this century have highlighted the need to decentralize operations. And the importance of mission command will increase in the future as armed forces confront both hostile military forces and nonstate armed groups as well as criminal and terrorist organizations. Different types of enemy organizations are likely to operate in concert, employing a broad range of capabilities and adapting tactics and operations to avoid strengths and attack weaknesses. Uncertainty stemming from military forces' interaction with adaptive enemies and the complexity of local conditions will require leaders capable of taking initiative and organizations capable of operating with a high degree of autonomy. As Shamir points out, conducting decentralized operations consistent with the doctrine of mission command demands not only common understanding but also an organizational culture that permits effective implementation.

It is important to note that Shamir's analysis and the doctrine of mission command itself contrast starkly with what might be described as the orthodoxy of defense transformation in the 1990s. Western militaries based defense transformation efforts mainly on the idea that emerging technologies had created a revolution in military affairs (RMA). RMA advocates asserted that emerging communications, information, surveillance, and technical intelligence capabilities would lift the fog of war and "allow unprecedented awareness of every aspect of future operations."[2] Common operating pictures displayed on computer screens, in combination with processes, such as system-of-systems analysis and operational net assessment, would permit omniscient headquarters to develop detailed plans, make perfect decisions, control organizations closely, apply resources efficiently, and direct operations linearly toward mission accomplishment. Indeed, defense transformation and RMA thinking seemed to be eclipsing the doctrine of mission command. The orthodoxy of defense transformation, however, considered war as mainly a targeting exercise and divorced war from its political, human, psychological, and cultural dimensions. Defense transformation and RMA thinking also neglected the continuous interaction with enemies determined to evade or counter sophisticated technological capabilities. The embrace of the orthodoxy of defense transformation and the associated neglect of the doctrine of mission command complicated greatly U.S. and coalition efforts in Afghanistan and Iraq as well as Israeli efforts in Southern Lebanon in 2006.

As Shamir points out, wartime experience often inspires a return to the fundamentals of mission command. While emerging communications and information technologies can help leaders command effectively and improve the capabilities of military organizations, recent conflicts have demonstrated that war is not and will not become "network centric," as some predicted in the 1990s. Communications and information technologies, therefore, should be employed in a way that permits effective decentralization of operations rather than as a means for centralizing control of resources and decision making.

The clear implication of this important book is that Western militaries would be wise to promote the doctrine and practice of mission command to improve military effectiveness and protect against the peacetime tendencies to simplify military problems and exaggerate the effect of technology on the character of war. Doing so will require leader development and education that emphasizes the study of war and warfare, as Sir Michael Howard suggested, in "width, depth, and context."[3] Leader development and education should promote an organizational culture in which higher-level commanders are comfortable with relinquishing control and authority to junior commanders while setting conditions for effective decentralized operations consistent with the doctrine of mission command. Junior leaders must possess a bias toward action and accept necessary risks associated with leading and fighting in complex and uncertain environments against determined and adaptive enemies.

H. R. McMaster, PhD
Brigadier General, U.S. Army

The views expressed are those of the author and do not reflect the views of the Department of Defense or any of its components.

THE THEORY AND HISTORY OF MISSION COMMAND

Part I

1 SETTING THE STAGE

THE GERMAN CONCEPT of *Auftragstaktik*,[1] translated here as "mission command," denotes decentralized leadership; it is a philosophy that requires and facilitates initiative on all levels of command directly involved with events on the battlefield. It encourages subordinates to exploit opportunities by empowering them to take the initiative and exercise judgment in pursuit of their mission; alignment is maintained through adherence to the commander's intent. The doctrine, firmly rooted in Prussian-German military culture and experience, presupposes the existence of trust in the subordinate's ability to act wisely and creatively without supervision when faced with unexpected situations. Essentially, it is a contract between commander and subordinate, wherein the latter is granted the freedom to choose unanticipated courses of action in order to accomplish the mission.

The primary objective of the current study is to explore the process through which mission command was adopted, adapted, and practiced in the U.S., British, and Israeli armies, since the concept's "rediscovery" in the 1980s. By so doing, the research also examines the broader issue of adoption and adaptation of foreign concepts into doctrine and practice.

While a number of works have investigated the adoption of mission command, this examination has usually been secondary to the study of broader themes, such as maneuver warfare or the operational level of war. In addition, earlier studies have focused on specific cases, such as the American reforms of the post-Vietnam era or the Bagnall reforms in Britain.[2] However, the relevance of mission command is not restricted to any one doctrine or historical period. Indeed, modern militaries endeavor to apply it regardless of continuous and significant changes in the nature and character of war. A study of mission command, pursued independently from an examination of other general doctrines, can provide a comprehensive understanding of this approach. It may also reveal the process through which new ideas and approaches are developed, introduced, manipulated, and finally implemented. Consequently, the current study will focus on the tension between the introduction and implementation of new ideas through the prism of mission command.

An investigation of mission command poses a serious challenge, as the concept is quite elusive. The meaning accorded to *Auftragstaktik* in nineteenth- and early-twentieth-century Prussian-German writings was different than that accorded to it today.[3] In a manner similar to Blitzkrieg, although mission command was practiced, the term itself was absent from official doctrinal publications.[4] Nevertheless, its principles were incorporated into German military doctrine during the nineteenth century. Many historians believe that mission command had reached its highest form when practiced by the Prussian-German Army. Some have gone so far as to assert that the *Wehrmacht* owed its effectiveness and achievements to its reliance on *Auftragstaktik*.[5] This concept was largely neglected by mainstream Western militaries until the second half of the Cold War. At that time the West began to seek means of offsetting the Red Army's quantitative superiority. The search led the Anglo-Americans to reexamine the fighting qualities of the Wehrmacht; they discovered the pivotal role played by mission command in securing Germany an edge over its rivals.

On a more practical level, the Anglo-Americans considered mission command crucial for the practice of maneuver warfare. Developed by Americans and the British and later adopted, maneuver warfare was the doctrinal response to the Soviet threat.[6] Though the Cold War has receded into the pages of history, and despite a shift in the focus of military operations, mission command has demonstrated significant staying power. Some argue that it is the method of command best suited for unconventional warfare scenarios, such as low-intensity conflicts (LICs), peacekeeping operations, and counterinsurgency.[7] Mission command is also believed to have retained its validity in the face of the new digital command and control (C2) technologies, which ostensibly increase micromanagement.[8]

A somewhat more cynical outlook views mission command as just another technical or managerial concept,[9] similar to a score of others examined and discarded, such as Management by Objectives (MBO), Total Quality Management (TQM), Reengineering, or Just in Time (JIT), all produced primarily by corporate America.[10] However, in contrast to these business-oriented concepts, mission command is firmly rooted in military theory. This foundation may account for its enduring popularity and near mythical canonization. These accolades notwithstanding, evidence suggests that modern militaries have encountered difficulties in the implementation and practice of mission command. The gap between theory and practice may stem from internal organizational factors as well as from external factors. This disparity, too, will be explored in the current research.

AIMS AND ARGUMENTS

Using the Prussian-German historical experience as a point of reference, this study examines three modern armies that adopted mission command in the 1980s and 1990s: the American Army, the British Army, and the Israel Defense Forces (IDF). In each of these cases, the analysis revolves around three primary concepts: adoption, adaptation, and praxis. The first, adoption, represents an organizational decision to embrace a foreign concept; the second, adaptation, covers the process of integrating this concept into the organization; and the third, praxis, focuses on the factors that affect the organization's ability to implement the foreign concept in combat. This book therefore aims to answer the following questions:

- What were the American, British, and Israeli traditions of command prior to the adoption of mission command?
- How did these traditions of command influence the adoption of mission command, and what other factors may have had an impact?
- How did these forces adapt mission command in theory and in practice?
- How similar are the American, British, and Israeli variants of mission command?
- Was the adoption of mission command successful from the perspective of doctrine and practice? Why or why not?

The main argument in this study is that a borrowed concept such as mission command, chosen for its promise to enhance operational effectiveness, will be interpreted and practiced differently by the adopting party due to the impact of particular strategic settings and organizational cultures. Consequently, the impact of the adopted concept on the organization and its effectiveness may be different than expected or intended.

THE CONCEPTUAL FRAMEWORK

The model presented in Figure 1, which demonstrates the process of adoption through adaptation and praxis, illustrates the main argument of this book. The process begins with the development of an approach to command within the framework of Organization A's particular cultural, strategic, and organizational circumstances. In the case of mission command, Organization A represents the Prussian-German Army. This approach is then adopted by Organization B, which represents the American, British, and Israeli Armies, each of which operates within a unique cultural context. Mission command is studied by each of these armies as a paradigm of and for excellence. It is then adapted and incorporated into official doctrine. The first gap, interpretation, develops at this stage, influencing doctrinal output, due to different cultural settings and diverse interpretations accorded to the concept within each army.[11] The accumulated affect is a de facto differentiation between the original idea and its adapted doctrinal form.

The second gap, praxis, develops during the implementation of the adapted doctrine. It occurs as a result of an interplay between external and internal

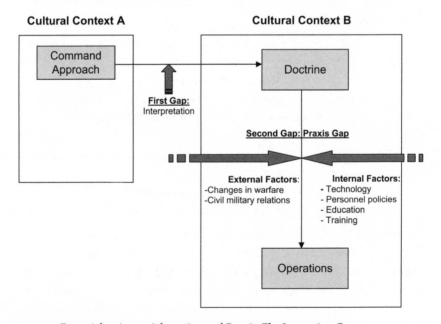

Figure 1. From Adoption to Adaptation and Praxis: The Increasing Gap.

factors governing the organizational culture of each army and their unique modus operandi. External factors include the changes in the nature of warfare and in civil-military relations, particularly from the end of the Cold War until the first decade of the twenty-first century. Internal factors include education, training, and personnel policies. Consequently, the main argument is that mission command, developed by one organization and adopted by others, has undergone at least two phases of transformation. These changes have breached an ever widening gap between the original concept and its application in combat operations, its raison d'être. Indeed, due to these gaps, mission command has mutated, a process resulting in the creation of variants more in congruence with local organization cultures.

The structure of this book is based on the theoretical model discussed above. It begins with an investigation of the Prussian army and the particular cultural context that bore mission command. This discussion will be followed by an exploration of the approach to, and culture of, command in each of the three armies. The interpretation gap in each of the case studies will then be explored through an analysis of the adoption process each army underwent; the praxis gap will be analyzed through recent operations and organizational practices. The discussion of these gaps will demonstrate the extent to which mission command has influenced local command cultures.

2 COMMAND AND MILITARY CULTURE

THE FOLLOWING CHAPTER discusses in depth both the concept of command and of mission command. The chapter will also make the link between these concepts and military culture and organizational theory. It expounds on the unique challenges posed by battlefield friction and on the manner through which mission command can mitigate it. The concept of mission command denotes decentralization of decision-making authority and empowerment of subordinates; therefore this chapter also discusses the rationale and the organizational theory at the root of both concepts. It then explores the cultural transformation required from, and the inherent difficulties faced by, military organizations endeavoring to practice mission command. The theories of organizational culture and empowerment are then examined in order to explain varied approaches to command and practices of command before and following the adoption of mission command. The concepts and methods discussed in this chapter will serve as the foundation for the discussion of the process of adoption and adaptation of mission command in the following chapters. The chapter concludes with an exploration of the basic cultural elements necessary for a successful implementation of mission command. The chapter thus demonstrates the significance of cultural elements to the process of adoption and adaptation of new ideas.

WHAT IS COMMAND?

What is command and how is it different from leadership? Command in battle is considered of such significance that it is widely assumed that if performed well, regardless of other shortcomings, it can ensure victory. Indi-

viduals have led, directed, and made critical decisions on battlefields throughout the history of war. When civilization first began to exploit the power of
organized violence through the military organization, the positions of leadership were regulated. The position of command came to represent a function transcending any individual occupying it. The function of command and
the existence of a chain of command differentiate between military organizations and tribal warriors. Modern British doctrine defines command as
the "authority vested in an individual for the direction, coordination, and
control of military forces" and states that leadership, command, and management are "closely related."[1] Management and command functions involve
the "allocation and control of resources to achieve objectives," only the latter
of which is "fully tested under the extraordinary stresses of war fighting." In
this extreme context, command is comprised of leadership, decision making,
and control.[2]

According to U.S. Army doctrine, leadership entails "influencing people by
providing purpose, direction and motivation," while decision making signifies
"selecting a course of action as the one most favorable to accomplish the mission."[3] In addition to leadership, command also includes authority, which is the
"delegated power to judge, act, or command, it includes responsibility, accountability and delegation of authority."[4] However, it is important to note that
delegation of authority does not absolve commanders of their responsibilities
or accountability; indeed, responsibilities cannot be delegated. The element of
control, crucial for the practice of command, is defined by the Americans as
the "regulation of forces and battlefield operating systems to accomplish the
mission according to the commander's intent."[5] These definitions emphasize
control of structures and processes over "creativity and will." According to
an alternate definition, commanders "invent novel solutions to mission problems . . . and [are] the source of diligent purposefulness." Command is thus a
combination of art and science, a "creative expression of human will." Control
is comprised primarily of the structures and processes enabling command and
risk management.[6]

Military organizations have been hierarchical for centuries in that authority, responsibility, and accountability devolve on one individual. Lower ranking individuals are both subordinates and commanders; they are required to
interpret the orders they are given and issue orders to their subordinates. The
difficulties inherent in this system were greatly compounded by the onset of
the French Revolution and the consequent expansion in both the size and

spread of armies. Technology has mitigated these difficulties but has also added an additional dimension of complexity.

The research devoted to command is still in its infancy.[7] Despite technological advances and the importance of the subject, little has changed since Martin van Creveld lamented the rarity of works on command two decades ago.[8] The broader discipline of warfare, too, is rather neglected, leading Jim Storr to characterize it as "poorly developed."[9] The literature devoted to command falls under three categories. The works comprising the first category focus on the personalities and behavioral patterns of great commanders. These include biographies and autobiographies as well as more systematic studies analyzing the actions and decisions of great captains in an attempt to unveil the secrets of their success or failure.[10] The second category includes social sciences–oriented studies, in which command is regarded as a subcategory of leadership and management, as it includes elements of both. Leadership is concerned with motivation, influence, and inspiration, whereas management focuses on the effective and efficient allocation and process of resources. Accordingly, much of the literature devoted to leadership and management is applied to the study of command. The third category includes technically oriented studies devoted primarily to command and control procedures and processes, such as information gathering, analysis, and dissemination. Recently, this field has centered around the impact of digital technology on command and control.[11] Few have endeavored to integrate the tools afforded by these disciplines for a comprehensive study of command. This deficiency may account for the primary stage of development of the theory of command.

In this study, command is identified as a collaborative, rather than individual, endeavor involving an entire system.[12] It assumes that command is an organizational activity exercised under the chaotic conditions of battle and that it both reflects and creates military and organizational cultures.[13]

THE CHALLENGE OF COMMAND

According to Carl von Clausewitz, war is the "province of uncertainty," imposing instability on, and hurling the unexpected at, military organizations practicing the art and science of organized violence.[14] Endeavoring to understand the dynamics of war, Clausewitz developed powerful interrelated concepts: friction, chance, and fog. Mission command was designed as a means of countering the impact of these forces on the performance of military organizations.

Friction, according to Richard Simpkin, was "Clausewitz's most important contribution to military thought."[15] Barry Watts noted that the idea "grew
over more than two decades into a theoretical concept that lies at the very
heart of his mature approach in employing this concept."[16] In war, Clausewitz
warned, situations rarely develop according to plan, and the concept of friction explains why. Superficially similar to the infamous Murphy's law, which
dictates that whatever can go wrong will go wrong,[17] friction denotes not occasional misfortune but rather a phenomenon structurally embedded in the
situation. Indeed, "everything is very simple in war, but the simplest thing is
difficult. The difficulties accumulate and end by producing a kind of friction
that is inconceivable unless one has experienced war."[18] Friction, according to
Clausewitz, is the "only concept which more or less corresponds to the factors
that distinguish real war from war on paper."[19] To illustrate the effects of friction, Clausewitz described the seemingly minor details that force one man to
alter his travel plans during the course of one day. All the more so:

> A battalion is made up of individuals, the least important of whom may chance
> to delay things or somehow make them go wrong. The dangers inseparable
> from war and the physical exertions war demands can aggravate the problem
> to such an extent that they must be ranked among its principal causes. . . . This
> tremendous friction, which cannot, as in mechanics, be reduced to a few points,
> is everywhere in contact with chance, and brings about effects that can not be
> measured, just because they are largely due to chance. . . . Action in war is like
> movement in a resistant element.[20]

Organizations are comprised of individuals driven by independent motives,
fears, and perceptions who produce friction. Consequently, what seems simple becomes infinitely more complex. On the basis of Clausewitz's theory,
Watts created an instructive taxonomy of the "unified concept of general friction," which includes:

1. Danger;
2. Physical exertion;
3. Uncertain and imperfect information on which actions in war are
   based;
4. Friction in the narrow sense of the resistance within one's own
   forces;
5. Chance events that cannot be readily foreseen;
6. Physical and political limits to the use of military force;

7. Unpredictability stemming from interaction with the enemy; and

8. Discontinuity between ends and means in war.[21]

This all-inclusive list demonstrates the dynamics that create the disparity be-tween war on paper and war in reality. Combined with violence and the pri-macy of politics, chance forms the Clausewitzian "remarkable trinity" consti-tuting the nature of war.[22] Accordingly: "If we now consider briefly the subjective nature of war—the means by which war has to be fought—it will look more than ever like a gamble."[23] As an example, Clausewitz says: "Fog can prevent the enemy from being seen in time, a gun from firing when it should, a report from reaching the commanding officer. Rain can prevent a battalion from arriving . . . ruin a cavalry charge."[24] Both fog and chance are included in Watts's "general friction theory."[25]

The concept of fog, represented in the expression "fog of war," is in fact comparatively less important than the other two concepts.[26] Moreover, ac-cording to Eugenia Kiesling, Clausewitz used the term "fog" only four times and never used the expression "fog of war," preferring the "twilight" metaphor instead.[27] The term "fog" was used twice to explain the source of friction and a third time in the context of information distortions in war. It was used only once to describe the erratic nature of war, leading Kiesling to argue that fog and friction are entwined rather than separate concepts denoting mental dis-tortions and physical difficulties, respectively. Consequently, it would appear that Clausewitz attributed friction to the mental and psychological rigors of battle (such as the effects of exhaustion and fear) rather than to information-gathering difficulties. Nevertheless, though the information gap may consti-tute a less significant component of friction, it remains a part of it.

In his essay on friction, Watts examined three principle questions: Is fric-tion an everlasting structural feature of war, transcending social and techno-logical transformations? Can it be reduced by technology or by other means? Can these concepts be described through modern scientific concepts? Based on an analysis of Operation Desert Storm (1991), Watts concluded that friction is in fact an inherent, structural feature of war. His analysis revealed an abun-dance of classic examples of friction such as the failure of the coalition to de-stroy the Iraqi Republican Guard. Synchronization of the intended envelop-ment maneuver had failed due to divergent perceptions of developments on the battlefield and the unexpected retreat of the Guard. Difficulties were com-pounded by adverse weather conditions and communication and coordination deficiencies.[28] Similarly, reports of an imminent flank attack by an Iraqi armored brigade forced an American armored brigade to alter its plans during the second Iraq War. As it turned out, the strength of the Iraqi force, which had actually lost its way in the desert, had been inflated due to confusion in reports and the weather conditions—which, incidentally, are categorized by Clausewitz under chance.[29] In light of these examples, Watts concluded that friction is inherent to war.

This conclusion is based also on the answer he provides to the third question: how can these concepts be described using modern scientific concepts? Watts adopted Alan Beyerchen's concepts of "nonlinear science" and specifically "nonlinear systems," which explain in modern terminology what Clausewitz understood intuitively. For a system to be linear, it must meet two basic conditions. The first is proportionality: changes in the system output must be proportional to the system input. For example, all other things being equal, a gallon of gas will always produce the same mileage, and an increase in gas will result in a proportional increase in mileage. This feature enables accurate input-to-output predictions. The second condition of linearity is additive: the whole is the sum of all its parts. This characteristic ensures that the origin of a problem can be traced to specific elements and corrected. In contrast, nonlinear systems do not obey the rules of proportionality or additivity. In these types of systems, "small differences of outputs can produce entirely different outcomes for the system, yielding various behavior routes to a degree of complexity that exhibits characteristics of randomness—hence the term "chaos."[30]

Clausewitz, according to Beyerchen, understood war to be a nonlinear phenomenon, therefore neither predictable nor controllable in the common sense. Watts accepted this interpretation, noting that the warring sides are in fact "complex adaptive systems"—that is, they process information nonlinearly. They attempt to identify "regularities or patterns that can be condensed into concepts or schemata describing aspects of reality."[31] In the military doctrine, this schemata is represented by standard operating procedures (SOPs). These arrangements serve as a mechanism for decreasing the information gap that develops between the system and the environment. Nevertheless, some gaps and errors are unavoidable as perfect information is never available during combat situations.[32] Watts also concluded that technologically enhanced information-gathering and processing capabilities can lift the fog of war and potentially reduce the effects of friction.[33] However, the human mind has limited information-processing capacities, which are further reduced under stressful conditions. Watts argues that the friction-reducing effects of information gathering and assessment technologies may be offset by their inherent complexity. Similarly, Jacob Kip and Lester Grau warned that even when technology lives up to its promise, it often requires greater resource allocation and attention for its maintenance, and therefore it creates new sources of friction.[34]

In view of the above, David Betz argues that friction will continue to challenge military organizations in the information age.[35] This challenge was demonstrated by the abortive 2003 Israeli assassination attempt on the life of Hamas spiritual leader Sheikh Yassin. Earlier, in 2002, the IDF had assassinated Hamas leader Salach Shchadeh by dropping a one-ton bomb on his house. The bomb caused collateral damage, killing innocent civilians, including children, and resulted in a domestic and international outcry. In 2003, the IDF had learned that the entire leadership of Hamas would be convening on the third floor of a Gaza building. Attempting to avoid previous mistakes, it decided to use a 250 kg precision-guided munition (PGM) bomb that would destroy that floor only. As it happened, the meeting was relocated to the first floor at the last minute due to technical reasons. Hence, although the bomb performed as advertised, Hamas leaders escaped nearly unscathed. Perfect intelligence, planning, and execution were all for naught due to friction caused by political constraints and unforeseen events.[36]

AN ORGANIZATIONAL SOLUTION

The origins of mission command are usually traced to the reforms instituted in Prussia following the humiliating defeat at Jena (1806).[37] The reformists concluded that the rigid, mechanistic army of the ancien régime was incapable of facing the challenges posed by Napoleonic warfare. The size, composition, and tactics of modern armies had rendered obsolete the traditions of old. New technologies introduced by the mid-nineteenth-century Industrial Revolution (primarily the rail, telegraph, and breech loading gun) also called for new agile and flexible military organization and command systems.

It was Helmuth von Moltke the Elder who recognized the need to revolutionize command and articulated the essence of mission command. According to Moltke, subordinates are told what to do, not how to do it, and are required to operate within the purview of the superior's intent. Superiors specify the mission objectives and constraints and allocate resources, leaving the rest to subordinates. The latter's skills, creativity, and commitment, or lack thereof, will ultimately determine the battle plan and its execution. *Auftragstaktik* is therefore not merely a technique for issuing orders but a type of leadership that is "inextricably linked to a certain image of men as soldiers."[38] Subordinates were not relegated to the status of robots, simply following orders, but rather were regarded as individuals capable of making independent judgments. Within a unique historical, strategic, and social context, the Prussian-German army combined military theory and praxis that enabled it to practice *Auftragstaktik*. Its conceptual tenets are as follows:

- The chaotic nature of the battlefield, the Clausewitzian chance, friction, and uncertainty trinity, are inherent to war and should be considered as such.
- Optimization of complex systems' subunit output requires an application of the concept of intent.
- Time is a critical factor: tactical command must practice short decision-making cycles.
- As the human capacity for information processing is limited, the process should include selected subordinates.
- Technology can improve communications and information processing, but it lacks the human capacity for creativity and snap judgments.
- Motivation and commitment are strengthened by active participation and responsibility.

These concepts seem to validate the belief that mission command will retain its relevance as long as the nature of both warfare and man remain unaltered.[39]

CENTRALIZATION VERSUS DECENTRALIZATION

The degree of centralization in an organization is primarily a function of its formal structural design. Structure designates the relations and communications between the comprising elements of an organization and is defined by formal reporting and communication lines.[40] The primary function of an organizational structure is motivating and coordinating the efforts of the various components toward a common goal. Although military organizations rely on a centralized, narrow span of control that creates tall structures, they are becoming increasingly differentiated due to the increasing number of specialized units.[41] Specialization in turn requires further coordination mechanisms, such as headquarters, procedures, and coordination officers, all of which contribute to inflexibility.

The concept of "division of labor" in organizational theory signifies the assignment of tasks and responsibilities, and the degree of specialization, within an organization. Extended "horizontal differentiation,"—that is, increased division and specialization—inflates communication difficulties and requires extensive coordination. Expanded "vertical differentiation"—an excessive number of hierarchical levels—introduces excessive intermediate levels in order to limit the number of mistakes. Tall organizations increase decision-making redundancy, or the reexamination of decisions made by lower-level individuals. The result is not only slower decision-making cycles but also loss of motivation and a sense of powerlessness in the lower levels. Increasing decentralization in tall structure organizations, or lower-level involvement in the decision-making process, requires a flattening of the structure.[42] Over the past few decades, many organizations have done so in order to extend the individual's sphere of responsibility beyond the job description.[43] Increased organizational division and specialization also requires powerful communication and coordination mechanisms in order to ensure organizational integrity or unity of purpose. In other words, greater horizontal differentiation necessitates greater reliance on coordination and integration mechanisms in order to ensure effective results. Coordination denotes the extent and the means by which an organization integrates or holds together its comprising elements to work together toward a common goal. This can be achieved through different methods:

1. Mutual adjustment: direct communication between organizational components. This model is less productive when instituted by large and dispersed organizations.
2. Direct supervision: coordination in military or civilian organizations is achieved through a "chain of command" that maintains "unity of command." Each commander is directly responsible for a number of units; the number of people reporting directly to him constitutes his "span of control." The size of the span of control is influenced by the degree of task complexity, physical distance, and type of supervisor-subordinate interaction. The standard span of control in combat units extends to three or four subordinates, mainly due to the dispersion of troops and the high quantity of information. Essentially, the smaller the span of control, the more attention a commander can

dedicate to each subordinate. Of course, decreased spans of control invariably increase the number of vertical levels. The commander's limited capacity for information processing and division of attention can be resolved by either reducing spans of control or decentralizing decision making.

3. Standardization of work process: coordination between specialized elements can be effected through standardized work procedures. This method yields the highest dividends when applied to the coordination of highly specialized, unskilled, and repetitive tasks. Military organizations employ SOPs for anticipated tasks or situations that can be dealt with effectively by using routine, structured responses. Decisions in this case are limited and programmed.

4. Standardization of outputs: specification of a desired output can serve as a coordination mechanism. This approach allows lower-level discretion in regard to the choice of means but requires increased communication or mutual adjustment.

5. Standardization of skills: this coordination mechanism concentrates on the degree of professionalism, expertise, and training required to accomplish the task. Professionals apply similar types of specialized knowledge and skills when approaching a task or a problem. In contrast to the use of SOPs, professionals apply heuristic-type thinking to particular problems, rather than relying on pre-set processes that share a common set of assumptions, methodologies, and knowledge. They utilize a particular jargon that enables communication and working together toward common goals across the organizational hierarchy.[44]

Mission command relies primarily on the last two methods, which are probably the most effective as they provide flexibility but are harder to obtain and require a certain culture and a large initial investment.

EMPOWERMENT AND DELEGATION

Delegation of authority, the core of mission command, is difficult to achieve, as commanders are required to relinquish control over events but retain responsibility for them. Additionally, it requires subordinates to initiate action without awaiting instructions. In order to mitigate the influence of these human tendencies and to facilitate the practice of mission command, a certain organizational culture must be developed. The psychological concept of empowerment implies strengthening an individual's belief in his ability to effect change and control situations.[45] The literature suggests that empowerment can be fostered through certain management practices. Albert Bandura conceptualized the notion of self-efficacy and its centrality to the individual's sense of personal power in the world. According to Bandura, empowerment can be achieved through positive emotional support during experiences associated with stress and anxiety, verbal encouragement and positive persuasion, and identification through incidental learning and actual mastery of a task—this last being probably the most effective means.[46]

Empowerment emphasizes the importance of a supervisor's attitude toward subordinates. Supervisors are required to subscribe to Theory Y, which implies that their subordinates are capable and motivated and accept greater responsibility, rather than to Theory X. The latter assumes that subordinates are unmotivated and require close supervision. By doing so, they initiate a Pygmalion effect, a self-fulfilling prophecy.[47] Conger identified several effective empowerment managerial practices, including offering positive and emotional support, manifest rewards and encouragement, frequent expressions of confidence and praise of accomplishments, and cultivation of initiative and responsibility.

In contrast, certain managerial practices can induce a feeling of powerlessness. These include a perceived lack of control over the situation and insufficient resources, capabilities, or discretion necessary to complete a task.[48] The bureaucratic top-down structure common to most militaries tends to encourage dependency and submissiveness.[49] Since they are controlled by rules and routines, little room is left for initiative and discretion.[50] The conduct of subordinates is often guided by rules over which they have no control and which prove ineffective in the face of a new situation or a changing context. Due to its obvious advantages, empowerment is being promoted as a powerful managerial practice.[51] However, it should be noted that empowerment may have adverse effects; unmonitored mistakes may very well induce a false sense of confidence.[52] In order to avoid this undesirable effect, organizations should establish effective mechanisms of coordination.

The second issue hindering decentralization is the fear of losing control over processes and situations. Here a solution was offered by the modern management theory of complexity. According to this theory, seemingly small changes can initiate a random chain of events, ultimately effecting a significant transformation. The most popular representation of this concept is the "butterfly effect." This metaphor tells of a butterfly flapping its wings in Tokyo and triggering a storm in America. According to this theory, the flapping of the wings caused a random chain of events that evolved incrementally and created a new pattern. The theory of complexity offers significant dividends for organizations, particularly in regard to the practice of control and hierarchy.[53] In this context, the concept of order in an organization receives a different meaning. It denotes an emerging process subject to fluctuations. The dynamic nature of the process negates preparatory planning or the possibility of achieving a predetermined end result. At most, leaders can be provided with a number of basic rules. Commanders are hard pressed to accept this concept, as it contradicts the natural inclination to impose order. Nevertheless, commanders have to understand that they are part of a flux and develop the skills to facilitate the process; they must go with the flow of change rather than control it in the traditional sense. The role of the commander is shifting from that of a planner to that of a designer. He is expected to create a context in which appropriate forms of self-organization can occur. According to Morgan, "Managers need to define the minimum specifications that can define an appropriate context, while allowing the details to unfold within the frame. In this way they can help to shape emergent processes of self organization, while avoiding the trap of imposing too much control."[54] Thus, commanders should set a general course by stipulating critical parameters and allow subordinates to exercise independent initiative, which then promotes a shift in system patterns and creates a much larger effect. Long before modern organizational theory had been developed, it was the nineteenth-century Prussian Chief of Staff Moltke the Elder who probably described it best when he defined strategy as a "system of expedients."[55]

THE ROLE OF ORGANIZATIONAL CULTURE

Adopted from anthropology, the concept of culture has, in recent years, become central to the study of organizations in general and military organizations in particular. Though its definition is subject to debate,[56] it has been instrumental in explaining organizational behaviors and outcomes,[57] as organizations interpret information and choose strategies through a prism of cultural assumptions.[58] A number of management studies have attempted to define the type of culture that contributes positively to overall organizational effectiveness.[59] Theo Farrell and Terry Terriff explained that culture is comprised of norms that are "intersubjective beliefs about the social and natural world that define actors, their situation, and the possibilities of action."[60] Additionally,

> Military culture is most often employed to examine a military organization's approach to or understanding of organizational ways of war with the aim being to explain anomalous behaviour. . . . Organizational culture thus can provide a compelling explanation why specific military organizations may continue to pursue ways of warfare that are incompatible with emerging or prevailing strategic and operational realities or why they resist change.[61]

For example, James Corum explained that technologies that were employed differently in interwar Germany and France reflected the distinctive culture of their respective general staffs.[62] Culture can also be used to explain the different approaches to command. In this regard, there are two levels of analysis: strategic culture and military culture.[63] The first encompasses variables relating to the entire national security level. According to Colin Gray, it shapes the context for behavior. Furthermore, while strategy and strategic behavior are comprised of more than culture, as "the dimensions of strategy are expressed in behaviour by people and institutions that have internalized strategic culture while at the same time constructing interpreting and amending that culture."[64] Gray argued that culture is the concept that "weaves together" or provides a context and meaning to strategic behavior. It is the frame of reference through which "ideas, attitudes, traditions, and preference for kind of action are considered."[65] Consequently, culture "shapes the process of strategy making and influences the execution of strategy."[66]

The second level of analysis is that of military culture. Military culture is influenced by the strategic culture (national-level variables such as geopolitics, religion, the economy, and civil-military relations) and the peculiarities, beliefs, and behaviors of distinct organizational cultures that develop traditions, practices, and technology. For example, though operating within the same strategic culture, the various U.S. military services boast distinct cultures.[67] Even when facing similar tasks or situations, the U.S. Army and Marines operate differently,[68] although some also argue that specifically in terms of their orientation toward maneuver, they are not that far apart. It is possible, then, that strategic culture accounts for some of the differences in styles of command between the American and British armies, while others can be attributed to military and organizational culture.

Another important aspect of culture is the link between organizational culture and organizational change and learning.[69] Farrell and Terriff noted that "Norms make meaningful action possible by telling military actors who they are and what they can do in given situations. In this way cultural norms define the purpose and possibilities of military change. For this reason we start looking at culture."[70] The organizational theorist Edgar Schein defined culture as "a pattern of shared basic assumptions that was learned by a group as it solved its problems of external adaptation and internal integration that has worked well enough to be considered valid and, therefore, to be taught to new members as the correct way to perceive, think and feel in relation to those problems."[71] Schein's understanding of culture has two distinct advantages in the context of developing approaches to command. First, it explains the discrepancy between the formal and declared and the informal and undeclared. In other words, this model accounts for the differences between everyday cultural manifestations in organizations, "the unwritten rules of the game,"[72] and the organization's official rules and regulations. The second advantage is that it explains the complex relationships between leaders and culture. It encompasses the leader's role in cultural change—the manner through which the attitudes and actions of leaders influence existing and emerging cultures.

According to Schein, culture consists of three distinctive levels—distinct to the extent that they are visible to an outside observer. The first and most visible level consist of artifacts. These include all visible products of an organization, such as organizational structure, procedures, and technology; rites and rituals; design of physical space; tales of important events and celebrated heroes; and formal statements, such as vision and mission. Though easy to observe, this level is difficult to decipher. To get to the deeper meaning of artifact, one must explore the next level, which consists of espoused beliefs and values. These are values, unwritten rules, and norms that govern and guide day-to-day behavior. These values serve as an integrating mechanism and often reduce uncertainty in key areas of a group's functioning. As Schein noted, these values are still very much on the conscious level and produce many observed behaviors and artifacts.[73] The third and deepest level encompasses the organization's basic underlying assumptions. These reflect a marked preference for certain solutions to problems, adopted on the basis of past experience. Often these are certain applications of beliefs that reflect a certain understanding of cause-and-effect relationships. Information technology provides a good example. The telegraph, field telephone, mobile radio, and the modern digital C2 technology were employed in accordance with a belief system that determined the command approach.[74]

Culture, as a set of basic assumptions, dictates what to pay attention to, its interpretation, and the emotional response to it. Since organizations are not always aware of these basic assumptions, it is difficult to challenge them and bring about comprehensive change. For example, an organizational assumption dictating that subordinates are incapable of independent judgment will be expressed through strong control procedures. Procedural changes will prove insufficient if unaccompanied by a corresponding change of the basic assumptions. According to Schein's model, the problems faced by military organizations attempting to adopt mission command can be traced to the second and the third levels: values and assumptions. As long as these remain unaltered, so will the organizational behavior.

According to Chris Argyris, professed values that represent organizational aspirations are frequently expressed in written statements.[75] Indeed, any statement made will be incongruent with these declared values, which he labeled the organization's "espoused theory." Actual operations and decisions, however, will reflect the organization's "theory in use"—implicit assumptions that are stronger than the former and that may reflect opposing values. Members of the organization look to the leader's actions and attempt to derive from these a "theory in use" or the "rules of the game." They must also learn the espoused theory in order to become accepted socially as members of the organization. Thus, they must master the correct organizational jargon, such as "we value our people," "the customer comes first," or "mission command is the best command approach." In the case of mission command, the "theory in use" can be a strong organizational reaction to mistakes, competing values such as zero defects, or obeying orders. These values might take precedence, thereby encouraging behaviour not congruent with official declarations. According to Argyris, "Any change which does not first change the meaning of effective action cannot persist, because it continues to expose individuals to potential embarrassment or threat. . . . This embarrassment or threat is what prevents organizational learning—the gap between intended actions and what actually happens."[76] Schein also noted that the basic assumptions in this model are rarely confronted and are therefore extremely difficult to change. In order to effect a fundamental change, an organization must effect change on this particular level, paradoxically the most difficult to change. It would necessitate what Argyris and Schön labeled as "double-loop learning," or frame breaking.[77]

Leaders play a crucial role in the process of culture change as they both shape and are shaped by culture. Leaders represent the culture in which they themselves matured; conversely, leadership is distinguished from management primarily by its capacity to generate cultural change. In situations where the gap between "theory in use" and "espoused theory" generate dysfunction, leaders must identify and steer a course for change. They are afforded multiple avenues through which to effect change:[78]

- What they pay attention to, measure, and control;
- Their reaction to critical incidents and organizational crisis;
- Resource allocation;
- Deliberate role modeling, teaching, and coaching;
- Awarding rewards and status; and
- Recruitment, selection, promotion, and communication procedures.

However, in order to effect a cultural change, the impact of these measures must be felt across all three levels of culture. In other words, the "espoused theory" such as the official command doctrine must therefore correspond with the "theory in use" lest a gap develop between intentions and behaviors. This would also explain the difference between command doctrine and the actual fruits of its implementation. According to this theory, if existing cultural elements contradict elements of mission command, leaders are required to effect change and reshape the cultural elements. They should reframe traditional cultural assumptions and embed alternative ones in their stead. Consequently, reinforcing the principles of mission command facilitates culture change. In contrast, reinforcement of existing defensive behavior may widen the gap between doctrine and behavior.

OLD CULTURE VERSUS NEW CULTURE

An examination of the adoption of mission command, an imported concept representing new cultural assumptions, requires an exploration of the relationship between the "old" and "new" cultures. While modern Western society attributes greater value to the "new" and the more recent as a representation of modernity, military organizations cherish traditions and allow historical memory to forge contemporary ethos and are essentially conservative and slow to embrace change. In most cases, they suffer from what Terriff described as a high degree of institutionalization, which results in a greater resistance to change.[79] According to Farrell and Terriff, there are three processes of change in military organizations. The first is a planned change that is tied to new visionary leaders mobilizing new ideas and behaviors and promoting a theory of victory. The second change involves an external shock, such as a defeat, which leads to a transformation of norms and beliefs. Change can also be effected through emulation, which Farrell and Terriff note is the process least studied to date.[80] In this regard, it is useful to review what the general organizational theory has found.

The continuous dilemma is how to balance the new and the old, as some traditions and practices retain their validity and usefulness. Also, commanders may mistakenly attempt to replace a culture as one would a technological platform or software. Alan Wilkins, an organizational theorist, related one anecdote about a CEO who asked him as his consultant to "install" a new culture. In another, he tells of an executive who, after listening to a presentation on culture, turned around and said to his staff, "I want one of those excellent company cultures, and Monday would not be too soon."[81]

After examining many failures to effect a cultural change, Wilkins concluded that organizations usually employed one of three processes: a piecemeal imitation of a successful organization, importing a new culture, or fostering a revolution. Organizations instituting the first option adopted a particular idea or practice from a successful organization, usually referred to in business jargon as "best practice." The result was often cynicism among members of the organization toward the adopted best practice and no indications of real improvement in effectiveness and productivity. Such was the case with the borrowed Japanese management practices of Quality Circles and Just in Time (JIT). These programs, efficient within their original settings due to historical context, specific skills, and shared values, did not fare well in the transfer. The economic term for this phenomenon is "imperfect imitability": the inability to identify, and consequently imitate, the sources of success. Moreover, even identification of the relevant variables does not ensure a successful implementation. This is due to the fact that these variables rely on tacit skills and knowledge found in the habits, memory, and commitments of the original organization. Moreover, it is impossible to imitate the key factor, which is execution; it has to be developed through trial and error. Wilkins is not against borrowing ideas, but he is against quick fixes and blind imitation. He believes that organizations require specific know-how in order to adapt a foreign practice to fit their own style, a process that requires considerable learning.[82] In most cases, it necessitates a fundamental change of the organization's values and sometimes even a change in its basic assumptions.

The second way, importing a culture, more prevalent in the business world than in the military, involves adopting cultures through mergers and acquisitions (M&A) or the hiring of executives of successful organizations. A successful example of culture importation through merger in the military is the 1950s merger in the IDF between Unit 101 and the Paratrooper battalion. The explicit intention of the merger was to imbue the army with the unique fighting culture developed by Unit 101.[83] An example of the second method of importing culture was the appointment of Israeli Air Force (IAF) general Dan Halutz as IDF chief of staff. It was hoped the appointment would facilitate adoption of IAF management culture by the ground forces.[84]

The third way of effecting cultural change is through a revolution. Studies have demonstrated that successful revolutions depend on a number of factors. First, there must be a crisis that shakes the belief in the methods of the "old guard" followed by the introduction of a new method by new leaders. These improve organization performance but also ensure that members of the organization attribute the success to the new methods. Finally, the new leadership institutionalizes the change through a reward system, hiring, promotion structure, and so forth. But more often than not, these conditions are not met; subordinates either do not experience the same degree of urgency, or they do not understand or know how to implement the new ways. As a result, performance does not improve and questions arise as to whether the old ways were indeed worse. The result is that people may learn "how to resist the new ways while appearing to support them."[85] Wilkins concluded that effective change requires "honouring the past" and involves developing "motivational faith"—that is, the faith in the fairness and the ability of members of the organization, their colleagues, and their leaders to be fair and able.[86] Hence, Wilkins recommended that introduction of a new culture include a "return to the past for inspiration and instruction." He suggested that the organization identify "principals that will remain constant," "promote hybrids," and find "current success examples within the organization."[87]

ESSENTIALS FOR MISSION COMMAND

A review of organizational literature reveals that empowerment and delegation of decision-making authority, the core of mission command, requires a change of organizational culture. Indeed, mission command is not merely a technique or procedure for issuing orders but a cultural phenomenon.[88] Successful implementation of this approach to command depends primarily on a cognitive understanding between commander and subordinate. This is then translated into the practice of decisions and behaviors on the basis of shared values. A number of authors have listed cultural elements necessary for mission command. The most common element is trust. David Schmidtchen found that mission command requires mutual trust, "respect between commanders and subordinates," as well as "understanding, acceptance of responsibility and acceptance of risk." Trust is acquired through professional development aiming at "developing leaders with self confidence who would not hesitate to exercise their initiative." Schmidtchen rightly argued that implementation of mission command can foster creativity and innovation. However, stating that mission command is largely dependent upon a culture that encourages creativity and innovation is equally valid. The question of cause and effect in regards to culture remains unsolved.[89]

Ad Vogelaar and Eric-Hans Kramer argued that mission command is based on "autonomy of action, clarity of objectives, adequacy of means to accomplish the mission and mutual trust."[90] Similarly, Walter von Lossow emphasized the "uniformity of thinking and reliability of action," which can be achieved through a long, common goal–oriented education and training process.[91] Antulio Echevarria opined that *Auftragstaktik* was enabled by a German military culture that strongly emphasized "initiative, aggressiveness, and subordinate freedom of action." Indeed, it valued personal initiative even at the cost of disobedience (though adhering to a higher intent). Subordinates were expected to demonstrate sound judgment grounded in military professionalism, inculcated through training and education.[92] A summary list of the necessary cultural requirements for mission command therefore includes the following:

- Understanding of and adherence to higher intent and the potential tension with the local mission.
- Mutual trust based on professional competence (and not necessarily on acquaintance or relationship).
- Excellent communication based on shared understanding of doctrine.
- High value on learning as expressed and emphasized in training and education.
- Tolerance for well-intended mistakes.

- A propensity for action and initiatives.
- Responsibility link to authority.
- Belief in the ability of individuals to make sound judgment calls.[93]

Some of these characteristics do not complement each other; indeed, they may even be contradictory. For example, an aggressive propensity for action and initiative does not bode well with control in the form of sound judgment and self-discipline. However, provided the process is managed properly, it is precisely this tension that can produce a positive yet delicate balanced dynamic.

MISSION COMMAND AND ORGANIZATIONAL THEORY

The purpose of this chapter was to define mission command and explore its relationship with a number of organizational concepts and phenomena. It began by discussing various definitions of command as an activity combining leadership, management, and decision making. However, more than simply being comprised of these, command is a unique activity conducted under the extreme conditions presented by war and battle. It was demonstrated that the uniqueness of command stems from friction and its related phenomena, inherent to war. Mission command was presented as an organizational solution aimed at minimizing the effects of friction and facilitating the pursuance of organizational objectives. It denotes decentralization and delegation of decision-making authority, allowing lower-level commanders to make quick independent decisions. In order to avoid the subsequent loss of organizational alignment toward an overall objective, mission command relies on adherence to higher command guidelines—the concept of intent. However, decentralization requires subordinate empowerment and ability. Subordinates must be equipped with the necessary knowledge and skills in order to make correct judgment calls; superiors must communicate their intent in the simplest and clearest manner. These conditions require a specific organizational culture wherein commanders and subordinates accept and share the risk of failure and where commanders feel able to grant their subordinates freedom to carry out missions independently. The literature demonstrates that in order to adopt successful practices, the adopting organization must undergo certain changes. Cultural change is neither quick nor a linear process; it is largely dependent on the example set by and the decisions made by its leaders. By establishing a theoretical framework and clarifying the central concepts, this chapter provided the necessary foundation for understanding the mechanisms employed in the adoption process of mission command. The next chapter will explore the historical origins of mission command and its development. The original historical context of mission command will then be used a yardstick against which to evaluate contemporary attempts to emulate this approach to command.

3 THE ORIGINS OF MISSION COMMAND (*AUFTRAGSTAKTIK*)

LEADING MODERN WESTERN ARMIES have adopted the historical concept of *Auftragstaktik* (mission command)[1] as an effective response to the challenges posed by modern warfare. However, as Martin van Creveld noted, "Command cannot be understood in isolation."[2] An understanding of the German experience can provide a contextual framework for the analysis of the contemporary concept of mission command and the process of adaptation it has undergone.

Hence, this chapter will provide an investigation of the historical concept and the sociopolitical institution that originally created it, the Prussian-German Army. I will begin by exploring Fredrick's eighteenth-century Prussian army, the changes wrought by Napoleon and the French Revolution, and the subsequent reforms instituted by the Prussians. The following sections will delineate Clausewitzian theory concerning the nature of war, the inherent difficulties it presents, and the idea of *Auftragstaktik* and other related ideas developed by German military theorists from Moltke the Elder through the Blitzkrieg era.

THE SEARCH FOR TOTAL CONTROL

From the eighteenth through the nineteenth centuries, scientific advancements were mirrored by developments in military theory.[3] Various schools of the Enlightenment, Newtonian science in particular, argued that objective reality can be controlled. The popular metaphor used to represent the world was that of a machine, signifying that the scientific perception of nature was one of control and synchronized harmony.[4] Military theorists proposed that mathematical tools could be used in order to quantify war as well and that such efforts would yield a corpus of universal rules and formulas guaranteeing victory. The application of these rules, the theorist stated, would depend on individual commanders. Success would depend on the level of their genius.[5] It should be noted that the ideas emanating from Enlightenment military theorists, and epitomized by Frederick the Great's army, continue to influence modern organizations. Thus, military organizations have maintained marching parade-ground drills as a means for instilling a sense of unity and cohesion.[6]

The eighteenth-century Prussian army that fought the Seven Years' War (1756–1763) embodied these ideas and established itself as the best army in Europe. Contemporary theorists recognized and admired Frederick's genius but felt it was uncontrollable, unpredictable, and therefore impossible to imitate. Turning to his army instead, the world focused on its organization and doctrine and especially on the automatic, robotic-like behavior it practiced and that Frederick had utilized so well.[7] This blind obedience was enforced through draconian discipline based on fear.[8] Soldiers, Frederick believed, "need to fear their officers more than the enemy."[9] Christopher Duffy explained that "This principle of subordination submits the soldier to his officer, the officer to his commander, the colonel to his general and the body of generals as a whole to the commander of the army."[10] Due to the limited size of the army and the battlefield, Frederick was able to conduct all the necessary planning, issue detailed orders, and monitor their execution.[11] The king would assign specific assignments to units, which were then expected to carry them out without deviation.[12] This system of command was partially successful at best, and only under the leadership of a military genius.[13] The staff during that period was an ad hoc organization formed for specific campaigns, enjoying limited responsibilities and precluded from the decision-making process. Prussian army tactics and organization were heavily influenced by technological capabilities and constraints. For instance, due to their weight, artillery guns remained stationary throughout the battle. In addition, the inaccurate, slow-rate infantry musket (two shots per minute) was only good up to about ninety meters. Breaking an enemy line required concentrated fire delivered by massed close-order formations. Battalions had to complete the complicated transition from marching columns to lines of attack without incurring any gaps and then march to within firing range. Massed volleys were fired following a march, thereby conferring crucial importance to the speed of advance; therefore, when the Prussians increased their marching rate from 90 to 120 paces per minute, they gained a valuable advantage and were considered the marvel of the world.[14]

The rigid structure and discipline were reinforced by the social divide that separated the aristocratic officers from the common folk of the rank and file. The officers were believed to posses, by right of birth, such qualities as independence of mind, chivalry, self-sacrifice, and courage, as had their knightly ancestors. Enlisted men were considered no more than raw material that needed to be molded and trained to become "a walking musket."[15] However, the limits of tightly controlled infantry bodies were already demonstrated in the French and Indian War (1756–1763).[16] Difficult terrain, reconnaissance, and skirmishing were best conducted by small, independent detachments of light infantry and cavalry, such as the European Hussars or the Rangers of the New World. Distinguished by, and despised for, their independence, similar units were soon adopted by other European armies.[17] This development notwithstanding, the armies essentially continued to fight in the traditional way.

NAPOLEON AND THE FRENCH REVOLUTION

A system based on hierarchy and blind obedience, such as that employed by the ancien régime, inhibits initiative, creativity, and trust; these proved a disadvantage in the face of a complex and changing environment. This system severely restricted the army's ability to conduct reconnaissance, skirmishing, and open-order combat and thereby greatly reduced the effectiveness of attack. It prevented major actions in broken terrain and barred commanders from seeking decision through surprise. Commanders avoided night operations, wooded terrain, and, most important, pursuit, for fear of losing control of the troops. These constraints were largely "social, political and organizational rather than technological."[18] By the beginning of the nineteenth century, the Prussian army was beset by narrow-minded officers, supply difficulties, and rigid tactics, which were no longer offset by an exceptional warrior king.[19] It was no match for *La Grande Armée*, driven by enthusiasm and motivation, led by officers promoted primarily for merit, and commanded by a military genius.[20] Napoleon exploited these when he inflicted the humiliating defeat of Jena (1806) upon the Prussians.

Imposing *Levée en Masse* in 1793, the French National Convention created the means with which Napoleon would usher in a new era in the history of warfare. Until that time, the size and maneuverability of armies was limited by four factors. First, a large proportion of the population was exempt from service in order to ensure continued tax revenues, necessary for the conduct of war and the avoidance of civil strife. Second, disciplinary requirements prohibited fast-paced, complicated maneuvers. Third, troops had to also be controlled outside the battlefield in order to prevent mass desertions. The fourth limiting factor was lack of divisional infrastructure and staff.[21] The ranks of the new French armies were filled by men fighting for a common cause, respecting one another as fellow citizens, and led by a new breed of officers. Desertion rates dropped significantly, and when soldiers did desert it mattered less. Skirmish tactic and columns formations, followed invariably by bayonet charges, proliferated.[22] Also, the Imperial Army developed the organizational structure of the Corps, in effect small independent armies, which greatly increased French strategic flexibility. During these years, Napoleon laid down his principles of "numerical strength, deep strategic penetration and rapid concentration of force."[23] These were designed to annihilate opposing military forces and force the capitulation of an enemy.[24]

Though Napoleon implemented a staff system,[25] his was nevertheless a "one man show."[26] His staff processed information, wrote reports, and assisted in the issuance of orders but neither developed plans nor participated in the decision-making process. Neither did the staff have the ability to make independent decisions within the framework of his strategic intentions. Hence, when Napoleon's unique but human span of control failed to cope with the size and number of fronts, control broke down.[27] Commanders in the age of Napoleon could actually see most of the forces employed on the battlefield. At Jena, Napoleon was able to issue timely orders down to the regimental level.[28] The advent of the Industrial Revolution would change that characteristic as it would expand battlefields immeasurably.[29]

Napoleon's centralized style of command was less than revolutionary. Van Creveld argued that from a tactical point of view, Napoleon differed little from Marlborough or Frederick the Great. Like them, he did all his planning by himself, sharing only fractions of the plan with his generals and technically oriented staff. Only toward the end was he willing to allow critical observations of his operational plans. Napoleon did, however, delegate authority to the independent Corps; by fielding multiple independent organizations, he actually promoted a degree of decentralization and was afforded strategic flexibility.[30] His success, and their independence, depended on the degree to which his intentions had been understood by his lieutenants. Napoleon's extraordinary information-processing skills enabled accelerated decision-making cycles. It was a system that Napoleon alone could master; it was a reflection of him and his exceptional capabilities.[31]

THEORETICAL SEEDS

The ideas of the German Romantic Movement, which began to emerge toward the end of the eighteenth century, served as a basis for a critical analysis of ancien régime military theory.[32] The Romantic theorists believed that the world is the province of chance and human creativity and cannot be reduced to a Newtonian paradigm.[33] Thus, in a book published in the late 1790s, Berenhorst argued that wars are subject to the known, unknown, and uncontrollable. He challenged the practice of employing troops as automatons given the demonstrated importance of morale and patriotic fervor.[34] The Prussian reformer Scharnhorst attempted to combine the Enlightenment principles of reason, knowledge, judgment, and education with the Romantic ideals of independent will and creativity.[35] He argued that there were no scientific rules for war, only "correct concepts that are grounded in the nature of things or experience," the application of which is an art acquired through historical study and exercise.[36] The best way to prepare an officer for the demands of the battlefield is to teach him these *correct concepts* and then encourage him to think and make independent analysis and decisions.

Scharnhorst molded the next generation of Prussian officers through the Berlin Military Academy.[37] He taught them a theory of war that encompassed "the complexity of the political human and military conditions that formed reality . . . free un-dogmatic principles."[38] His disciples were of a new breed, possessing scientific and historical knowledge, self-confidence born of battlefield experience, sound judgment, and a critical mind. His most famous protégé was Carl von Clausewitz, whose ideas were significant to the future development of *Auftragstaktik* and the German command culture.[39] Clausewitz believed that war is the realm of human activity and therefore an art rather than a science. Indeed, dominated by the dynamics of actions and reactions, war resembles other social phenomena, such as commerce or politics.[40] Clausewitz concluded that due to its reciprocal nature and the significance of moral forces, warfare is governed by the unknown and the unforeseen. Hence, an invariable gap develops between planning and actual events.[41]

Clausewitz introduced the concept of friction in his seminal *On War*,[42] in order to analyze the uncontrollable and unforeseeable factors that dominate war.[43] Whereas his contemporaries, such as Lloyd and von Bulow, dreaded the accidental and the coincidental, Clausewitz believed that friction and chance afforded the genius commander invaluable opportunities.[44] The term "genius" in this context denotes not the exceptional but rather the ordinary individual possessing the qualities necessary for command.[45] The qualities he thought necessary for great commanders included boldness, initiative, and a propensity for risk taking balanced by education, imagination, and intellect.[46] Clausewitz believed, as did his mentor Scharnhorst, that the nature of war requires quick decision and flexible plans:

> Since all information and assumptions are open to doubt, and with chance at work everywhere, the commander continually finds that things are not as he expected. This is bound to influence his plans, or at least the assumptions underlying them. During an operation decisions have usually to be made at once; there may be no time to review the situation or even to think it through.[47]

Peter Paret argued that friction was one of the two Clausewitzian concepts adopted by the German army. Its centrality to the German culture of command has led some to attribute the origins of *Auftragstaktik* to Clausewitz.[48]

CONVERTING IDEAS INTO PRACTICE, 1806–1819

The Prussian reforms that gave rise to *Auftragstaktik,* especially the adoption of the concept of the Nation in Arms, occurred within a wider social and political context. The army became comparatively socially heterogenic, utilizing open-order tactics more suitable for untrained masses led by better educated and increasingly independent NCOs and officers. Acceptance of these reforms was far from universal as some feared the revolutionary ideas of La Grand Armeé more than they did its military might.

Though he had already begun to spread his ideas through the newly established military academy in Berlin (1801), it was the Jena-Auerstedt defeat that facilitated the acceptance of Scharnhorst's ideas in the army.[49] A special committee for reorganization of the military was formed in 1807, shortly after the war. Chaired by Scharnhorst, it soon demonstrated that it intended not to reinvigorate but rather to provide a substitute for the Fredrician system.[50] As part of these reforms, a general staff was established. Destined to be the most influential Prussian-German corps over the next century and a half, its origins were humble indeed. It was charged with preparing war plans, researching, and educating officers (primarily through historical case studies). Though given no formal command, the general staff soon became a clearinghouse for military knowledge.[51] Scharnhorst's Berlin academy played a significant role in these reforms. It was redesigned to prepare officers for higher staff positions; therefore, selection for it became gradually stricter, and written exams were introduced. Similarly, cadet schools were reformed and began accepting middle-class applicants. The selection and promotion process within the army began to favor merit over class. Moreover, many of the officers held responsible for the defeat were retired. Special attention was given to the training and education of NCOs, who were to become the backbone of the Prussian army. Here, too, selection was based on merit, and selected NCOs were even encouraged to apply to officer schools. Due to the special status conferred to officers and NCOs in Prussian society, the new system also increased social mobility.[52]

Tactics and training also were improved, and the number of elite *Jäger* light infantry regiments was increased. Field exercises and target practice replaced some of the old parade-ground drills, and new infantry drill regulations were issued in 1812.[53] These regulations advocated a "mixture of old linear formations with battalion columns and *tirallieur* tactics as used by the French."[54] The company, instead of the battalion, became the basic tactical unit. A new education system was designed in order to develop imaginative and independent leaders capable of leading these small units.[55] The regulations, reaffirming Scharnhorst's ideas, provided only general guidelines, leaving the rest to experience and common sense.[56] Though politically conservative and opposed to some of Scharnhorst's reforms, Yorck understood the necessity of granting soldiers greater latitude and independence on the battlefield.[57] Indeed, he was instrumental in introducing this concept in the new regulations.[58] In the 1810 Instructions for Light-Troops, he stated: "written directions cannot cover all details and the elaboration is left to the light brigade commanders."[59] That same year and under Yorck, the army performed a series of realistic maneuvers, which introduced ambushes and night attacks, requiring initiative and independence from junior commanders.[60] This attitude explains why and how the conservative Yorck and the reformer Scharnhorst could agree on the need to decentralize command:

> The tactical doctrine . . . was in agreement with the new dynamics of strategy and with the changed nature of war. If skirmishes and columns meant a loss of mechanical control, they also provided the commander with a new means to exploit the unforeseen. . . . Now, after a century and a half in which military

absolutism had neared perfection, some of the commander's tactical authority was again delegated to his subordinates, who passed on the increased freedom to the common soldier.[61]

Gneisenau took over Scharnhorst's duties in 1813. A veteran of the American Revolutionary War, he understood the importance of sharpshooters, small units, and the inherent motivational value of patriotism.[62] As chief of the general staff, he continued to perfect a command system that was based on concise general directives and emphasized subordinate initiative and independence.[63] The new foundations of the Prussian army designed by the reformers from 1806 through 1819 emphasized the power and importance of the individual.

However, the following decades saw the rise of counterrevolutionary forces, which endangered these achievements. For instance, since regiments were entrusted with officer selection, the aristocracy was able to circumvent the new selection and promotion standards. Similarly, the curriculum and acceptance standards to officer schools, with the exception of the Berlin war academy, remained basically unchanged. In addition, these counterrevolutionary forces successfully fought the campaign to abolish physical punishment and the new attitude toward discipline.[64] Nevertheless, reformists successfully converted the outdated Prussian military organization into a modern organization; its effectiveness was demonstrated in the Battle of the Nations (1813) and at Waterloo (1815). This success was due in part to the introduction of the earliest version of *Auftragstaktik* and the cultural changes it has brought. New ideas concerning war coupled with organizational change created a new military culture.

INSTITUTIONALIZING *AUFTRAGSTAKTIK*

Designated by some as the Father of *Auftragstaktik*, it was Helmuth von Moltke the Elder[65] who institutionalized the new approach to command.[66] His impact has been so significant that some have suggested he "invented a new system of command."[67] Others prefer to award the title to Scharnhorst, adding that Moltke merely promoted this style of command.[68] Yet, it was under Moltke's watch that "the system of directive command [mission command] was established as coherent theory . . . and enforced as official doctrine."[69] Moltke possessed great intellectual ability and is regarded as a true successor to the original reform movement. A moderate sociopolitical conservative, Moltke believed in change, modernization, and technology. He was sympathetic to the objectives of the liberal movement but believed that change should come from above and be carefully regulated.[70] Above all, Moltke was interested in pursuing practical aims rather than contemplating pure theory. Two questions emerge with regard to Moltke and *Auftragstaktik:* Where did his conviction in the concept originate from? How did he create a culture that enabled it?

Some explain that the origins of his convictions were both theoretical and practical. Military theory during the mid-nineteenth century had to adapt to larger armies and technological advances, such as the telegraph and the railroad, which affected mobilization and deployment. He endeavored to harness technology to support doctrine.[71] A limited number of rail lines and scarce rail facilities necessitated dispersion of the forces; consequently, the army was spread over hundreds of miles. This dispersion greatly diminished the ability to observe the battlefield in its entirety from any single command post.[72] Moltke's solution was to decentralize command. Essentially he marched his forces separately and united them on the battlefield. Moltke's ideas on decentralized command were integral to his overall concept of warfare and strategy. He considered himself a disciple of Clausewitz.[73] Like the master, Moltke recognized the importance of friction and chance in war and therefore rejected attempts to restrict individual initiative.

In the fashion of Napoleon, he sought a decisive battle of annihilation; unlike Napoleon, his plans never depended upon the abilities of a single genius commander. Moltke strove to create a local numerical superiority through envelopment maneuvers practiced by fast-moving converging armies. He also believed that mobilization and deployment could and should be carefully planned and that friction at this stage was manageable. Nevertheless, Moltke did not consider these ideas gospel; he was willing to employ any and all means in specific cases. Moltke also believed that once fighting has begun, planning gives way to general directives and subordinate initiative. Strategy, according to Moltke, was but a "system of expedients."[74] Strategy provides for and is dependent upon tactical opportunities. Victory depends on the ability of tactical-level subordinates to identify and exploit fleeting opportunities for the benefit of the strategic objective:

> Strategy affords tactics the means for fighting and the probability of winning by the direction of armies and their meetings at the place of combat. The demands of strategy grow silent in the face of a tactical victory and adapt themselves to the newly created situation. Strategy is a system of expedients. It

is . . . the continued development of the original leading thought in accordance with the constantly changing circumstance.[75]

The tactical result of an engagement forms the base for the strategic decisions . . . because victory or defeat in battle changes the situation to such a
degree that no human acumen is able to see beyond the first battle. Therefore
no plan of operation extends with any certainty beyond the first contact with
the main hostile force.[76]

Moltke saw *Auftragstaktik* as a key process in the complex dynamic between
strategy and tactics. Therefore, corps and even division commanders "must
judge the situation for themselves and must know how to act independently in
consonance with the general intention . . . taking the initiative is of the ut-
most value."[77] And

Prearranged designs (schema) collapse and only a proper estimate of the situation can show the commander the correct way. The advantage of the situation will never be fully utilized if subordinate commanders wait for orders. . . .
It will be generally more advisable to proceed actively and keep the initiative
than to wait to the law of the opponent.[78]

Moltke preferred decentralized command from a theoretical point of view but
also resorted to it out of practical considerations since, as in 1813, he too commanded a coalition army.[79] Such was the case in the Franco-Prussian War, when
Prussia fought alongside the armies of the North German Confederation.[80]
After that war, Moltke sought to combine the German armies, as he understood
that pursuance of a common objective and purpose were dependent upon unity
of doctrine, training, and logistics. His efforts were only partially successful, as
significant decisions were made in Berlin while the Saxons, Bavarians, and
Württembergers retained considerable autonomy.[81]

An additional practical consideration was the introduction of breech-
loading rifles, which had intensified infantry firepower and necessitated a
transformation of tactics. The new screen of rapid fire gave rise to a debate
concerning the conduct of future infantry offensives. The primary tactical
unit, once the battalion, became the company; company commanders were
consequently highly independent.[82] Though he did not advocate allowing them
the same degree of autonomy granted to corps and division commanders,
Moltke acknowledged that such a development would become necessary before too long. Moltke's enthusiasm for decentralized command may have also

stemmed from the comparatively weak status of the general staff. Until the 1866 campaign against Austria, the wars of Prussia were directed by the kaiser, with the general staff serving in an advisory capacity. It was during that war that the status of the general staff was strengthened and Moltke was authorized to issue orders to the army. His obscurity is manifested through the famous story of a divisional commander, who upon receiving an order from Moltke exclaimed: "It all seems in order, but who is General von Moltke?"[83] Though Moltke had orchestrated the campaign against France, his authority still derived primarily from his reputation, and his directives were ignored on more than one occasion. Thus, it could be argued that in contrast to Napoleon, Moltke did not actually choose his style of command; it was dictated to him by the realities of his era.[84]

A successful implementation of Moltke's ideas concerning command depended on the general staff; consequently, its size and purview were greatly expanded. Officers of the Great General Staff (*Grosser Generalstab*) were assigned to corps and divisional staffs (*Truppengeneralstab*), which was the Field General Staff. Though designated as advisors, their expertise and prestige ensured that field commanders would rely on their advice regarding planning and operations. The commander and general staff representative were expected to function as a team and complement each other. However, if disagreements arose, the latter could have their objections officially recorded and even resign. Also, though relatively junior in both age and rank (major/captain) to the commander, this experience actually served as a test of their leadership skills.[85] Through this network, Moltke ensured that units could grasp and follow the intent of the general staff. Subordinates were given nothing but the necessary information, a statement of intent, and a mission. They were allowed freedom to realize these objectives and were trusted to conduct themselves as the commander would.[86] This genius system allowed for local initiative while ensuring unity of purpose; the German army could enjoy the benefits of decentralization while maintaining control.

The general staff was a relatively small organization. The officers assigned to it were intimately acquainted and enjoyed prestige and rapid promotions. Mistakes often led to constructive criticism, allowing the officers freedom to experiment and learn.[87] This atmosphere was nurtured in the school for general staff officers, the famous *Kriegsakademie*. During the tenure of von Peuker as Prussian chief of military training in the 1860s, the academy became an intellectual center, "the seat of higher military learning that would originate new ideas and spread them throughout the army."[88] Academy graduates served six months in a branch other than their own and were then posted to the general staff for a one-year trial period. Many *Kriegsakademie* instructors were considered "rising stars," as the German army did not subscribe to the famous dichotomy between "those who teach and those who do."[89] Also, classes were composed of students from all branches in order to facilitate communication and transcend the traditional branch boundaries.[90]

Communication was another central issue for Moltke, who considered the flow of information "between headquarters and units . . . absolutely necessary for proper cooperation of all for a common purpose."[91] Consequently, the manner and technique of issuing written orders was given a high priority in the academy. Using an order template, officers were trained to include only a mission statement, a statement of intent, disposition of enemy and friendly forces, and special instructions (when necessary). The academy emphasized clear and concise orders that dictated little and left the details of execution to subordinates.[92] However, written orders were issued only to corps and divisions, which had *Generalstab* representatives and had sufficient time for staff duties. Battalions and companies were to be issued verbal orders.[93] Moltke distinguished between operational and tactical command, believing that the former should be conducted from headquarters:

> In a large battle it will usually be irrelevant whether the supreme commander views any single part of the battlefield or not. He must act on the basis of reports and will often have a clearer conception of the situation if he receives his information from all parts of the battlefield in the same manner. He can then calmly reach his decisions far from the confusing effect of the fighting.[94]

Gone were the days of Napoleon and Fredrick, when commanders could observe the whole battlefield from their command post. Therefore, Moltke opted for delegation: "Commanders of units to be committed must receive definite tasks (*Aufträge*) but not be limited in the choice of means to accomplish them."[95] In order to assimilate these concepts in the army, Moltke published a series of essays on tactics and operations and cultivated personal relationships with key army commanders.[96] For the same purpose, he also recounted instructive stories. One often-repeated story told of a major who justified a bad decision by claiming to having been following orders, to which Prince Frederick Charles replied: "His Majesty made you a major because he believed you would know when not to follow orders."[97] Moltke's influence increased gradually, and by the end of the Wars of German Unification his ideas were well rooted. By 1870, it could be said that by and large the army had been molded in accordance with his ideas.[98] No discussion of Moltke's style of command would be complete without the extraordinary description of him lying on a sofa calmly reading a book while the army mobilized to fight Austria. J. F. C. Fuller found this image disturbing, stating that Moltke had "abdicated his command."[99] Moreover, Fuller faulted Moltke for relying so heavily on subordinates' initiative: "On August 31 and September 1 [1870] he never issued an order except for a few suggestions to General Blumenthal. . . . He never foresaw the encirclement of the French which was due to their stupidity and the initiative of the Prussian army commanders. . . . Moltke is not a general to copy but to study."[100] Alternatively, it could be maintained that Moltke facilitated Prussian initiative and exploitation of French mistakes; in that regard, chance was actually an integral part of his plan.

TRAINING AND SERVICE IN MOLTKE'S ARMY, 1870–1914

The German general staff led the *Kaiserheer* by setting standards, educating, and injecting new ideas into its ranks. However, the army came under its purview only in times of war; in peace, authority over the army devolved on Corps commanders and the War Ministry. It is therefore necessary to examine the Prussian army independently. What were its qualities? And how well did it prepare for war?

A dramatic population increase in the mid-nineteenth century enabled the army to apply strict selection criteria and still recruit 600,000 men annually, double the necessary number of recruits. The army instituted a high-standard, intensive training program in order to maintain its combat readiness. Commanders were given free reign over training, so long as they followed the regulations.[101] Though this freedom diversified tactics and doctrine, it encouraged independence.[102] Most officers were products of mediocre cadet schools that provided a broad education but neglected their military education. Those graduating at the top of the class were commissioned while the rest enjoyed another nine-month study period in one of the war schools. Upon graduation from these schools, they were posted to regiments on temporary commission and, if vetted by their colleagues, finally commissioned. The pressure to perform continued even after a commission was granted, since their training skills were closely and continuously monitored. In addition to this duty, officers were expected to serve in another branch for a period of time in order to obtain a multibranch attitude. Also, they were expected to be able to perform the duties of their superiors. Promotion was based on performance and proven abilities; if removed from the promotion lists, they were expected to retire.[103] The conduct of large-scale field maneuvers simulating battlefield conditions served to both hone their skills and provide a testing ground for new ideas.[104]

The 1881 testimony of one Graham Lumley, a British national who had served as a German cavalry officer, before a committee of British officers offers a glimpse of that life. His account provides a detailed description of the rigorous training and difficult examinations candidates underwent in order to earn a commission in the cavalry *(Cavalrie)*. Lumley told of the independence squadron commanders (captains) enjoyed in training their men and making their units "military efficient."[105] According to Lumley, a commanding officer (colonel) interferes only if he thinks that "the efficiency and uniformity of the regiment is threatened by the system adopted in his squadron by any particular Captain."[106] Captains adopted the same approach toward their subordinates, and "when handing over classes to the respective officers, laying down certain principles which he wishes them to carried out, he seldom interferes, unless some egregious incapability, or want of military principles is displayed."[107] Lumley's testimony provides a vivid account of how *Auftragstaktik* was practiced during the training of junior officers:

> The Commander is handed a letter containing the particulars. . . . How the orders are carried out is entirely left by the officers receiving them. The officer who had set the work with other superior officers ride about and observe the doing of each party, and when he thinks operations have reached a climax . . . he . . . assemble[s] the officers engaged. Criticism of what has taken place is then held. . . . Superior officers . . . pass their remarks upon what was done, and very clearly demonstrate whether the way the operation has been conducted was in accordance with their views or not. . . . The officers are able to form a very concise opinion of the success they have had.[108]

In addition, Lumley describes the issuance of orders during brigade-level maneuvers, demonstrating how mission orders were used:

> The General assembles all the officers, reads them his orders and acquaints them with the way he proposes to carry them out. He then disposes with his advance guard arrangement and gives to each Colonel his special instruc-

tions, who like wise inform their officers of their intentions and allot to the Captains their specific duties; these in the same manner instruct Lieutenants, and they, again inform the men of the general object in view and give instruction to the NCOs.[109]

Both passages suggest that *Auftragstaktik* had been institutionalized through order-issuance and communication procedures as well as a system of training that encouraged officer independence and initiative. This system was strengthened by close relationships among officers, characterized by Lumley as "members of family."[110] The contrast between some of the German and the British practices surfaced in a debate that followed the testimony. The following conversation demonstrates one of the conceptual gaps between the two organizations:

> *Colonel Blundell, Grenadier Guards:* May I ask whether the junior officers have to personally drill the squads?
> *Captain Lumley:* Yes they do; every command is given by the officer personally on different occasion.
> *Colonel Blundell:* Is not the excessive cultivation of the junior officer somewhat against the cultivation of the NCO?

Captain Lumley responded in detail, explaining that while NCOs train new recruits and oversee basic training and discipline, officers instruct them in critical battle skills and tactics. His puzzled audience remained unconvinced, questioning:

> *Colonel Blundell:* I must say, unless you give responsibilities to NCOs on minor matters you seem to lose one of the strongest elements of discipline. . . . If the NCO is practically eliminated there is a danger of losing discipline.
> *Captain Lumley:* No, quite the contrary. NCOs have more influence over the men with the duties allotted to them. . . . [He goes on to provide a detail description of NCO daily duties—au.]. But the instruction of drill is personally done by the Officer. I think an NCO disciplinarian . . . can do that much better than an officer whose capabilities should be as a leader and instructor. . . . I never saw in Germany what I saw in France during the war, there every prisoner that was taken put the blame on the incapacity of the officer. . . . You never would hear a Prussian say that. He could never say so as the officers teach the men everything personally, they (the officers) are expected to know every man personally where he comes from, who is his father.[111]

The British officers' inability, in this case, to comprehend a system that required its officers to know and train their men, serves as a strong indication of the uniqueness of German military culture. Lumley's observations are validated through the experience of another British officer, Captain Henry Hozier, who rode with the *Cavalrie* in the Franco-Prussian war. He was struck by the "intellectual capacity" of the Prussian officer and the efficiency and flexibility of the cavalry units.[112]

THE TACTICAL DEBATES, 1870–1914

After the dust settled on the Wars of German Unification (1864, 1866, 1870–1871), it became apparent that the continuous technological advances were going to change the face of war. The increased range, accuracy, and capacity of both artillery and infantry weapons made the old offensive tactics prohibitively costly and forced all three branches back to the drawing boards.[113] Several studies offering a critical analysis of contemporary warfare were published following the Franco-Prussian war. Captain Albrecht von Boguslawski published a book titled *A Tactical Deduction from the War of 1870–71*. Another important work on the topic was Major Wilhelm von Scherff's *Studies in the New Tactics of Infantry*. Both stressed the importance of breechloaders, predicted the end of mass infantry attacks, and recognized the increasing effectiveness of the defensive. More conservative authors, such as Alexander von Pape, wartime commander of the First Prussian Guard Division, missed no opportunity to oppose attempts to allow junior officers to exercise initiative.[114]

Toward the turn of the century, revisionists formed another group that was further subdivided into proponents of *Normaltaktik* (standardized tactics) and supporters of *Auftragstaktik* (mission tactics). The latter emphasized independent action and wide troop dispersion when traversing an open battlefield; the former sought synchronization of movement and firepower, which depended on maintenance of control and therefore argued in favor of standardized formations. Both agreed that the new battlefield put a premium on the combination of firepower, movement, and the final effect of a bayonet assault; both rejected the reliance on masses marching in battalion-size close-order formations or on firepower alone. They disagreed on best way to control fire and movement during an attack.[115]

Supporters of *Auftragstaktik* believed that force composition should always be determined by situational factors, such as the mission, terrain, and enemy. However, the great freedoms they afforded junior commanders required trained troops, cohesive units, and superior leadership.[116] The most distinguished of the *Auftragstaktik* proponents was Colonel Sigismund von Schlichting. As a commander, he largely ignored the regulations and trained his troops to spread out and fire at random from a distance. Schlichting's troops specialized in using terrain for cover against frontal attacks and deep infantry formations. He believed in large flanking maneuvers and in the critical role of tactics to decide battles. In that respect, he saw himself as a disciple of Moltke; also like Moltke, he was a firm believer in delegating authority to junior officers. His extreme approach was contested by traditionalists such as Jacob Meckel and von Pape, who feared that his methods would have a negative effect on discipline. They believed that battlefield discipline depended on standard formations.[117] However, opposition notwithstanding, the 1888 infantry drill regulations were an affirmation of Schlichting's ideas.

The 1888 regulations discontinued the use of company and battalion columns. They "would shift into skirmish lines at about 1,500 meters and then dispersed into battle groups at 600 meters firing at will."[118] Tactical decisions were delegated to junior officers and NCOs. The regulations allowed commanders to choose a formation based on specific battlefield requirements; many conservative officers preferred to employ close-order platoon columns.[119] Ironically, the decentralized training system that encouraged the independence of the officer corps and allowed commanders' freedom in the conduct of training also facilitated their circumvention of the new regulations.[120] A gap developed between the official position represented by the regulations and the actual practices in the army. The majority of the officers serving from 1870 through 1890 were staunch traditionalists who rejected social reforms. Despite the regulations, they continued to practice massed columns formations and parade ground tactics and devoted little or no time to skirmishing. Also, they rejected both technological advancements and the tactical implications derived from them. For example, in the late 1880s, a committee comprised of traditionalists turned down rifle magazines, arguing that soldiers would consume their ammunition at too early a stage and lose heart soon after. The attitudes toward the machine guns also reflected the army's resistance to change.[121]

The rejection of tactical innovation and new technologies, despite the experience of the Franco-Prussian War, may have stemmed from the sociopolitical structural transformations rocking the army. These changes had a negative impact on the attitudes of the two primary branches, the cavalry and the infantry. The cavalry, the citadel of nobility, clung desperately to old traditions.

Bourgeoisie infantry officers seeking social acceptance also adopted traditional positions. Consequently, the tactical debate carried on through the turn of the century. Foreign military attachés observing German maneuvers noted that "they are old as the wars with Napoleon."[122] The kaiser himself complained on one occasion that "When I am in East Prussia I find one tactic, when in Metz another, and when I go to Hanover I find something else entirely, which is in itself different from Silesia."[123] The combined effect of the lessons drawn from the Russo-Japanese war (1904–1905) and the chaotic state of training resulted in the issuance of the 1906 infantry drill regulations. The new regulations reaffirmed the importance accorded to *Auftragstaktik* in the 1888 edition, albeit in a new technological environment. Efforts to standardize doctrine and training during that year on the basis of the new regulations were only partially successful. Moreover, it would seem that the German infantry attacking the Belgian fort of Liege (1914) either ignored or forgot these regulations and the teachings of Moltke and Schlichting. The infantry attacked in mass, shoulder to shoulder, suffering many casualties and attained only some of its objectives. The failure of the infantry to practice uniform, open-order tactics contributed significantly to the failure in Belgium and therefore to that of the Schlieffen Plan itself.[124]

STOSSTRUPPEN, 1916–1918

Scholars have long debated the principles of command at the root of the famous Schlieffen Plan. Some opined that the plan constituted a significant deviation from Moltke's principles of *Auftragstaktik* as it enforced too many constraints on the field commanders and left little room for friction and local initiative.[125] Others have faulted Schlieffen for failing to maintain control through available communication technology, in contrast to the tradition of Scharnhorst and Moltke.[126] In contrast, some have suggested that the plan merely represented a statement of intent, never intended to restrict the manner of execution. Also they argued that the risks it carried were no greater than those taken by Moltke the Elder.[127] However, the Schlieffen Plan was indeed rigid and detailed; moreover, as Robert Foley noted, Schlieffen himself had often criticized Moltke for not exercising sufficient control.[128] Though he encouraged subordinate independence, he believed that higher command must dictate more detailed directives.[129]

For various reasons, at the Eastern Front the Germans were more successful at developing their traditional mobile warfare and expressed *Auftragstaktik* more clearly. For example, historian Citino recalls a story told by Major General Francois, the brilliant cavalry commander most responsible for victory at the decisive Battle of Tannenberg:

> In January 1915, I arrived on the western front and reported to the Kaiser in Charleville. The Kaiser received me in the garden of the villa. He said some very appreciative things about Gumbinnen, Tannenberg and the Masurian Lakes and the defense against the second Russian offensive in October and November 1914. . . . He explained to me how things stood on the western front, and then told me, with a friendly laugh, "Now with God's help, Francois, you'll do a good job here too. But rein yourself in. You're too independent." Francois' punishment for repeated disobedience to orders that made no sense amounted to promotion to command 8th Army in the fall of 1915.[130]

As mobile operations gave way to trench warfare in the west, the German army strategic command lost some of its flexibility, as did its opponents, and became rigid and centralistic.[131] Communication technologies such as the telephone and radio facilitated greater interference in the execution of missions.[132] However, as opposed to their opponents, the Germans did not propose to break the stalemate by using technological marvels such as the British tank. Instead, they exploited a cultural emphasis on learning and experimentation with new tactics. New technologies served new tactical concepts; small, highly trained infantry units enjoying unprecedented firepower were unleashed against the enemy trench lines. While technology was instrumental, the decisive edge was attained through a daring new approach to command and control. For the first time, German tactics relied on quality rather than quantity, striving for victory through superior skills, tactics, and leadership at the junior officer and NCO level.

The efforts to breach the stalemate of World War I trench warfare had been ultimately successful due to general staff sponsorship of new initiatives, such as those of the relatively junior Major Kaslow and Hauptmann (Captain) Rohr. The result was a new type of infantry unit: the Stosstrupp (Shock Troops). Employed on a large scale in 1918, the new tactics achieved the (arguably) most successful tactical breakthrough of the war. These assault squads were small, specialized units of eight men commanded by an NCO. Instead of the rifle and bayonet, they were equipped with a variety of weapons that enhanced their firepower by an order of magnitude. Their arsenal included mortars, machine guns, grenades, flamethrowers, pistols, carbines, and later also submachine guns. Highly maneuverable, they acted independently, exploiting fleeting opportunities. Squad leaders were trained to take the initiative within the framework of the overall mission and the commander's intent.[133] Thus, this system expanded the Moltkean system. Moltke had instituted formal *Auftragstaktik* to senior command and merely encouraged it in the lower levels. The development of assault squads, which expanded its use all the way down to the NCO level due to the tactical reality, was a revolution from below, one that emerged at the tactical level.

Bruce Gudmundsson has explained that the German army's ability to institute change and innovation was a result of a unique military culture and a decentralized tradition—also, a high degree of trust, education, and professionalism enjoyed by officers and NCOs.[134] Martin Samuels has opined that the speed of adaptation and change exhibited by the German Army of that period suggests an existence of efficient learning mechanisms and effective communication between frontline units and higher command.[135] Nevertheless, the German high command proved unable to convert hard-won tactical breakthroughs into operational and strategic victories.[136] The failure resulted from the German army's inability to offer corresponding developments in strategic planning, logistics, and mobility in order exploit the tactical success. After the war, the reconstructed German army conducted a thorough analysis of the war and internalized the key lessons from the 1918 campaign.

THE BLITZKRIEG ERA, 1918–1945

Two competing narratives have emerged concerning the development of the German Blitzkrieg during the interwar period.[137] Since *Auftragstaktik* is an essential component of this doctrine, it is important to understand this debate and its implications.

The first school proclaims Blitzkrieg to be a revolutionary military doctrine combining advanced communications technology and new weapon platforms with new tactical concepts. Proponents of this school single out Heinz Guderian as the driving force behind the creation of the German armored forces and its doctrine. Further, they hold that, inspired primarily by the British military theorists J. F. C. Fuller and B. H. Liddell-Hart, Guderian had to struggle against a reactionary military establishment. Indeed, so entrenched was the establishment that it took Hitler's far-sightedness and enthusiasm to realize Guderian's groundbreaking concept, the panzer division.[138] Proponents of this narrative concede that certain Blitzkrieg characteristics, such as offensiveness and envelopment, may have been inherited from traditional German doctrine. However, they argue that the emphasis on disruption of command and control rather than on physical annihilation was innovative and even revolutionary.[139]

The second, revisionist, school considers Blitzkrieg a representation of German military theory, encompassing both the teachings of Moltke and lessons of the Great War. It is based "on a very old and very traditional view of war."[140] According to this narrative, the development of Blitzkrieg was a collective effort that even included men labeled Old Guard by Guderian. One such individual was von Seeckt, who was instrumental in the development of the interwar German army and doctrine. Another was von Beck, who issued the famous *Truppenführung* (1933–1934) regulations that served as the basis of Wehrmacht doctrine. Revisionists acknowledge Guderian's significant contribution to the creation of the panzer division but deny his claim for exclusivity concerning the advocacy of mobile and combined arms warfare or his struggle against an old-fashioned institution. The proponents of this school argue that Blitzkrieg objectives were congruent with the principles of German strategy as far back as Clausewitz: mobile warfare endeavoring to encircle and envelope the main enemy force followed by its physical annihilation. They consider Blitzkrieg a technologically advanced application of *storm troop* tactics.[141]

Like its *Stosstrupp* predecessor, the panzer division represented a new type of maneuver-based combined arms formation; only this time it enabled decisive victory on the operational level. Its reliance on speed and surprise was on a different order of magnitude requiring a corresponding flexible system of command and control. *Auftragstaktik,* the unique German cultural development reconstituted at the end of the Great War, was chosen and played a central role in Blitzkrieg doctrine and success. However, due to the speed and muscle of the panzer forces, tactical command was expected not only to exploit opportunities but to create them. This marriage between mobile warfare and *Auftragstaktik* came naturally to the Wehrmacht, as Seeckt's interwar army taught and practiced the principles of mobility-based offensives and the traditional *Auftragstaktik*. Seeckt's field service regulations *Leadership and Battle* (1921–1923) emphasized subordinate initiative as well as the effects of fog and friction.[142] *Reichswehr* training programs were designed to create a professional cadre; thus, it provided the necessary skills, knowledge, and practice for NCOs and officers to command one or two levels above their rank. Also, the army adopted the general staff practice of cross-branch training and made it mandatory for all soldiers.[143] The size and composition limitations imposed on the army by the Versailles Treaty strengthened already existing *Auftragstaktik* tendencies. In addition, it was intended to serve as a *Führerheer*, an army of leaders, in an eventual expansion of the German armed forces.

The regulations issued a decade later, which would serve the Wehrmacht, were based on the foundations of the 1923 regulations. The 1933 *Troop Leadership* (*Truppenführung*) is considered by one author to be "one of the most important military expressions of doctrine in modern history."[144] It combined the best of the German military tradition with the new dimensions of maneuver warfare. *Troop Leadership* carried *Auftragstaktik* through another evolutionary step. The regulations detailed the expected approach to command extending its application to the lowliest private. Although the term *Auftragstaktik* was still not used, ten paragraphs were devoted to its principles.[145] The following comments made by senior Wehrmacht officers after World War II are illustrative:

> It has always been the particular forte of German leadership to grant wide scope to the self-dependence of subordinate commanders—to allot them tasks which leave the method of execution to the discretion of the individual. From time immortal, certainly since Moltke the elder's day—this principle has distinguished Germany's military leadership from that of other armies.[146]

> Generally, the German high commanders rarely or never reproached their subordinates unless they made a terrible blunder. . . . They left him room for initiative and did not reprimand him unless he did something very wrong. This went down to the individual soldier, who was praised for developing initiative.[147]

The Wehrmacht was able to implement these regulations due to the modified and improved Prussian organizational system. This system reinforced values such as trust, professionalism, and initiative through processes of selection, training, promotion, reward, and education designed to enhance familiarity and cohesiveness.[148]

The fast-paced decentralized nature of mobile armored warfare posed a significant communication and coordination challenge for which the radio proved a magical solution. It was a classic example of technology employed in the service of doctrine, rather than the all too familiar and unfortunate reverse dynamic. By 1939, radio technology had advanced sufficiently to be of tactical use; it could facilitate communications between large formations and between individual vehicles.[149] The Germans developed the principles necessary for a radio-based command. Radios were instrumental to the practice of *Auftragstaktik* as they not only expedited decision-making cycles but afforded lower levels of command a more comprehensive understanding of the larger picture. To the panzer generals, it served as an instrument of control without relegating them to the confinement of headquarters. Just as in the days of Napoleon, they could assess the situation firsthand and exercise leadership by example or boost troop morale by their mere appearance. This development led historian Martin van Creveld to remark cynically that: "a hefty pair of binoculars slung over one's shoulder was elevated into a status symbol that no commander could afford to be without."[150]

Blitzkrieg panzer commanders, such as Rommel and Guderian, exercised their own unique version of command, one that can be described as a combination of *Auftragstaktik* and forward command. Some writers have praised this style as an effective approach allowing commanders to monitor situations closely without having to relinquish control. Others, such as Jonathan House, have opined that the presence of higher commanders inhibits subordinate initiative while tempting the former to micromanage situations. In addition, it exposed the commander to undue risk. More important, a breakdown in communications would render commanders impotent and ineffective.[151] Harsher criticism was offered by Shimon Naveh, who labeled this style "command from the saddle." He concluded that it substituted strategic understanding for sheer opportunism, overstretching field commanders' independence and ultimately collapsing the entire German command system, which was based on a delicate balance.[152] A more evenhanded analysis was offered by Richard Simpkin, who pointed out that commanders must strike a balance between the need to assess situations firsthand and the aforementioned disadvantages of leaving the command post.[153]

There is, however, a consensus among authors concerning the contribution of *Auftragstaktik* to the Wehrmacht tactical and operational excellence during the initial stages of the war.[154] Nevertheless, bad strategy that led to setbacks on the Eastern Front and increased resistance on the Western Front soon put Germany in a difficult strategic predicament. Hitler gradually lost what little trust he had in his generals and began to exercise closer control over the field units through a directive that forbade divisions to attack or withdraw without consulting first with the Führer.[155] The death of German *Auftragstaktik*, on the strategic and perhaps operational levels, occurred on the Eastern Front in December 1941. After the Red Army halted the Germans at the gates of Moscow, Hitler issued his famous "stand fast" order and assumed command of OKH (*Oberkommando des Heeres*), the headquarters responsible for the entire front.[156] His first order of business was to demand detailed reports from all commanders down to the divisional level. Hitler asked to be informed of any failure to follow orders or complete missions and then fired some generals for effect, including Heinz Guderian. The latter was dismissed by the commander of Army Group East, Gunther von Kluge, for having exercised his professional judgment and ordering a tactical retreat.[157] This marked the beginning of the end of the German way of war. Though on the tactical level *Auftragstatik* would weather Hitler and the war, it simply ceased to exist on the strategic level, and to some degree on the operational level.

Auftragstaktik suffered also from a steady decline in combat effectiveness as mounting casualties necessitated lower recruitment standards and shorter periods of training.[158] However, despite quantitative and qualitative manpower difficulties, withdrawals, and defeats, the German army never ceased to exist as an effective fighting force. Its decentralized tradition facilitated organized and effective resistance even while the supreme command had all but collapsed and its field units comprised a ragtag collection of soldiers. The ability of junior officers and NCOs to transform individuals into effective fighting units and lead them successfully into battle was a final demonstration of and tribute to the power and effectiveness of *Auftragstaktik*.[159]

CONCLUSION: THE GERMAN WAY OF COMMAND

Though decentralized command was practiced by many commanders throughout history, it had been a reflection of an individual style. The Prussian-German army systematically developed it into a comprehensive body and integrated it into doctrine and practice. *Auftragstaktik* was the German response to both the genius of Napoleon and the unavoidable friction and fog inherent to the phenomena of war. By successfully adapting these ideas into their military culture, the Germans were able to transcend personal style, units, and time.[160]

Auftragstaktik was a product of specific Prussian and German historical circumstances and forces that produced a unique strategic mind-set and military culture. It has developed top-down as well as bottom-up almost in parallel. It would be wrong to assume that the final outcome was predetermined; mission command was developed through the collective efforts of capable individuals who understood the nature of warfare and command and devised a system best suited to meet the challenges they presented. Daniel Hughes was probably correct in stating that "*Auftragstaktik* was more than a system of command; it was part of a particular life style typical of Prussian officers for more than a century."[161] This latter point is crucial to understanding the difficulties faced by contemporary modern Western militaries, possessing different traditions of command and historical experiences, attempting to revive and adopt this style of command.

THE PURPOSE OF CHAPTERS 4–6 is to identify the distinct traditions of command in the U.S., British, and Israeli armies prior to the adoption of mission command. For that purpose, Part II will chart the circumstances that shaped the strategic and military culture that led to the emergence of these different command approaches. The charting of these traditions of command will afford a better understanding of their influence over adaptation of the local variant of mission command.

In order to explore the unique culture of each army, this section examines significant events and individuals throughout the evolutionary process. Specifically, the historical inquiry focuses on battles, prominent leaders, and critical institutions, such as the general staff. The underlying assumption is that the creation of a tradition of command was influenced by these as well as by other factors, such as national character and geostrategic position.

Part II therefore includes three chapters, each of which is dedicated to a different army. Each of these chapters includes a historical analysis of the evolution of command in its respective army. Part II concludes with a comparison of the data using Schien's model for understanding organizational culture. This analysis will include a comparison of the three armies against the ideal type of mission command in regard to basic assumptions, values, and artifacts.

4 INSPIRED BY CORPORATE PRACTICES: AMERICAN ARMY COMMAND TRADITIONS

THE CONTINENTAL ARMY was born on June 14, 1775, with the passing of a reso-
lution by the Continental Congress authorizing "ten companies of expert
riflemen" earmarked to assist the New Englanders besieging Boston. Congress
then appointed George Washington to command the new army. A veteran
British officer of the French and Indian War, he sought to create a regular army.
Though it fought well, by the battle of Yorktown (1781) and the end of the War
of Independence, the Continental Army had been reduced to some 600 men.
Its numbers would swell again to fight the British, Mexicans, and Indians during the first half of the nineteenth century, but it would remain relatively small
until the Civil War.[1]

Like the British, the new American republic was averse to a large standing
army, preferring instead to rely on militia.[2] A professional army was rejected
because the Founding Fathers believed it would pose a threat to liberal ideals
and because they abhorred the central (federal) authority it served. These ideals were sustained for nearly a century: following the 1812 war against Britain,
the U.S. Navy protected American shores while land campaigns were fought
against the relatively weak Indians and Mexicans.[3] Indeed, until the end of the
nineteenth century, Americans considered the military profession a necessary evil. The army was expected to conduct operations other than war; major
conflicts would be fought by citizen soldiers. The underlying assumption was
that the military profession required no specialized education and could thus
be carried out by anyone. Individual initiative was considered superior to the
traditional military discipline; the militia system that encouraged it was believed to embody the American ideals. Since militia units were sponsored by

the various states, the system also achieved the purpose of weakening the power of the federal government. Indeed, these sentiments nearly resulted in the elimination of West Point in 1837.[4]

Established in 1802, West Point was an engineering school modeled after the French *École Polytechnique*.[5] A small enclave representing the closest thing to military professionalism America had, it too reflected antimilitary professionalism. The French influence was manifest also in the military theory taught in the academy. Dennis Mahan, its most famous teacher and scholar, was a student of Napoleonic warfare. The most popular and influential military theorist in the academy was the Swiss officer Antoine Jomini.[6] Mahan taught the generation of officers who would later lead both sides of the Civil War. Though advocating "seizing initiative through aggressive action," Mahan was critical of Napoleon's costly battles, preferring instead less costly tactics.[7] Though the academy trained cadets as engineers, they were also given basic military education and were consequently in high demand in the war with Mexico (1848–1849) and in the Civil War (1861–1865). West Point emphasized character building and such virtues as loyalty, honor, and courage. Cultivated from above, West Pointers were an elite group sharing a common worldview and a strong sense of commitment similar to British aristocratic Etonians. However, "there was no intellectual questioning, no real curiosity . . . or curiosity to seek out new fields of knowledge." Mathematics was by far the most important subject; other topics were studied through memorization.[8] Indeed, even the acclaimed Civil War tactician and strategist Robert E. Lee concentrated predominantly on engineering studies at West Point.

Some of the difficulties encountered during the Civil War stemmed from an absence of a shared doctrine and knowledge of proper staff work necessary to support the decision-making process. Unlike in the Prussian army, ingenuity and creativity remained local and uncoordinated until General Ulysses S. Grant established the General Headquarters (GHQ) in 1864.[9] This was so because even the professional officers had learned "how to lead a 50 man cavalry squadron in the West, but nothing else."[10] Staff work was conducted by amateurs who were forced to learn the hard way.[11] Neither General Robert E. Lee nor George Mead enjoyed the benefits of operational planning or information-processing functions at Gettysburg (1863).[12]

During the Civil War, factors such as terrain, size of armies, and weapon technologies complicated control. Commanders were therefore forced to resort to Napoleonic decision-making and control methods. Essentially, brigade-level commanders could influence an engagement only through manipulation of reserves. Due to the absence of staff work and common doctrine, the war was "determined by local expedients and improvisations rather than by the master plan of the commander in chief."[13] Nevertheless, West Pointers formed a small group whose shared experience and education, however limited, enabled trust and understanding and allowed for a primary form of decentralized command.

Both sides managed their resources admirably, but the North enjoyed tremendous resource superiority. The South fell back on the skills of its men and officers. It was Grant who transformed the attrition nature of the war by consolidating his resources and pressuring Lee on multiple fronts simultaneously. While he slowly crushed Lee, he unleashed General William T. Sherman in the West in order to destroy the Southern interior.[14] The Civil War was the first in which Americans fielded large armies and is considered the first war to combine Napoleonic warfare with the means afforded by the Industrial Revolution.[15]

During the following two decades, the strength of the army was reduced to a mere 30,000, charged primarily with policing the West and subduing the Native American tribes.[16] The Indian Wars in the West marked the return of the American army to familiar patterns of overcoming the elements and fighting guerrilla and counterinsurgency warfare. Officers such as George A. Custer were granted near complete autonomy in the vast Western territories. It was Custer's image, bravely leading his Seventh Cavalry into catastrophe, which came to symbolize late-nineteenth-century American romanticism.

CREATING A MODERN MILITARY

At the onset of the Spanish-American War (1898), the American army suffered from "slow promotions and the dispersed state of the Army, which had created over 70 operational posts during the various Indian campaigns [which] discouraged interest in military innovation and created little opportunity to practice handling larger numbers of troops at the divisional, brigade or even regimental levels."[17] Its commander, the famous Indian fighter Nelson A. Miles, was a conservative who had little interest in European military ideas or in reforms. He believed in the militia system and preferred to leave things the way they were.[18] However, the army performed poorly. The Dodge Committee established to investigate the failings of the army during that war recommended a number of reforms, including the formation of a general staff system.

Influenced by Emory Upton's survey of the Prussian general staff, Secretary of War Elihu Root accepted these recommendations.[19] With the support of President Theodore (Teddy) Roosevelt, he introduced the 1903 General Staff Act, which "strengthened executive control over the army and promoted greater professionalism."[20] The purview of the new general staff included planning for national defense, coordination, preparation of readiness reports, and advising the secretary of war and the field commanders. However, the new system proved ineffective because "no one knew what to do."[21] The effectiveness of the general staff was further reduced by the 1916 National Defense Act, which restricted its activities to war planning.[22] Thus, the new act served to widen the gap between the American general staff system and its Prussian equivalent.

The Root reforms also introduced a new combined arms education system for officers and reorganized the Fort Leavenworth General Service and Staff College. Selection to the Staff College, in the period following World War I, was based on recommendation and efficiency reports rather than an examination system. It was intended that the college would prepare officers for divisional and higher staff positions. But attendance was considered only important rather than crucial for one's career. The curriculum was based on French materials and doctrine adopted during the Great War. Despite its efforts, the college failed to reach the Prussian level of training, and its graduating captains were considered "pale copies of the lieutenant colonels produced by the *Kriegsakademie*."[23] Another institution established by the Root reforms was the Army War College in Washington, DC. It was designated as a "preparatory general staff" school designed to afford students with supervised general staff tasks. Initially founded as a "high visibility high prestige institution that would attract the Army's best," the college became a posting for retiring officers.[24] During the interwar period, lectures began to substitute for independent work. Also, the school began to emphasize broader themes, such as international relations, economics, industry, and management, which in later years proved to be invaluable. However, the American colleges were also encouraging contemporary industrial management ideas, emphasizing efficiency through centralized control processes. In contrast to the *Kriegsakademie*, American higher military education institutions did not require entrance exams nor did they offer an intensive three-year military studies program. Similarly, they did not become a screening tool for promotion and failed to attain the high status required for attracting the best candidates.[25]

COMMAND DURING THE WORLD WARS

The American army prior to 1917 has been described as a "work in progress." However, within a year and a half, it expanded from a mere 213,557 to a staggering 3,685,485 enlisted men and officers.[26] The Americans believed that the infantry would retain its prewar dominance, agreeing with the Anglo-French conclusion that "the stalemate in the Great War was due to the lack of aggressiveness of both sides."[27] The successful Meuse-Aragon engagement fought against the shattered *Kaiserheer* reinforced their belief that "combined arms should be avoided. . . . Infantry must be self reliant. . . . Too much reliance [of infantry] on auxiliary tend to destroy the initiative."[28] The newly introduced tank and airplane would best serve as supporting elements in infantry actions.[29] These ideas were represented in the 1923 Field Service Regulations (FSRs), which proved remarkably resilient, as they were altered only in 1939.

In addition, the Americans adopted the five-section French general staff system (G1–G5). The section chiefs were directly subordinate to the chief of staff.[30] Divisional staffs had only three sections: operations, intelligence, and supply. However, "The [French] divisional chief of staff in particular, rather than being an operations officer first and foremost was a manager whose function was to coordinate and supervise the functioning of the assistant chief of staff."[31] In contrast, the German organizational structure subordinates all activities to operational planning. The status of the operations officer (*Ia*), *first among equals*, reflects the German emphasis on operational planning and combat activity, relegating other staff responsibilities to the status of support.

The social status of the army also changed during the interwar period. The 1920s and 1930s were ruled by an ethos of business liberalism, which marginalized the conservative ethos of the army. In reaction to the liberal onslaught, the army closed ranks and reinforced conservatism and loyalty. Officers were expected to adhere to "the same body of doctrine" and to conform to "army policies and mainstream culture."[32] Interwar American military academies devoted little time to the study of large unit leadership. Rather, they concentrated on managerial tasks, such as mobilization, organization, and supply. Consequently, graduates understood the science of management rather than the art of war.[33] World War II also strengthened American reliance on business-oriented techniques. Army Chief of Staff General George C. Marshall patterned army organization on the ideas of American business.[34] The managerial focus allowed the Americans to excel at such aspects of war as large-scale mobilization, logistics, and deployment; it was less helpful in the realm of combat command.

By 1941 the Americans had recognized the advantage of the German practice of command and based the new FSRs on the German 1933–1934 *Leadership of Troops*. Nevertheless, the Americans failed to capture the essence of the German approach, centered as it was on friction and chance and considering war a free creative activity. The American approach was influenced by Fredrick Taylor's principles of scientific management.[35] They sought to control war through efficient planning and execution processes. Thus, for example, the regulations emphasized loyalty as opposed to independent action.[36] The regulations reflected a society assured of its material superiority and an understanding that success depended on the ability to bring it to bear against an enemy. A German commentator stated after the war that these regulations reflected a "tendency to underestimate the importance of surprise, maneuver and improvisation."[37] Though ostensibly aspiring to mission command, the overly detailed regulations attempted to "foresee many different situations."[38]

The managerial orientation was evident also in army practices such as the mechanized, centralized, and mathematical nature of American personnel management. The preferred solution for most problems came in the form of improved managerial control based on reports or statistics.[39] Processes such as selection were conducted as an assembly-line operation. Training was conducted en masse, disregarding the needs of parent units. It was based on engineering principles, breaking each task into smaller components and emphasizing automatic drills. The replacement system was also based on mathematical optimization models. A higher priority was given to administrative requirements than to the psychological dimension of war.[40] Essentially, the American approach attempted to streamline core processes through industrial principles striving for efficiency while sacrificing the human-moral dimension. War was not regarded as a clash of wills but as a contest of machines and resources. The impact of individual judgment was set aside.[41] Accordingly, the Americans constructed a centralized organization requiring vast amounts of information in the form of statistical reports. Reliance on superior resources and firepower often resulted in mediocre tactical performance.[42]

Some forces, such as the Ranger and airborne units, demonstrated superior tactical capabilities. Similar to the *Stosstruppen* of the Great War, these elite units could boast of higher individual motivation and training and greater reliance on initiative. However, many regular American units were plagued by mediocre tactical command and merely ordinary operational level command. American generals lacked the knowledge necessary for leading divisions and larger formations.[43] The Germans often exposed their flanks and took risks knowing that the Americans lacked the skill to exploit such opportunities. On the whole, the American army proved neither aggressive nor flexible enough to exploit several opportunities to destroy the Wehrmacht. General James Gavin noted: "Our American Army individually means well and tries hard . . . but it is untrained and completely inefficient."[44] General George C. Patton was the exception who proved the rule. A natural leader of large formations, he inferred enemy intentions intuitively and constantly strove for decisive results. He was tactically innovative and believed in speed, shock, and surprise.[45] In a sense, Patton had more in common with Guderian and Rommel than with Allied generals.[46] In France he refused to halt his advance, constantly pushing forward, exploiting opportunities, and lamenting the cautiousness of the planners. Patton argued that his detractors failed to grasp the principles of mission command.[47]

THE IMPACT OF THE VIETNAM WAR

The first significant postwar military challenge faced by the Americans was the Korean War. Following the initial mobile and amphibious operations, the conflict degenerated into attrition warfare "at the expense of *maneuver*."[48] The Korean War was the first limited war fought between the Cold War powers, both directly and by proxy. However, "the commanders and the tactics as well as many of the troops and the weapons were largely from the global war of 1941–1945." This conflict "incorporated many similarities to the previous war. . . . Due to their training and experience, the civilian and military leadership of the United States was especially prone to see the Korean emergency from the perspective of the 1939–1945 ordeal."[49] Tactical command in the Korean conflict also resembled that of World War II. Moreover, both MacArthur and his air chief, George E. Stratemeyer, falsely believed they could defeat the enemy through strategic bombing. During the last two years of the war, following the termination of the mobile phase, the frontline resembled the First rather than the Second World War.[50]

By and large, the American approach to command during the Cold War was influenced by the experience of the decade-long Vietnam War. In that war, the managerial approach became dominant. Although it was advantageous during World War II, due to the size and scope of forces and operations, the extreme application of the scientific managerial approach during Vietnam created an absurdity.[51] The driving force behind the shift was Secretary of Defense Robert S. McNamara, a former corporate America executive. He believed that the army had to adopt corporate procedures in order to succeed in the modern world. McNamara embraced statistical and quantitative measures for better control. Consequently, the officer corps adopted a managerial ethos, at the expense of the unique military experience. One indication of this trend was the number of officers who took business degrees during that period. American officers adopted corporate jargon, attitudes, and values, substituting the ethos of shared responsibility and self-sacrifice for the greater good with self-serving practices designed to promote individual careers. This trend was shared by most of NATO, but the Americans embraced it most enthusiastically. War was viewed through the prism of balance sheets and accounting principles; quantitative methods and models were used to assess unit effectiveness. For example, daily statistics were submitted concerning the ratio of enemies killed and captured daily against number of enemy units operating in a given area.[52] In a manner resembling the Great War, the Americans instituted a "body count" as part of an overall attrition strategy.

This approach also dominated tactical and operational command and leadership. Centralized control was practiced and decisions were made on the basis of quantitative information gathered through the new communication and information technologies.[53] Signal and communications units grew exponentially. Satisfying system requirements for analysis necessitated vast amounts of information. The result was at times absurd:

> A helpless company commander engaged in a fire fight on the ground was subjected to direct observation by the battalion commander circling above, who was in turn supervised by the brigade commander circling a thousand or so feet higher up, who in turn was monitored by the division commander in the next higher chopper . . . watched by the Field Force (Corps) Commander. With each of these commanders asking the man on the ground to tune in his frequency and explain the situation, a heavy demand for information was generated that could and did interfere with the troops' ability to operate effectively.[54]

The hunger for information at the top produced an information overload resulting in long lead times needed in order to prepare and launch operations. Hence, the Americans' ability to respond quickly to the fast-paced guerrilla warfare was severely curtailed. The obsession for quantitative data across the chain of command resulted in indiscriminate loads of information being transmitted between hierarchal levels and an eventual paralysis caused by information overloads.[55]

Centralization and managerial command were also fostered by an increasing dependency on firepower. The availability of artillery and air power support made it standard practice to call for fire support at the beginning of an engagement. During the inevitable tactical pause, commanders focused on coordinating fire support and answering to superiors instead of directing troops and consequently losing the initiative.[56] Also, commanders came to prefer rearward positions, which facilitated communications with superiors, rather than forward positions, which afforded a better sense of the unfolding situation.[57] The following anecdote illustrates this point. While visiting troops in Vietnam, Moshe Dayan joined a patrol of the famous First Cavalry. The patrol was soon pinned down under hostile fire, and the captain was horrified to learn that his guest had disappeared. He located him atop a grassy hill and asked him what he was doing. "What are *you* doing? Was Dayan's answer, get you're a** up here, and see what this battle is all about."[58] According to Dayan, B-52 bombers were often called upon when soldiers met resistance, not for lack of courage but due to faulty doctrine and command. As a result of micromanagement, officers were less inclined to exhibit initiative and originality.[59] This situation was compounded by other issues. A six-month tour of duty as opposed to the thirteen-month tour of enlisted men and NCOs did not increase officer popularity and hindered the creation of organizational memory and lessons learned. Administrative policies impeded officers' attempts to develop esprit de corps and trust within their units. As the popularity of the war declined, so did the quality of the officers, and the number of assaults against officers (*fragging*) increased. Between 1969 and 1971, the army reported 730 instances of confirmed assaults, 83 of which were fatal.[60] Reflecting contemporary America, many junior officers suffered from drug abuse or ignored its use in the ranks.[61] The experiences of Vietnam served to strengthen American inclination toward business management methods rather than the Moltkean style of command. One historian summarized the "American Way of War"[62] as a

grinding strategy of attrition: the strategy employed by Ulysses S. Grant to destroy Robert E. Lee's army in 1864–65, by John J. Pershing to wear down the German army in 1918, and by the U.S. Army Air Force to pulverize all the major cities of Germany and Japan in 1944–45. In this view, the Civil War,

World War I, and World War II were won not by tactical or strategic brilliance but by the sheer weight of numbers—the awesome destructive power that only a fully mobilized and highly industrialized democracy can bring to bear. In all these conflicts, U.S. armies composed of citizen-soldiers suffered and inflicted massive casualties.[63]

On the tactical level, it meant using superior firepower to suppress the enemy.[64] The command approach derived from this way of war sought efficient ways to manage American resources in order to bring them to bear and exhaust its opponent.

Generals such as Sheridan and Patton were the exceptions to an institutional culture that was based on the assumption that war is all about the efficient utilization of resources and engineering and scientific techniques. With the advent of the twentieth century and the rise of the business theory, the military adopted also quantitative management and scientific management tools. The Vietnam War was merely its most extreme version. It should be noted that American society believed that the individual is capable of making a difference, as is reflected in the ethos of the lone cowboy who rides into town at high noon and saves the day. However, while the American social and economic system does reserve a place for individuals, it must also manage large-scale business organizations. These require striving for efficiency through methods such as mass production and centralized control. This understanding was adopted by a military that enjoyed resource superiority and sought means of exploiting it to the fullest. The obvious solution was to turn to the business environment that had already developed appropriate management efficiency methods.

5 CAUGHT BETWEEN EXTREMES: BRITISH ARMY COMMAND TRADITIONS

THE BRITISH ARMY, usually smaller than its continental adversaries, probably carries the oldest military tradition in the world, as some of its regiments trace back to the mid-seventeenth century. Despite its diminutive size and comparative lack of resources, it has continuously proved itself a resourceful organization able to secure one of the largest empires the world has ever seen.[1] When called upon, it has been able to expand quickly and play a decisive role in continental conflicts. One of the factors affecting the evolution of British military culture has been the fact that Britain is an island, essentially isolated from the Continent. The resulting strategic culture favored the navy over the army. The maintenance of a strong navy diminished the fear of invasion; it was the navy rather than the army that was regarded as Britain's first line of defense.[2] A second imperative influencing the British Army's Way of War was its imperial role. Since the mid-eighteenth century, it was spread in small garrisons fighting numerous small wars and skirmishes. In fact, during the century between Waterloo (1815) and World War I, it participated in only one European war, the Crimean War (1853–1856). The colonial experience had a decisive effect on the British military culture and style of command.[3]

A third factor was the lack of a doctrine of command, leading the British army to rely instead on certain individuals being in the right place at the right time.[4] According to Brian Holden Reid, the British have no tradition of conforming to doctrine:

But there are certain features of British generalship which recur and have done so throughout our history. If there is one word that sums up the British

Command style, it is *improvisation*. A universal exception prevails, almost operating like a law of nature, that a Wellington or a Montgomery will turn up and . . . turn defeat into victory.[5]

Indeed, talented and self-taught leaders often carried the day, leaving behind a lasting legacy that shaped the British army command approach. With the absence of a "great captain," it often suffered major defeats, whether in colonial or continental wars.[6] However, the British army always demonstrated sufficient tenacity and adaptability to carry it through until victory was secured. After most of his column was annihilated during the French and Indian War and before succumbing to his own mortal wounds, General Edward Braddock remarked that "we shall know better how to deal with them another time."[7] This probably best reflects the British army mentality. Protected by an ocean and a dominant navy, the British army could afford local tactical defeats without risking strategic crises. One of the first commanders in the long line of great captains was Oliver Cromwell, who had probably set the precedent:

> In many ways . . . like Frederick he became a national exponent of efficient military, but unlike Frederick, Cromwell has shown little indication of possessing an appreciation of the intellectual preparation required for the maintenance of a truly professional military force . . . [and consequently] founded no schools devoted to military learning and training of staff officers.[8]

The next "great captain" was the Duke of Marlborough, who, together with Frederick the Great, epitomized the ancien régime style of warfare. Both "accepted the existing system but so resolved its limitations and perfected its techniques as to gain the tactical advantage."[9] According to Strachan, though the British were influenced by Frederician discipline and uniforms, they were less eager to accept his ideas concerning officer training.[10] Similarly,

> Marlborough, like his contemporaries, was his own operations officer in all important matters. . . . British military history after Marlborough will arouse a strong suspicion that those individuals who achieved successes on the field of battle did so as individuals, and not as products of the military system.[11]

Wellington's legacy was perhaps most significant. Michael Howard noted that his "calm, understated style of command perhaps set the pattern of British leadership for two hundred years."[12] His was the "antiheroic" style of leadership; at Waterloo he chose a position sufficiently forward to personally survey the battle but rearward enough to minimize risk of injury.[13] Wellington carefully matched tactics to terrain, sought to minimize casualties by sheltering his closely supervised troops, and refused to "delegate any responsibility central to the outcome of the engagement."[14]

His was a style of command that emphasized strategic and tactical deployment and incredible resilience. To a request for reinforcement, he replied, "tell him what he wishes for is impossible, he and I and every Englishman in the field must die on the spot which we now occupy."[15] Wellington created a staff system capable of providing the assistance he required to perform his duties of command. But in keeping with Marlborough's traditions, his command echelons were primarily the products of his own effort, and he too failed to establish a school for staff officers. In contrast with the French bureau system, Wellington's staff included only an adjutant general and a quartermaster general. Most of the operational and intelligence functions came under the purview of the adjutant. This lean division of staff personnel into two basic components remained a predominant feature of British staff organization and had its distinct advantages.[16]

Contrary to popular belief, Wellington held his army in the highest regard, believing that "there are no men in Europe that can fight like them" and that "we have mutual confidence and are never disappointed."[17] Though a strict disciplinarian and a firm proponent of severe punishments, he believed in motivation through the army's "secret weapon," the regimental system, which provided intimacy and familiarity for the rank and file. In contrast to this lenient attitude toward the soldiers, he was less forgiving toward his own staff, to whom and of whom he routinely complained "Must I do everything myself?" during the Spanish Peninsula campaign.[18] He felt that many of his officers were simply incompetent and wrote that "We shall do no good until we shall so far alter our system as to force the officers of the junior ranks to perform their duty and have some mode of punishing them for their neglect." He acknowledged that aristocratic officers could be trusted to display leadership and bravery at the onset of battle. The difficulty lay in reaching that point.[19] Wellington's influence was felt for many decades following Waterloo. In his later years, he became a reactionary and resisted any reform that would change what he believed to be a successful system.[20] In 1837 the army was still very much the same Napoleonic-era organization dominated by the duke and a clique of officers serving under him.

British army officers and enlisted men were worlds apart socially. Most officers were aristocrats who had purchased their rank and position. Though hardly a profitable occupation, the military was considered a career suitable for real gentlemen imbued with a sense of a "serving elite." They were educated, socially powerful, and privileged and maintained their traditions and codes of honor and conduct. In contrast, the men of the ranks held no "individual worth or influence," and the two never mixed. Usually, officers encountered the men only on parade grounds, and even then most duties fell to the senior NCOs. In terms of combat motivation and leadership, much was dependent on the attitude of individual commanders. Traditionalists were strict disciplinarians who believed in blind obedience and felt that soldiers should never think independently. Increased social liberalism combined with technological developments facilitating dispersed formations slowly undermined this view, but it was a slow change.[21] In battle these commanders led the charge and demonstrated remarkable personal courage. This characteristic, combined with regimental loyalty and a "broad sense of national superiority," was at the heart of British military dominance.[22]

From the end of the Crimean War (1856) until the beginning of World War I (1914), the army did not participate in a continental war; its experience was limited to conflicts of the type identified today as counterinsurgency. These experiences shaped the British army's approach to warfare and more specifically to command. Despite its conservatism, the army proved rather flexible in these engagements. It fought various peoples with differing warfare traditions through extreme climates and over difficult terrain. Lessons learned in one campaign were often irrelevant to another. At the beginning of a given engagement, the British would normally have insufficient resources and knowledge of enemy and terrain. After suffering initial defeats, they would readjust and emerge victorious.[23] The units participating in these conflicts were relatively small. The largest force fielded between the Crimean and South African (1899–1902) Wars was 35,000 or so in what might be termed the Egyptian theater in 1882. Nevertheless, professional demands were made of commanders and their staffs. It was an experience, as one historian noted, "much beyond anything a Moltke or even a Grant who fought Mexican and Indians had."[24]

It was a reality of independence and even isolation in which commanders were forced to improvise and seek unconventional ways to defeat their enemies. However, these short and limited campaigns did not necessitate staff officers and other mechanisms necessary for the management of a large army.

In this respect, despite the experience gained in the Crimea, the situation was little improved by the time of the Boer War.[25]

COMMAND IN THE WORLD WAR I ERA

Prior to the Great War, the British FSRs stipulated that orders issued to large units should include only that which clarifies the object to be attained rather than the method by which it should be attained.[26] In practice, during the Great War, the British army maintained two "mutually contradictory, command systems which have been termed as 'umpiring' and 'restrictive control.'"[27] The latter is a highly centralized and tightly controlled system in which subordinates are given detailed orders and are expected to carry them out regardless of circumstances. Local initiative is subdued in favor of the central plan and is regarded as interference. This highly centralized approach developed despite the prewar regulations for a number of reasons: an engineering approach to war that reflected the scientific spirit of the age; the need to train masses of new recruits; and the routine of peace, which supported the illusion that war could be reduced to a science.[28]

The British initially fought in dense linear formations, utilizing bayonet-based tactics. Attacks were set-piece battles endeavoring to capture enemy trenches.[29] Training was decentralized, entrusted to divisional commanders rather than to staff officers schooled in similar modes of thought. The doctrine seemed to fit the rapid expansion of the army and was based on time-table tactics that required soldiers little in the way of thinking, other than obedience. They were supervised by an increasing number of officers and NCOs who ensured that discipline was maintained and orders were followed. The emphasis was put on drills and physical exercise.[30]

In contrast to life in the trenches, higher headquarters were positioned in "comfortable locations selected for the office space and ease of communications that they offered, sometimes dozens of miles behind the front. . . . [Staff officers] tended to fall into bureaucratic routine and lose touch with the troops in the slimy holes." As the Great War dragged on, the task of "day-to day management gained an importance to the point where it often overshadowed the military side of things."[31] Douglas Haig's chief of intelligence remarked that "one of the greatest difficulties of everyone at GHQ is to get away from the office often and long enough to get in close touch with the front."[32] The reach of command often corresponded with that of the radio signal, and operations were planned with this restriction in mind. The final preparations for the

Battle of the Somme "proceeded with a clockwork precision that was made possible only by meticulous staff work, excellent communications, and centralized control." The dominant notion was that Kitchener's armies were too green to do anything but follow rigidly prescribed orders. "Haig had his Chief of Staff, General Kiggel, issue an order for the attack consisting of thirty two sections on fifty seven pages, excluding appendices."[33]

For example, forward artillery observers did not accompany the infantry since their usefulness was limited. Changes in the firing tables could be authorized only by Corps Headquarters. The system was designed so as to minimize confusion, and therefore each unit was "assigned a patch of front of standard length across which to advance slowly and deliberately . . . towards prescribed objectives to be reached within a prescribed period of time." Having reached their objectives, "the troops were to halt, consolidate, re-establish communications, and wait for the second wave to catch up . . . and the entire process to start afresh." With such detailed orders, battalion commanders and those upward were redundant and in any case forbidden from taking initiative. A few miles behind, the corps commander had little knowledge of progress made. Division or even brigade commanders were only slightly better informed. Despite grave conditions, plans were "carried out with a vengeance, displaying that discipline for which they were famous. . . . Battalions marched slowly and almost shoulder to shoulder, and forbidden to break into a run or take cover."[34] Successful attacks, rare though they may have been, were not exploited. Troops were controlled rather than commanded, left to their own devices, unable to alter the plan.[35] This harsh judgment notwithstanding, according to Strachan the thinking of the armies was not static. Both sides studied each other, emulated each other, or negated each other.[36]

Umpiring, at the opposite of the spectrum of command, denotes the abdication of command responsibilities.[37] While in both detailed and mission command the commander imposes his will, the umpire provides a general objective and then completely withdraws. Neglecting to specify clear objectives, constraints, or intent, the commander is essentially practicing an extreme form of delegation, an excessive "hands-off" and "laissez-faire" approach. The roots of this practice can be traced back to the British colonial experience, where middle-ranking officers commanded small campaigns practically autonomously. Senior commanders remained farther away and had therefore much less knowledge of and influence over battlefield occurrences. The regimental system increased the tendency toward umpiring, especially on the operational level. The British army before the Great War could be described as a "collection of fiercely independent battalions each with its own sense of identity and tradition."[38] Overseas deployment in small garrisons reinforced cohesiveness and a sense of independence. The effects of this independence were felt strongly in operational level commands. Operational level commanders hesitated to impose their will on battalion commanders, who regarded their units as their own personal possession. Operational command was therefore practiced through suggestion and request.[39]

This tendency was strengthened by the underdeveloped nature of the operational level in the British army. Prior to the Great War, the army lacked sufficient divisional and corps headquarters. Furthermore, it offered fewer than half the number of senior positions offered by the Germans. The army was confident in its understanding of the concept of leadership, "the highest of virtues." Command, however, is a more complex issue. Few understood the meaning of a command structure for a unit larger than six infantry divisions, and fewer still had commanded such a force.[40] Command opportunities were limited, and the major wars that took place between 1870 and 1914, with the exception of the Boer War, involved small units. Hence there was little opportunity to develop operational-level expertise. Moreover, the British misunderstood the German *Auftragstaktik*. Although both armies allowed subordinates freedom of action, there were critical differences between the two. British commanders avoided interfering out of respect for the feelings and reputation of subordinates. Maintaining relationships was more important than achieving the objective. Decentralization therefore became an end in itself rather than a means to an end. In addition, the British offered little training in the form of maneuver or war games.[41] Consequently, the inexperienced commanders of large formations often resorted to one of the two extreme approaches described above.

The proportion of officers commissioned from the ranks swelled from a mere 2 percent prior to the First World War, to 41 percent during the war.[42] In addition, due to rapid wartime promotion, operational-level positions were filled by individuals whose experience rarely surpassed that of regimental officers. Also, the British, unlike the Germans, did not train officers for the tasks of the next higher rank.[43] British army culture during the Great War cultivated the "cult of the rank," according to which senior officers possess more knowledge and better solutions. Criticism and debate from junior officers was unwelcome and was considered a challenge to their authority. Senior officers were expected to always have the best solution at hand and to never waver. It was assumed that once an officer reached the rank of a general, he had nothing new to learn.[44] It was said of General Haig that he "demonstrated a variable command style, sometimes intervening and meddling and sometimes standing aloof even as mistakes were made."[45]

Nevertheless, the British system was a learning one. As Bourne points out, much of the criticism discussed above has been directed toward British generals.[46] Lower ranks, in contrast, enjoyed a more flexible and evolutionary progression during the war. Battlefield practices improved through the efforts of the men at the front. They depended "on their training, their experience, and the willingness of their superiors to trust their judgment."[47] By 1918, infantry tactics were improved, limited initiative was approved, and authority was delegated to experienced junior officers and NCOs.[48] Corresponding changes were also felt in the attitude of generals. Indeed, as the ability of the army grew, so did Haig's confidence in his subordinates and his level of interference decreased.[49] It was battalion- and brigade-level officers who recognized "that there is more to command than issuing orders down a telephone line."[50]

GENERAL STAFF, DOCTRINE, AND OFFICER EDUCATION

The British allowed Wellington's staff mechanism to regress in the decades following 1815. British military thinking stagnated for almost forty years, and army doctrine on the eve of the Crimean War was much as it was in Waterloo.[51] The only doctrinal publication was a text from 1852 encompassing current British thinking. It argued that the absence of staff education in the British army was due to "the assertion that knowledge of staff duties can only be acquired in the field."[52] Wellington himself believed that the importance of practical experience surpassed that of formal education. Contemporary British society viewed war as neither an art nor a science but rather as a type of extreme sport. This notion was fostered in public schools, where the vast majority of future officers were educated.[53] A staff school was established only in 1858 as a lesson from the Crimean War. Though a progressive step in itself, the British staff system did not progress.[54]

It was Spencer Wilkinson who eventually awakened British interest in the general staff through his 1890 exposé of the Prussian *Generalstab*.[55] He explained that the British were grossly uninformed as to the workings of the staff in general and the Prussian staff in particular. Wilkinson demonstrated that the Prussian staff relied not only on systemized functions but primarily upon professional training and the benefits of "the mature wisdom which the higher education of the general staff is directed."[56] However, interest in the topic was translated to practical measures only as a result of the Boer War. An investigation of army command deficiencies led by the Lord Esher Committee found that insufficient staff training had gravely harmed operations in South Africa. Its recommendation to establish a general staff forthwith was implemented and was followed by the establishment of a field staff. In practice, however, the Edwardian army remained similar to its Victorian predecessors. Esher and his colleagues succeeded in changing the personalities but not the process. Indeed, although promotions and appointments were no longer purchased, they still depended upon connections rather than seniority or merit.[57] Shortly afterward, the War Office translated Schellendorff's *The Duties of the General Staff* (1905).[58] Nevertheless, the adoption of German concepts was a "highly selective procedure by which efficient military concepts were discarded."[59]

The increased awareness of the importance of military education led to the opening of Staff College at Camberley. Many basic staff procedures were developed there and later published under the title "Staff Manual" (1912). This publication, which would serve the British army until after the Second World War, was a hybrid of Prussian and British ideas. Hittle described it as a "Prussian variation on the British theme."[60] Before the Great War, the school attracted an excellent faculty, but tuition proved too expensive. Additionally, the newly established General Staff Corps (1906) had yet to develop a strong enough regimental affiliation.[61] The college therefore attracted middle-aged officers whose careers had stalled, rather than rising stars. In addition, reading was not considered necessary to advance one's career and professionalism. This approach was fostered from the top when the Duke of Cambridge remarked that the regimental officer was the best staff officer. It did contribute to social cohesion; as van Creveld noted, quoting Sir William Robertson, "the greatest achievement of the nineteenth century Staff College was probably that it had provided mutual agreement and excellent comradeship. Another contribution was the emphasis on developing the ability to summarize complicated situations in brief messages."[62]

The Esher report proposed to recruit general staff officers mainly from Staff College and grant them an accelerated promotion track. However, it was decided to allow accelerated promotions to any staff positions. Selection for the Staff College was hindered by regimental loyalty, the quota system, an entrance examination, and the system of nominations. Consequently, the students were not the crème de la crème as in the German case. For example, while four to five candidates competed for a place in Staff College in 1913, there were more than eight competing for a place in the *Kriegsakademie*.[63] The school focused on administrative tasks, leading Henry Rawlinson (1908) to urge its directors to include training for command in war.[64] A 1911 supplement to the 1909 field regulations stated that "it is outside the scope of the staff to interfere with the exercise of command. . . . Only one man can Command." Thus, neither the school nor tours in staff positions were required for high command. Also, many staff positions were not filled by Staff College graduates.[65]

The British general staff never functioned as the German organization upon which it was modeled. Unlike the *Generalstab*, it was not an independent intellectual powerhouse enjoying enormous influence over the army. The British staff's apparent disinterest in training of the part of GHQ may be contrasted with their general insistence upon discipline.[66] Its officers did not enjoy the high status accorded to their German counterparts, which facilitated their advisory role in the field units.[67] Moreover, in reality, "for most regimental commanders the existence of general staff remained a dead letter."[68] In summation, the British general staff was unable to assert the degree of authority, independence, and leadership exercised by its German equivalent and was therefore in no position to provide the professional support so vital to the development of mission command.[69]

COMMAND DURING THE SECOND WORLD WAR

The concepts of armored warfare developed in Britain during the interwar period had the potential of changing the philosophy of command. After all, similar ideas served the German Blitzkrieg, which relied on mission command.[70] However, this was not to be. This may have been due to what Liddell-Hart labeled the "British Way of War." Liddell-Hart was also the principal advocate of the "limited liability" policy, which meant that Britain should concentrate on its imperial role.[71] Consequently, Britain was to rely on its air force and navy for its future continental wars. The army remained small and relatively undeveloped. Liddell-Hart objected to the concentration of mass against decisive points, preferring instead the famous "indirect approach"— that is, the use of maneuver and surprise against weak points. He proposed the "expanding torrent" in order to effect deep strategic penetrations through speed and moral superiority. This system necessitated a flexible command approach.

Fuller, the other famous proponent of armored warfare, foresaw a swarm of tanks punching through enemy lines, aiming to demoralize the enemy.[72] Brian Holden Reid suggested that Fuller "drew a remarkably accurate picture of the nature of future warfare, as it developed until 1941," or the German Blitzkrieg.[73] According to Reid, Fuller had also recognized the importance of the operational level of war.[74] He supported battlefield opportunism and therefore also flexible plans. Nevertheless, he warned that conferences ". . . should not be used as excuses for seeking ideas and letting people do what they please, a commander's role in short is to command."[75] Fuller believed that technological advances would allow commanders to exercise close control while still affording a degree of opportunism.[76]

The Second World War expanded the small British regular army once again. As in the Great War, centralized control and umpiring abounded. According to one historian, "junior officers were only allowed to change their actions if circumstances changed, and needed authorization to do so, which led to delay. Initiative was effectively banned."[77] Similarly, "the rigidity of the doctrine was loosened for senior officers. Orders became treated as suggestions."[78] Owing to a lack of practice and common tactical doctrine, there was no shared situational understanding. The outcome was a "deadly combination of strict central control and a free expression of opinions in the middle ranks [that] led to sluggish, uncoordinated and unimaginative performance."[79] The regimental system facilitated the transition of the British army from a small regular force to a large conscript army. It served as an effective mechanism for quickly integrating civilians into army life. This system provided a sense of belonging and group cohesion while old regimental rivalries proved effective means of motivation. This transformed the regiment into a cohesive and effective unit.[80] Conversely, the regimental system was remarkably inflexible. While the Germans derived great tactical advantages from amalgamating remnants of units, British units were hard pressed to cooperate with one another. German flexibility was due partially to a modular structure. The basic organic unit was the company, while larger formations were essentially ad hoc task forces. The Germans could assemble and dismantle units using the company as the basic building block. In contrast, British regiments, battalions, and brigades were permanent units less inclined toward mergers and regrouping.[81]

While the Allies relied on superior firepower and conducted slow set-piece attacks in order to minimize casualties, the Germans relied on infiltration by small groups led by NCOs utilizing imagination and initiative. The Germans often exposed their flanks, believing that their adversaries lacked the skill and imagination necessary to exploit such opportunities. For example, the Germans effected an orderly retreat from the Bulge as the Allies made no attempt to cut them off (1944). In contrast, Allied commanders refrained from following suit even when the Germans no longer possessed the sufficient resources or mobility to intervene with conviction.[82] While the generals of the First and Second World Wars shared a similar social and professional background, the generals of the latter had been regimental officers on the Western Front during the former. Having lived in the trenches and experienced the remoteness of high command, they were more sympathetic to their troops. They understood the significance of personal contact for effective leadership and endeavored to make it whenever possible. Mobile warfare and improved communications facilitated avoidance of unnecessarily casualties, and extreme caution in the conduct of operations became the hallmark of British command.[83]

Of course, the men serving under their command had every reason to be grateful. Offensive operations were carefully planned and conducted with full air and artillery support. Additionally, soldiers were advised as to the nature and purpose of operations. As Howard noted, "even at the lowest level of command we felt that we were being treated as intelligent human beings, and were expected to treat those under our own command accordingly."[84] Conversely, according to German intelligence, "British officers could be expected to fight gallantly. . . . The higher level commanders would . . . retain their laborious methods of issuing orders." They also noted that "their orders were schematic and went into the smallest detail. The middle and lower command were consequently allowed little freedom of movement."[85]

Commanders down to the divisional level were fiercely independent, though few demonstrated a capacity for higher command. World War II British commanders reflected the characteristics of the prewar regular army. They looked after their men and excelled in small-scale warfare but proved unequal to the professional Wehrmacht and unprepared for higher command. General Alan Brooke remarked in 1942 that "half our Corps and Divisional commanders are totally unfit. . . . They lack character, imagination, drive and power of leadership."[86] No British general possessed the experience in maneuvering great armies enjoyed by their German and Russian counterparts. Indeed, only two of its corps commanders were considered competent.[87] After the war, General Gerd von Rundstedt noted that the British were more cautious than the Americans and that British infantry tactics had advanced little from 1916.[88] The director of military training of the Fifteenth Army Group, stationed in Italy, stated that

> Our tactical methods are thorough and methodical but slow and cumbersome. In consequence our troops fight well in defence and our set piece attacks are usually successful, but it is not unfair to say that through lack of enterprise in exploitation, we seldom reap up the full benefit of them, we are too flank conscious, we over insure administratively, we are by nature too apprehensive of failure, and our training makes us more so.[89]

Field Marshal Bernard Law "Monty" Montgomery proved the rule; like Wellington, his legacy was to shape British command for decades to come. An autodidactic student of military theory, he was a consummate professional. Goronway Rees, who served on his staff, said that Monty thought about war as a scientist or a scholar. A meticulous planner, he designed complex operations for limited objectives relying on firepower and careful staff work, leaving little for chance or subordinate initiative.[90] Monty's command approach also reflected his understanding of the men under his command: intelligent, literate, unmilitary, and homesick citizen soldiers in need of motivation.[91] He treated them as men who had to complete an unpleasant but necessary job before they could go home.[92] Monty "fought the battle the army could win and created the army to win the battle he needed."[93] Though a superb planner and trainer, he failed repeatedly to exploit successes.[94]

Despite practicing centralized command through a "master plan," in accordance with British doctrine, he insisted on clarifying his intentions to subordinates. He brooked no debate concerning his intentions. But instead of micromanaging, he chose individuals who understood his intentions and granted them a degree of latitude. Montgomery relied on his chief of staff in his absence and entrusted to him the responsibility of working out the details. He believed that the duty of "commanders is to make plans and give decisions and for staffs then to work out the details."[95] An autocrat, Monty favored imposing order through a unified doctrine. He knew that battles do not develop as anticipated and was flexible enough to adjust his plans, though rarely his original intent, in accordance with battlefield occurrences.[96]

THE POST–WORLD WAR II ERA AND THE SOURCES
OF DISSATISFACTION (1945–1990)

In the postwar period, the British army was forced to prepare for both colonial and continental conflicts. The force realignment included stationing a large continental force facing the Soviets, the British Army on the Rhine (BAOR). Other forces participated in small wars around the globe: from constabulary actions in Northern Ireland to limited conventional conflicts in Egypt or the Falklands.[97] Due to the varied geographical locations, missions, and threats, two types of culture developed. Anticipating a Soviet attack, the heavily armored and mechanized units of the BAOR adopted a defensive posture according to NATO doctrine. The defensive doctrine coupled with the absence of actual combat experience led to stagnation.[98] One Israeli field commander who participated in a training exercise in Europe in the early 1980s said, "we were told exactly what, where and how, there was no leeway whatsoever. . . . I was astounded by the rigidity. . . . It was very different from how I used to train in the IDF."[99]

Forces operating outside the continent, mainly conducting counterinsurgency operations, were primarily special units and elite forces, such as the Special Air Service (SAS), paratrooper regiments, and the Royal Marines as well as some light infantry regiments. They proved determined and quick to learn and adapt in a manner similar to the Victorian British regular army. They combined the principles of minimum force, civil-military relations, cooperation, and tactical flexibility with a highly decentralized small-unit approach.[100] Fighting in the Falklands, this force performed well, and its command was typical of the British historical experience. Commanders improvised, led by example, and stuck to their objectives despite significant difficulties.

However, mission command was not universally practiced. Thus, when PARA 2 attacked Goose Green, where it lost its battalion commander, its plan had several significant shortcomings—not least of which was a complex and detailed thirteen-stage plan of attack. By the time the battalion attacked Wireless Ridge, these shortcomings were corrected. The plan of attack was shortened to four stages.[101] Some commanders attempted to control the chaos of war and their subordinates through detailed plans and centralization while others displayed greater flexibility.[102] The forces that participated in the Falklands demonstrated various degrees of performance. Indeed the Falklands campaign exposed the fact that a gap existed between various British army units and the need to bring them all to a higher standard of agility and flexibility. Moreover, due to the absence of a comprehensive doctrine of command, some officers reverted back to strict training habits and employed a detailed command approach. It became obvious to some that a significant change in army doctrine, education, and training was overdue.[103]

6 MOLDED BY NECESSITY: COMMAND IN THE IDF

THE UNIQUENESS OF THE IDF

The military capabilities demonstrated by the IDF between 1948 and 1973 led some to declare it successor to the Wehrmacht. According to one British brigade commander, "The IDF came to be regarded as the most effective fighting force in the world; paradoxically its closest rival in fighting power in the twentieth century is the *Wehrmacht*."[1] Robert Citino noted that the IDF "became the mobile force *par excellence*, and irony of ironies, the heir to the German *Wehrmacht*."[2] However, despite similarities in the geostrategic parameters and operational conduct, the origins and traditions of these two forces are very different.[3]

The Israeli Defense Force represents a unique case in terms of mission command. It was never too keen on developing military theory or publishing written doctrine. Continuous combat operations, which often required the participation of command course trainees, resulted in an emphasis on field practice rather than theory and doctrine. During its formative years, the IDF had no agencies dedicated to institutionalized learning, the study of military theory, or theoretical investigations. Therefore, it lacked the traditions created by *Kriegsakademie*-like organizations. Instead of theoreticians, academies, and research institutions, the IDF had autodidactic officers, familiar with military theory and open to new ideas. The immediate reality faced by the IDF demanded that all available resources be concentrated on praxis. Since its beginning and throughout its history, the IDF has demonstrated a marked preference for praxis over theory. Its founders adopted a decentralized command approach in order to facilitate strategic initiative and maneuver warfare as a means of dealing with Israel's basic strategic challenges. In fact, Israel's basic geostrategic parameters were similar to those of historic Prussia: a small country with no natural borders surrounded by larger powers significantly richer in resources. As we shall see, some of Israel's military solutions were indeed very similar to those of the Prussians.

Mission command was consistent with the *Sabra* ethos—the "new" archetype Zionist Jew who was born and raised in Palestine. As a result, the IDF developed its own version of mission command. However, as much as it was part of the culture, due to the absence of formal doctrine, mission command was never institutionalized or even fully understood. Following strategic and social changes occurring in the 1970s, the practice and principals of the IDF version of mission command—there was never much of a theory—began to fade with the people who understood it in a tacit form, only to be "rediscovered" in recent years.

CHAOS VERSUS ORDER, 1929–1948

In establishing the IDF, its founders drew from two distinct traditions dating to the period of the Second World War. The first was that of the *Palmach* (storm companies), the elite units of the *Haganah* (the underground Jewish defense force). The second was the British professional tradition, imported by Jewish officers who served in it during the war. In some issues, these traditions (and the individuals who represented them) complemented each other; in others they clashed.[4] British army veterans contributed significantly to the transformation of the Jewish armed forces from a militia to a regular army in such areas as organization, structure, and procedures as well as basic tactics.[5]

During the first few decades, the IDF was dominated by veterans of the Palmach and by the ethos of that organization. Two individuals were paramount in the shaping of the Palmach and through it the IDF: the British officer Charles Orde Wingate and the former Red Army officer Yitzhak Sadeh. Until the arrival of Sadeh onto the Palestine scene in the mid-1930s, the *Yishuv* (Jewish settlement in Palestine) practiced passive resistance against the Arab irregulars. Sadeh advocated active resistance through unconventional guerrilla tactics and campaigned successfully to establish mobile units.[6] Sadeh's version of mission command is amazingly similar to our modern understanding of the concept. He described it as part of an entire philosophy:

Our people were slower in transporting units (there were simply not enough vehicles . . .), however our maneuvering in the field was always faster. Commander's intent cascaded from one observant person to another. . . . Our military was extraordinary. We always took into consideration that the enemy will outnumber and outfire us, and we will not be able to achieve a decision in our favour through physical power alone, but through maneuvering and operating against the enemy's weakness.[7]

Sadeh was soon to be joined by the *Yadid* (Friend), Charles Wingate, an exceptional British intelligence officer. Wingate encouraged *Yishuv* leaders to adopt aggressive tactics emphasizing the following:

Leadership based on personal example, purposeful yet meticulous discipline, high focus on the practical and operational aspects, careful planning to assure that every man understood the purpose of the plan, full delegation of authority to subordinate commanders; allowing improvisation with accordance of the changing situation of the battle . . . and the exploitation of surprise mobility and night manoeuvres.[8]

Wingate, a passionate supporter of the Jewish cause, founded the Special Night Squads (SNS) in 1938. Years later, Israel's first prime minister and minister of defense, David Ben-Gurion, would say that "Wingate's doctrines were taken over by the IDF."[9] When Wingate was transferred from Palestine, his work was carried on by Sadeh, who established the underground *Fosh* (field companies). During the Second World War, he was instrumental in establishing the Palmach, a joint Jewish-British venture. His company commanders, former members of Wingate's SNS, included Moshe Dayan and Yigal Allon. The Palmach was established during the summer of 1941, when Rommel's *Afrikakorps* seemed unstoppable. In preparation for an evacuation of Palestine and a retreat to Egypt, British intelligence sanctioned the formation of storm companies trained in guerrilla tactics to harass and delay the German panzers.[10] When the winds of war changed at Alamein, the British sponsorship was retracted and the Palmach went underground.

Perhaps it was its pseudo-guerrilla nature or socialist ideology that made the Palmach's approach very different than that of the British army. Members of the Palmach formed a special brotherhood. It abhorred the formal routines associated with regular armies, such as parades and drills, salutes and uniform appearance. The men were a disorderly and informal bunch who addressed commanders by their nicknames. The Palmach emphasized independence and combat leadership at all levels.[11] The squad leader course that many underwent trained its participants for independent command. It was a force that emphasized initiative above all, internal discipline, and maintenance of objective and out-of-the-box thinking in all ranks.[12] One famous Palmach slogan, "the smallest unit is the single rifled man," reflected this approach.[13] During the Israeli War of Independence (1947–1949), the ranks of the Palmach swelled considerably with the influx of new recruits. It formed a number of elite brigades that spearheaded the fight against the invading Arab armies and performed countermaneuver attacks.[14] Ben Gurion, however, preferred to promote British army veterans rather than members of the Palmach, as he desired a professional army modeled on the British army. Additionally, the British veterans were politically unaffiliated and represented no immediate threat to his rule.[15] All the same, most IDF commanders during and following the war had been educated in the Haganah and the Palmach. Moreover, most IDF chiefs of staff and generals serving between 1953 and 1983 were Palmach veterans.[16] Consequently, the IDF was imbued with Palmach values.

Initially, the absence of a military tradition and doctrine allowed the IDF to experiment with new ideas and methods. Military problems were approached in an intellectual and open-minded manner. Operational plans were open to debate in which experience and innovative solutions counted for more than rank. Discipline was maintained through internal motivation rather than external formal coercion.[17] The leadership qualities displayed by the IDF and the development of the unique Israeli variant of mission command are best understood against the background of the underground command courses. During the last decade of the British Mandate, the Haganah and the Palmach held courses designed to train platoon commanders and NCOs. Pertinent to this discussion are three significant factors: the instructors were autodidactic individuals who studied military theory and doctrine independently; the course material was derived primarily from British and German military sources; and the graduates were exposed to the leadership of battalions and brigades.

For example, the German guerrilla campaign in East Africa during the Great War captured the imagination of Haganah leaders already during the 1920s.[18] The German commander of that campaign, von Lettow-Vorbeck, provided personal instruction in military theory and training methods to one member of the Haganah in Germany. Also, a few Austrian officers acted as instructors in one of the first command courses in Palestine. The training was primarily tactical, though students received some lectures on the operational level.[19] Institutionalization of the officers' course was begun in 1937 under the command of Yosef Avidar. An autodidact, he kept abreast of European military thought and lectured on it to his students. He envisioned a small professional leaders' army, similar to the *Reichswehr*, in which every trainee was a potential commander. "The best material was German," said Avidar, "but we tried to combine the best from different sources, Soviet, British and Polish."[20] It is noteworthy that many of the future leaders of the IDF participated in this course, including Moshe Dayan and Yigal Allon. According to historian Anita Shapira, cadets in this course actually simulated command of battalion and brigade formations.[21]

Trainees were encouraged to demonstrate initiative and to shoulder responsibility. The courses emphasized an open approach to problem solving rather than standardized text-book solutions. They were designed to prepare platoon commanders for higher command, affording them the necessary tools for independent thinking and planning. Platoon commanders were trained to plan and to execute plans for anticipated and unexpected situations. Preferred battle plans were those that emphasized maneuver and relied on initiative and independent thought. Decisions were made on the basis of an "estimate of the situation," which included an assessment of the situation and possible courses of action. As the methodology is essentially similar in large formations, it facilitated the transition to higher command.[22] Illustrative of the contemporary style of command is the following anecdote. In preparation for the Australian attack against Vichy Syria in 1941, the designated reconnaissance force, a Palmach unit, held a briefing. Platoon commander Yigal Allon briefed the men on the mission, the general political-strategic context, and the tasks of neighboring units. He then approached the Australian commander and suggested altering the plan of attack in favor of a surprise night attack. His recommendation was rejected against the excuse that the operational plan had already been set and the preparations for the attack had begun. Both Dayan and Allon later argued that greater flexibility on the part of the Australians would have changed the course of the campaign.[23]

IMPLICIT MISSION COMMAND, 1948–1956

Due to the narrow borders of the new state, Israeli strategic doctrine of the 1950s advocated preemptive strikes, transferring the fighting to enemy territory, and a quick battlefield decision in anticipation of an internationally imposed political settlement. This type of strategy required maneuver warfare capabilities, decentralized command, and maintenance of objective in light of the aim.[24] The details of a battle plan were left to subordinates on the basis of the mission objectives.[25] They could thus risk bold and aggressive operations without having to sacrifice creativity and unconventional actions.

The archetype commander was Yigal Allon, who designed and commanded some of the key operations of the War of Independence.[26] Toward the end of the war, Allon commanded Operation Yoav against the Egyptian army. The operation was carried out by a division-size task force relying on maneuver and the indirect approach.[27] The plan involved deep powerful thrusts behind Egyptian lines. The mission directive, penned with operations officer Yitzhak Rabin, was only one page long. The "method" section consisted of one word: *Beatzmecha* ("at own discretion").[28] Dayan was another legendary war figure of that war who inspired his men and encouraged initiative and risk taking.[29] This culture of independence was strengthened by the fact that the IDF was in the process of transformation from an underground organization to a regular army. The general staff had yet to assert its authority over the traditionally independent territorial forces. Hence, many operations were dependent on local initiative. Toward the end of the war, the general staff began exercising more centralized control, though it confined itself primarily to coordinating resources and intelligence.[30]

The outstanding young officers who emerged during those formative years had gained their knowledge through the trials of war rather than in the halls of military academies.[31] For example, the founders of the Armored Corps learned their trade by trial and error and "endless debate."[32] Some military literature was available, and officers such as Lieutenant Colonel Uri Ben-Ari, who later commanded the famous Seventh Armored Brigade, reportedly read and experimented with German panzer tactics. Nevertheless, limited access to the experience of foreign militaries forced the IDF to devise its doctrine nearly from scratch. This turn of events allowed the IDF to tailor fighting methods to its specific needs and encouraged experimentation. Thus, while the Prussian-British model of the general staff was adopted, various modifications were made. For example, the general staff was given operational control over all three branches (services).[33] This unique configuration had its faults; it naturally favored the land forces component but also greatly facilitated jointness and combined arms warfare.[34]

However, the IDF also carried some fundamental weaknesses. For example, in accordance with the Zionist ethos, it preferred the notion of citizen soldiers to that of military professionals. It rejected military intellectualism and the idea of establishing military academies.[35] It decided to institute a dual career system whereby officers would be discharged at the age of forty-five and begin a second, civilian, career. The proponents of this system felt that it would also revitalize command continuously.[36] Coupled with excessive reliance on field experience, this ethos would impede strategic and doctrinal development later on.[37]

Following the end of the War of Independence and the dismantling of the Palmach, the quality of the IDF deteriorated significantly. During the early 1950s, the IDF conducted a series of unsuccessful reprisal raids. Time and again, units were lost in the dark or retreated at the first sign of danger.[38] Furious at the dismal results, Chief of Staff Dayan (1953–1958) reiterated the importance of "maintenance of objective" and stipulated that no attack was to be suspended unless casualties exceeded 50 percent.[39] Even more important, he authorized the formation of the elite Unit 101 (1953) under the leadership of the young and charismatic Major Ariel Sharon. The small unit reinstituted the Palmach emphasis on physical stamina, endurance, navigational skills, innovation and daring, small unit tactics, and above all maintenance of objective. Their daring exploits boosted the morale of the IDF.[40] After only five months, the unit was merged with the paratrooper battalion, imbuing the latter with the ethos of the Palmach.[41]

Unit 101 emphasized aggressiveness, initiative, and tactical innovation and took nothing for granted.[42] Its commanders led by example, shouting the famous "follow me" motto, and suffered a high casualty rate.[43] Dayan preferred aggressiveness and initiative; hence when the men went beyond—and sometimes against—their authorized objectives, he let them off the hook. For example, following a raid that had caused substantial collateral damage, Dayan defended Sharon's unit by stating: "Depending upon the instance, I prefer excessive initiative and action, even if it involves some mistakes here and there, to the passivity of 'sit and do nothing' and covering yourself with paper and seven authorizations for an operation before its execution."[44]

From 1953 to 1956, units under Sharon's command conducted more than seventy reprisal attacks, most of which were initiated by the young battalion commander himself.[45] A reconnaissance by force through the Mitla Pass during the Suez War (1956) conducted by Sharon's paratroopers had turned into a heroic but ultimately senseless battle. Dayan, nevertheless, defended him, re-marking again: "I regard the problem as grave when a unit fails to fulfil its battle task, not when it goes beyond the bounds of duty."[46] He reacted in a similar fashion when the Seventh Armored Brigade rushed into Sinai twenty-four hours ahead of plan; he affirmed that it was "better to be engaged in re-straining the noble stallion than in prodding the reluctant mule."[47] Dayan's approach led to development of what some observers have termed a *bitsuism* culture in the IDF.[48] A *bitsuist* ("doer") is an action-oriented individual capa-ble of conducting many tasks swiftly and successfully. A former commander of the IDF officer candidate school (*Bahad-1*) stated that "The term officer is re-lated to performance. . . . An officer is one who makes things happen."[49]

The Suez campaign was not conducted on the basis of detailed plans; Dayan essentially unleashed the forces to fight their way independently to the Suez Canal. The plan sacrificed preparatory arrangements in favor of the ele-ment of surprise, and there was no attempt to coordinate the advance of vari-ous task forces. The aim was not to annihilate the enemy but rather "bring about its collapse." In a sense, the difficulties encountered during the Sinai campaign stemmed from excessive independence and insufficient control and coordination. This was characteristic of Dayan's style of command.[50] To some extent, these deficiencies were solved by the 1967 Six Days' War.

In 1958 Sharon was sent for a "cooling off" period at the Camberley Staff and Command College. Interestingly, his final course paper was titled "Com-mand Interference in Tactical Battlefield Decisions: British and German Ap-proaches." During his stay in Britain, Sharon held a series of meetings with B. H. Liddell-Hart, with whom he discussed the Indirect Approach.[51]

THE ERA OF BLITZKRIEG, 1956–1973

Chief of Staff Chaim Laskov (1958–1960) was a former British officer who bal-anced the culture of *bitsuism* and improvisation with military education based professionalism.[52] He emphasized the need for planning and control through the staff, though not at the expense of subordinate independence.[53] Interestingly, his work was continued by Palmach veteran Chief of Staff Yit-zhak Rabin a few years later.[54]

It was Rabin who, as head of the IDF Doctrine Branch, revised and unified IDF doctrine and training. He thus created a common professional language, a prerequisite for mission command.[55] Rabin emphasized quick decision mak-ing and the ability to plan and issue orders on the move, skills necessary for maneuver warfare and mission command.[56] In contrast to Dayan, who had commandeered a light plane and could usually be found at a divisional headquarters during the Sinai campaign, Rabin issued his orders to the army of 1967 from his underground headquarters in Tel Aviv. The IDF had struck a balance between detailed planning and improvisation, independence and control; operational plans were devised and revised on the move, allowing commanders to seize fleeting opportunities.[57] Indeed, only the first day of the fighting on the Southern Front had been pre-planned; the fighting over the remaining three days was essentially improvised by local command.[58] The conduct of the 1956 and 1967 campaigns led Luttwak and Horowitz to observe that IDF commanders can "change plans in the midst of combat" and that willingness to shoulder responsibility had been "the key to this flexibility. Purposeful action was achieved by focusing the confused energies of loosely organized forces and not by a meticulous execution of brilliant plans."[59] One officer later recalled: "It is hard to find even one commander in Tal's Ugdah [division] who operated according to a preconceived plan. Almost all the plans were foiled during the fighting but all objectives were attained in full—and faster than expected."[60] The IDF system of command was based upon trust and subordinate initiative within the framework of higher objectives.[61] The popular contemporary IDF slogan, "plans are merely a platform for change," reflects this approach.[62] It was developed "without reference to a foreign model . . . if only because the German *Auftragstaktik* could never be acknowledged."[63] Similarly, after visiting the battlefields and interviewing the Israeli generals, American military historian S. L. A. Marshal summarized what he perceived to be IDF tenets of command:

> When your orders have not gotten through assume what they must be; When in doubt strike; Keep up the pressure until your troops are worn down, but when they are near exhaustion pull back and have them rest; Supplies are on the way: do not wait for them: they will catch up with you; Keep your sense of humor; The battle will never go as you planned it. Improvise; Surprise is your most effective weapon.[64]

FROM PREEMPTION TO COUNTEROFFENSIVE, 1967–1973

The victory of 1967 dramatically altered Israel's strategic position. The newly acquired strategic depth allowed the IDF to adopt a defensive strategic doctrine. Containment and counteroffensive were substituted for the preemption doctrine.[65] When Egyptian president Nasser declared the opening of the War of Attrition (1969–1970), the IDF was busy conducting routine security operations. While small commando and paratrooper units performed special operations,[66] regular units conducted routine duties, such as long patrols and static observation. Consequently, operational planning and execution began to stagnate.

The decisive results of the 1967 war led to a sense of superiority. Consequently, the IDF became complacent and neglected its traditional combined arms doctrine. It adopted instead an all-tank doctrine, referred to by one Israeli general as "tankomania."[67] This transformation occurred despite a massive Arab rearmament program that concentrated on Soviet anti-tank and anti-aircraft weapons, which could (and would) neutralize the IDF Blitzkrieg.[68] According to the new doctrine, an early warning delivered by army intelligence (*Aman*) would trigger a mobilization of reserves. While the regular forces delayed the enemy, the reserves would organize and conduct a powerful counteroffensive. This offensive would be conducted by means of a concentrated armored attack designed to annihilate the enemy. However, the counterattack made by Southern Command on 8 October 1973, on the third day of the Yom Kippur War, resulted in one of the worst disasters in the history of the IDF.[69] Nonetheless, despite the obvious shortcomings of both IDF doctrine and high command, Israeli forces eventually stopped the invading Egyptians. The victory was due primarily to the tenacity, sacrifice, initiative, and maintenance of objective of small unit commanders.[70]

The army was forced to adapt quickly to a new battlefield, and the reserves (primarily Six Days' War veterans) led the way. In one crucial incident, the Eighty-seventh Reconnaissance Battalion (reserve) located a gap between the two Egyptian armies deployed east of the Suez Canal. Although in a position to destroy several enemy artillery batteries, the battalion commander understood the magnitude of his discovery. The force retreated undetected, and the information was transmitted to divisional headquarters. A few days later the IDF exploited the gap, crossed the Suez Canal, and encircled the Third Egyptian Army.[71] In Northern Command, it was Major General Musa Peled who challenged his orders to bolster the defense of the Golan Heights piecemeal; instead he lobbied for a counterattack assignment for his division. His operational concept was approved by the general staff, in a large part due to his persistence; the maneuver proved decisive.[72]

THE DECLINE OF MISSION COMMAND, 1974–1990

The committee formed to investigate the war, which included former Chief of Staff Laskov, was critical of the decision-making process in Southern Command. It found that senior command failed to form a correct situation analysis and convey intent properly. The committee found grave deficiencies in staff work procedures. Radio recordings and transcripts revealed that orders were issued using unclear and unprofessional terminology, which resulted in confusion and misunderstandings. For example, units were ordered to "tread ahead carefully" or to "press on."[73] In an addendum to the report, Chaim Laskov noted that an unwritten doctrine had developed, parallel to the formal doctrine.[74] The committee concluded that many of the failures stemmed from improper implementation of doctrine rather than from the doctrine itself.[75] According to the committee, the IDF had become overconfident and had underestimated the enemy in the aftermath of the Six Days' War.

Unfortunately, some of these lessons, especially those pertaining to command culture failures, were not rectified.[76] In reaction to the wartime manpower shortages that had severely limited IDF operations, the decision was made to increase the size of the armed forces.[77] The dominant view was that technology and numbers could compensate for the shortcomings exposed in the war. As a result, the lean and agile IDF was transformed into a complex bureaucratic machine with overinflated staff and support units.[78] In addition, the image of the IDF had been dealt a severe blow in the eyes of the Israeli public. Consequently, it experienced difficulties in recruiting top candidates and retaining its most talented officers. Also, due to the dual career concept, it was discharging the generation of officers that had led the campaigns of 1956 and 1967. The new generation of midlevel and senior commanders had not received a similar military education; moreover, for the most part, their experience was limited to routine security functions rather than large-scale and high-paced maneuver operations.

The lack of institutional learning capabilities was now reinforced by an inadequate officer education system. In contrast to the original Haganah platoon leader's course, IDF officer courses merely prepared cadets for small unit command. In addition, the Staff and Command College (1953) failed to attract the best and the brightest students or instructors. Attendance was not a prerequisite for promotion but rather a period of rest and preparation for a second career.[79] Thus, the valuable lessons of the war, born of the baptism of fire, were forgotten. The outcome of these various difficulties was demonstrated in the 1982 Peace for Galilee campaign in Lebanon. The IDF had prepared for that campaign for over a year and enjoyed considerable quantitative and qualitative superiority. Nevertheless, with the exception of IAF squadrons and a few elite brigades, most units demonstrated mediocre capabilities and failed to meet their objectives.[80] In part, this was due to the political controversy surrounding the war objectives and the sensitivity toward casualties in a war that was not one of *ein brayra* ("no choice"). However, as one American observer noted, "Although the IDF has historically espoused . . . the practice of tasking commanders then allowing them to fulfil their missions with little outside interference, the Lebanon War marked a departure from that practice. . . . Commanders on the scene were often visited by senior officers who tended to make decisions on the spot."[81] Indeed, many critics argued that IDF commanders lacked at that point in time the professionalism necessary to lead brigades, divisions, and corps. They had been unable to properly articulate and communicate their intent to the lower echelons.[82]

LOW-INTENSITY CONFLICTS, 1982–1993

During the decade following the First Lebanon War, the IDF devoted its resources primarily to low-intensity conflicts. In Southern Lebanon, it faced a situation akin to guerrilla warfare and proved slow to adapt to the new circumstances.[83] The unpopularity of its continued presence in Lebanon on the home front coupled with an emphasis on force protection led to micromanaging and constant intervention by senior command.[84] According to one Israeli officer, "if at the beginning of our presence there NCOs commanded reconnaissance patrols or ambushes, by the latter years these actions were commanded by Captains and sometime even Majors."[85] An additional challenge was posed by the first Intifada (1989–1993), the large-scale Arab civil uprising. In this situation, too, the knowledge base and skill sets of the IDF proved insufficient. During this conflict, the IDF was forced to deal not only with its immediate rival but also with new powerful actors, such as the world media, nongovernmental organizations (NGOs), international observers, Jewish settlers, and public opinion. The political nature of the civil uprising introduced the IDF to the "Strategic Corporal" syndrome,[86] whereby junior tactical command decisions have a (often adverse) strategic impact.[87]

Demonstrations and riots, barricades, rocks, and even Molotov cocktail bombs and light firearms (in the latter years) were for a time defeating the

IDF. Its vaunted mobile warfare capabilities were irrelevant for missions such as chasing and arresting rock-throwing youths, imposing curfews, forcibly opening striking businesses, and manning static check points in Judea, Samaria, and Gaza.[88] The constant contact with the civilian population led to friction. Many soldiers and commanders were confused as to the rules of engagement (ROE) and mission parameters. Indeed, they felt leaderless, forced to make difficult decisions with little direction from above, particularly when these resulted in operational blunders. Media-assisted domestic and international scrutiny often transformed tactical errors into strategic ones, further galvanizing Palestinian opposition.[89] Due to the desire to uphold the principle of *tohar haneshek* (Purity of Arms), the IDF advocate general investigated and indicted soldiers accused of abusing Palestinians during policing operations. However, these indictments had a detrimental effect on the morale of soldiers and commanders.[90] Fear of prosecution for carrying out ambiguous orders under uncertain rules of engagement led to risk aversion, the *rosh katan* (shirking from responsibility) syndrome. Often soldiers and junior commanders failed to perform missions of questionable legality. The poet and Palmach veteran Chaim Heffer remarked that "The IDF will not be the same IDF if in the wake of every accident or mistake officers become so afraid of Parents that they jeopardize the main thing: initiative; the willingness to take risks; comradeship and ingenuity."[91]

The IDF became embroiled in constabulary operations for which it was unprepared, untrained, and ill equipped.[92] This resulted in what one observer labeled schizophrenic behavior: training for conventional warfare but practicing police work.[93] The IDF was charged with controlling the lives of dissenting civilians instead of fighting an enemy. Continued frustration borne of the nature of these operations led to instances of brutalization, badly damaging the moral character of the IDF and its cohesiveness.[94] The practice of mission command requires clearly defined objectives, resources, and constraints. However, IDF objectives during that period were ambiguous and subject to public debate. As a result, the Israeli army began to experience widespread distrust and lack of initiative. The implicit form of mission command it had practiced in its mobile campaigns was lost by the First Lebanon War and the Palestinian Intifada.

7 COMPARISON

PART II OF THIS BOOK has charted the dominant cultural characteristics and command approaches of three armies prior to their adoption of mission command.[1] It was demonstrated that each organization developed a consistent and distinctive approach to command, though certain individuals or events proved exceptions to the rule. The historical analysis revealed a number of common themes that influenced the command approach; these are summarized in Table 1. The table is loosely based on Schien's model of primary cultural building blocks: basic assumptions, espoused values, and artifacts.[2] The table depicts the culture of command in these three armies and in the ideal type of mission command.

The American, British, and Israeli armies developed different command approaches based on distinct military cultures. Deconstruction of these cultures uncovers different assumptions concerning such issues as the nature of war, the role of the army, risk taking, and the military profession and education. These differences stem from national character, historical experience, and geopolitical circumstances. As culture is shaped also by leaders, these cultures represent the legacy of past influential leaders.

Schien argued that congruence between espoused beliefs and values and the underlying organizational assumptions will lead to the "articulation of those values into a philosophy of operating [which] can be helpful in bringing the group together, serving as a source of identity and core mission."[3]

The basic assumptions and values are reflected in the next level, observable artifact, in the form of educational institution and programs, technology, human resources practices, and staff organization. Consequently, it is easy to see

Table 1. A Comparison of Organizational and Command Cultures

Characteristics	American Army	British Army	IDF [a]	Mission Command Culture
		Basic Assumptions		
Attitude toward war	Similar to business	A sport or a game for the aristocracy	Necessary evil, "no choice"	A social phenomenon, clash of wills produces friction
Attitude toward the army	Undesired, but if needed should be large and powerful	Limited basis, to secure and police the empire	Necessary to secure existence	Central institution, "an army that has a state"
Attitude toward risk	Should be avoided if possible	Should be well calculated if taken	Unavoidable	Necessary in all levels
Attitude toward the military profession	Acceptable but not desirable	A lifestyle rather than a profession	A calling but not a proper profession	A distinct profession
Main inspiration for military education	Managerial knowledge	Traditions and practical experience	Field experience	A balance of theory and practice
		Espoused values		
Social source of military elite	West Point graduates	British serving aristocracy	Kibbutz and Palmach members	A blend of aristocracy and professional elite
Command doctrine	Managerial principles	Umpiring	Optional control	Friction, chance, and uncertainty
Uniquely emphasized principles of war[b]	Mass, simplicity, unity of command	Maintenance of aim, moral, surprise, flexibility	Initiative and stratagem	Reciprocal and dialectic principles
Inspiring figures	Grant, Lee, Sherman, Eisenhower, Patton	Marlborough, Wellington, Slim, Montgomery	Wingate, Dayan, Allon, Sharon, Tal	Fredrick the Great, Moltke the Elder
		Artifacts		
Higher military academies	Focus on managerial aspects	Focus on staff administration	Marginal influence or importance	Produces military professionals elite
General staff corps	Low status and influence	Medium status and influence	Medium status, but integrates all services	"Brain of an army," high influence
HQ's staff organization	French bureau system, operations equal to other bureaus	Similar to German structure, operations are "first among equals"	Adapted a version of the British/German structure	All staff functions revolves around operations
Technology	Heavy reliance on technology	Conservative and suspicious	Improvised	A tool to serve doctrine
Human resources policies	Managerial efficiency	The regimental system	High cohesion	Maintenance of unit cohesion and tactical flexibility

NOTE: The table relates to the historical period covered in Part II.

[a]The information concerning the IDF relates mostly to the years 1948–1973.

[b]This list includes only the unique principles. For a comprehensive listing, see Zvi Lanir, "The 'Principals of War' and Military Thinking," *Journal of Strategic Studies* 16:1 (March 1993), 1–17.

why the U.S. army developed a relatively centralized command approach. The British army was caught between the traditional independent nature of the regimental system and the need to manage a large conscript army. Historically it existed on a continuum between extreme laissez-faire and strict centralization.

Paradoxically, though it maintained a defensive ethos, the IDF had adopted an offensive strategy, believing it has "no choice."[4] Similar to Prussia, Israel was forced to fight quick decisive wars on multiple fronts. In addition, its original cadre of leaders was imbued with the egalitarian values of the *Kibbutzim* as well as a sense of independence and sacrifice. The implicit mission command practiced by the IDF was based on Palmach, autodidactic learning, and wartime experience rather than institutional knowledge. As the relevance of acquired experience declined and circumstances changed, so did the practice of mission command.

TRANSFORMING COMMAND　　　　　　　# Part III

8 ADOPTING AND ADAPTING MISSION COMMAND

THIS CHAPTER discusses the process through which mission command was adopted and adapted by each of the three armies under investigation. Each of the three sections is further divided into two subsections: the first describes the context and circumstances that led to the rediscovery and adoption of mission command up to the point of its incorporation into official doctrine. The second follows the debates and interpretations of this approach, which constitute part of the adaptation process. The existence of this intellectual exploration in the armies signifies an attempt to understand mission command within a unique cultural context.

The rediscovery of mission command reflects the perception shared by all three armies that it is essentially a "best practice." Subsequently, all three armies believed it should be adopted. Following this realization, in some cases in parallel, came an attempt to understand mission command in its original historical context and provide a modern interpretation that corresponds with current circumstances. Each army encountered different challenges and devised its own unique solution for integrating mission command into it. This process resulted in the emergence of very different views and interpretation of mission command and its place within the overall doctrine and theory of each army.

THE U.S. ARMY

Adoption and Adaptation of Mission Command

Adoption of mission command by the American army was carried out as part of the reforms of the 1970s and 1980s. The epicenter of these reforms was the development of a new doctrine designed to combat Soviet quantitative superiority. The 1976 field manual (FM) 100-5 *Operations*, though still espousing the principles of active defense, was the first such attempt. Its successor, the 1982 FM *Operations*, advocated the principles of maneuver warfare and the new "AirLand battle" doctrine. Inspired by the Germans, Israelis, and the Red Army, the new doctrine substituted mobility for attrition. It also marked the introduction of mission command into the American army command doctrine.[1] Indeed, mission command was a central tenant of AirLand battle and a prerequisite for its execution.

The AirLand battle was an intellectual reaction to the 1976 field manual, which many believed to be inadequate. When the former was first introduced by commander of Training and Doctrine Command (TRADOC) General Starry, it was described as merely evolutionary in order to minimize resistance to it.[2] Today, however, many agree that the doctrine posed a greater break than hitherto assumed.[3] According to Richard Lock-Pullan, the new doctrine emphasized "out-thinking instead of out slugging. . . . [The reforms] were aimed to develop a culture of a highly skilled sophisticated and capable army."[4] The 1976, 1982, and 1986 editions of FM 100-5 *Operations* were tailored to unique characteristics of the European battlefield and the Soviet adversary. The experience of Vietnam proved irrelevant in the face of Warsaw Pact numerical superiority.[5] Recognizing their numerical inferiority, planners sought a qualitative advantage. Consequently, the army began instituting a series of reforms, one of which was the establishment of a joint body for training and doctrine (1971). The new body, TRADOC, was created in order to facilitate integration of doctrinal developments, training, force structure, and weaponry.

Even prior to this, Chief of Staff General Creighton Abrams (1972–1974) stated that the army's objectives included "building more combat strength into the force . . . bolstering the responsiveness and strength of the Army's reserve components" while maintaining readiness.[6] He also emphasized the importance of the human element, stating that "People are not *in* the Army, people *are* the Army."[7] To support this vision, the first commander of TRADOC, General William E. DePuy, endeavored to "quickly produce a conceptual product that would suit the new conditions facing the American Army, the move from one theatre in Asia to a very different one in central Europe."[8] DePuy understood that the army might be forced to fight a short decisive war while outnumbered and outgunned. His primary objective was to reestablish fundamental tactical skills that required highly trained soldiers capable of forming maneuver-oriented combined armed teams.[9] Reinforced by the experience of the 1973 Arab-Israeli War, DePuy implemented these ideas in his 1976 manual.[10] It was meant to provide practical guidance to combat leaders on the modern battlefield. Though the term "active defense" was coined by others, it was an apt description of the manual's central themes.[11]

In the chapter titled "Defense," the manual stated five fundamentals of defensive operations: "understand the enemy; see the battlefield; concentrate at the critical times and places; fight as a combined arms team; exploit the advantages of the defender."[12] Active defense depended on the ability to concentrate sufficient combat power against Soviet attacks executed "on very narrow fronts in great depth."[13] Attaining a favorable force ratio required commanders to make timely decisions, expose their flanks, fight without reserves, and achieve a rapid lateral concentration of forces. It also relied on secure communications. In addition, commanders had to maximize the advantages afforded by terrain and to "understand completely the capabilities and limitations of friendly and enemy weapons."[14] Finally, defensive operations were to be elastic in nature in order to retain force cohesiveness and objective conformity in the face of large-scale attacks. The challenge, according to DePuy, would be "to destroy many targets in a short period of time."[15] Soviet numerical and resource superiority combined with the lethality and rapid pace of the modern battlefield would preclude national mobilization following the outbreak of hostilities. The army had to be prepared to "win the first battle of the next war" or face dire consequences.[16] Hence, defenders had "to move their units and improve the force ratio at critical points. The doctrine is neither an attempt to defend static lines nor a call for mobile defence, using territorial depth."[17]

Some observers believed that active defense marked the beginning of a doctrinal renaissance and praised it for refocusing attention on the defense of Europe.[18] Others criticized its basic tenets. Some of the arguments were misplaced, reflecting selective reading or ignorance of the army's constraints. More pertinent were the arguments against the emphasis on the defensive and the first battle; the preference of firepower over maneuver and of physical over psychological aspects of war; an oversimplification of Soviet doctrine; a lack of tactical reserve; and the feasibility of DePuy's "concentration tactics."[19] The most vocal opposition was voiced by civilian experts such as William S. Lind, Edward N. Luttwak, Steven L. Canby, Paul Bracken, and Jeffrey Record.[20] They argued that the manual reintroduced the traditional American preference for head-on collisions and reliance on superior resources. They considered army officers:

"hidebound bureaucrats cultivating managerial skills over leadership, being wedded to archaic methods, ignoring the study of military history and theory, and turning to safer technology instead of innovative military art." They concluded that the "Army compensated for lack of imagination with high technology and a tendency to treat military challenges as if they were simple engineering problems."[21] Lind, who developed a theory of maneuver warfare on the basis of Air Force Colonel John Boyd's ideas, was probably the most influential of the group. He emphasized the psychological benefits of "creating an unexpected and unfavorable operational strategic condition, not to kill enemy troops or destroy their equipment."[22] Lind advocated "Boyd cycling the enemy ... until he can no longer fight as an effective organized force,"[23] explaining:

> Conflict can best be understood as time competitive cycles of observing, orienting, deciding, and acting. . . . Whoever can go through this "Boyd Cycle" or "OODA Loop" consistently faster gains a tremendous advantage primarily because by the time his opponent acts his action has already changed the situation as to make the opponent's action irrelevant.[24]

According to Lind, effective fighting within the chaos of battle requires combatants to be consistently faster than their adversaries through the practice of operational art: "battles and refusals to give battle, to strike directly at the enemy centre of gravity ... [which] if shattered will bring him down."[25] Achieving the necessary tempo of operations requires decentralization of command and not only accepting but rather generating chaos.[26] Central to his theory are the following interdependent concepts: *Auftragstaktik* (mission command), *Schwerpunkt* (main effort), and *Lucken und Flachen* (surfaces and gaps).[27] The use of German terminology reveals Lind's intellectual inspiration and signifies his recognition of the origins of these concepts.

Lind described a dynamic environment wherein enemy strong and weak points cannot be predetermined as they are temporary and changing. Authority must therefore be delegated "down to the lowest level, so that small unit commanders can find gaps and immediately exploit them without delay."[28] Once the main effort is conveyed through the commander's "intent," reconnaissance forces locate and create gaps between enemy surfaces. Once identified, the main force is pulled through these gaps. Crucial to this process are subordinate initiative, boldness, and quick decisions.[29] Exploitation of gaps and maintenance of primary effort depends on effective execution of mission command, rapid decisions, and quick actions. In Lind's theory, mission command is a

Series of contracts between superior and subordinates. The superior, in his contract, pledges to make the result he desires crystal clear to his subordinates . . . to leave the subordinate maximum latitude in determining how to get the result, and perhaps the greatest change—to back him up when he makes mistakes.[30]

According to Lind, the subordinate ensures that his actions serve the commander's intent; self-discipline is substituted for imposed discipline, and initiative is constantly rewarded. The focus is on the situation, the enemy, and the final outcome rather than on processes and procedures. Missions are defined in terms of the desired effect on the enemy. When changed circumstances preclude the realization of the commander's intent through the original mission, subordinates are expected to revise their plans accordingly.[31]

Lind was inspired primarily by the historic Prussian-Germans and the British military intellectuals Liddell-Hart and Fuller.[32] Indeed, twelve of the twenty books he recommended for further reading were written either by German generals or about the German military.[33] Also on this list was Edward Luttwak's book on the Israeli army, which Lind considers "the most maneuver-minded post-World War II armed service."[34] In addition to introducing readers to the Israeli version of mission command, which he labeled "Optional Control," Luttwak's book emphasized the significance of the operational level and operational art. The latter he defined as a "higher combination that is more than the sum of its tactical parts."[35] At the same time, Lind's ideas were labeled "maneuver warfare." These radical ideas were first adopted by the Marine Corps, which was then undergoing transformation. Initially a light infantry unit, it was incorporating armored formations capable of sharing the burden of European defense with the army. Maneuver warfare and mission command afforded the Marines a means of punching "above their own weight."[36]

As Robert Doughty has suggested, *Active Defense* "became one of the most controversial field manuals ever written."[37] Field tests raised doubts concerning the actual effectiveness of the new doctrine, and its tenets were never accepted by the majority of officers.[38] It nevertheless reawakened interest in doctrine leading to a "renaissance of professional discourse" concerning army fighting methods.[39] The transition from tactical to operational doctrine is credited to TRADOC commander General Don A. Starry.[40] Starry, who replaced DePuy, adopted the aforementioned criticism and revised the doctrine.[41] According to General Huba Wass de Czega, one of the developers of the new doctrine, "army commanders became convinced as a result from their field training and war games that they would be unable to defeat the Soviets using the doctrine of 1976."[42]

Starry revisited the lessons of the 1973 Yom Kippur War through the prism of operational art. He was particular impressed by General Musah Peled's counterattack deep behind the Syrian lines, on the third day of the war, which had thrown the Syrian and Iraqi forces completely off balance.[43] The war "reaffirmed his operational idea that without initiative the outnumbered forces are doomed to lose."[44] Starry's ideas were inspired by his experience in World War II and Korea. From retired Wehrmacht generals he garnered a more comprehensive understanding of mission command, maneuver, and the operational art. For example, he held a four-day conference (1980) exploring Wehrmacht experience in Russia with Generals Balck and von Mellenthin.[45] The purpose was to derive lessons for a modern defense of Europe against a Soviet invasion.[46] The Germans told him that they had emphasized the human element and expounded on mission-type orders and the culture prevailing in the Wehrmacht that had enabled reliance on them. They explained that the Germans' superior battlefield performance derived from "the individuality of the German fighting man, his freedom to take initiatives and the system which engendered these policies and attitudes."[47] According to Balck, "independent action along the line of the general concept was praised and accepted."[48] Mission command, he explained, depended on shared experiences, doctrine, and training. Mellenthin remarked that "Commanders and subordinates start to understand each other during war. The better they know each other, the shorter and less detailed the orders can be. To follow a commander or an order requires that it is also thought through on the level from which the order was given."[49] In order to enable operational-level initiative and develop maneuver warfare doctrine, Starry adopted the concept of depth in relation to time, space, and resources. By analyzing the battlefield through the prism of these concepts, he hoped to acquire the flexibility and elasticity necessary to outmaneuver the larger Red Army. The new doctrine shifted the focus from terrain to the opposing enemy force; it regarded the battlefield as holistic rather than as lines of engagement.[50]

The new mode of fighting was centered on seizing and maintaining initiative rather than the traditional attrition strategy. The army had to learn how to confer operational-level significance to independent tactical engagements. FM 100-5 *Operations* (1982) stated that the operational concept stands at the very core of army doctrine. The focus was shifted from battles to campaigns, thereby signifying a conceptual shift from sequential linearity to holistic complexity. Attrition through superior technology and tactics was substituted by operational maneuvers utilizing interrelated tactical engagements designed to produce a strategic effect. Instead of concentrating on leading enemy formations, the new doctrine targeted rear echelons and command and control centers.[51] Its four basic tenets were "initiative, depth, agility, and synchronization."[52] Fighting depended on maintenance of tempo and aggressive execution relying on superior command and training rather than on resources or technology. The new doctrine developed, AirLand battle, required skilled and adaptive forces and leaders capable of recognizing "critical events as they occur and act to avoid enemy strengths and attack enemy vulnerabilities."[53]

A revised edition of the manual appeared in 1986 wherein the technical "operational level" was replaced by the more dynamic term "operational art." It instructed practitioners to identify an opponent's operational center of gravity and concentrate combat power against it.[54] Thus, the Clausewitzian center of gravity became the focal point of maneuver theory. Contrary to popular belief, the theory does not advocate maneuver over firepower but rather a balance between the two in the spirit of the maneuverist approach. This involved identifying and attacking key weak points, affecting and disintegrating the enemy's center of gravity. Commanders were instructed to ensure "a unified, aggressive quick, precise, agile and synchronized effort throughout the force."[55]

Maneuver warfare advocates believed that the necessary characteristics were embedded in the American national character and had to only be rediscovered.[56] This style of command emphasized high-quality, flexible, and fluid command, in contrast to the traditional top-down approach. The theory advocated rapid completion of OODA loops as a means of disrupting the enemy's decision-making capabilities. Central to the new 1986 manual were the mission command principles of clear intent, brief communications across the chain of command, and synchronization.[57] The latter denoted "the unity of effort of all forces towards single aim via a clear intent."[58] It depended on implicit rather than explicit coordination achieved if "all forces involved fully understand the intent of the commander."[59] Synchronization thus reflected "the essence of the operational art."[60]

Despite the innovation it represented, the AirLand battle doctrine was not universally accepted. Some complained it was merely an updated version of the traditional attrition mind-set. Robert Leonhard concluded that the changes were not radical enough:

> The developers of *AirLand Battle* flirted with maneuver but have been unable to shake American military traditions of the past. While *AirLand Battle* represents an attempt to break with doctrinal problems of the Vietnam era, the irresistible song of technology, fire and mass destruction continue to lure American thought back to battle calculus of attrition.[61]

Debates and Interpretations

The decision to adopt mission command led to debates concerning three major issues. One issue debated in the years following the adoption was the morality of adopting a technique employed by the Nazis. The second concerned the feasibility of adapting a foreign concept developed within a specific historical context.[62] It devolved from the broader issue of whether German military performance warranted emulation.[63] The third debate concerned the translation and interpretation of the concept as well as identification of its various comprising elements and their relation to a broader theory.

The debate concerning German military excellence, in which both officers and academics partook, raged over the pages of practitioner journals, such as *Military Review, Infantry,* and *Armor*. The issue transcended the mere historic; it had a direct impact on the practice of the profession. For instance, Roger Beaumont challenged the American and British fascination with the Wehrmacht performance. He argued that not only had the German army been greatly influenced by Nazi ideology but even its early victories were "more image than substance."[64] Moreover, he simply asked, if they were so good, how come they lost? Similarly, Daniel Hughes cautioned against borrowing German concepts of warfare, as "not all professionals share this respect for the *Wehrmacht*."[65] In contrast, Martin van Creveld held that the Wehrmacht was more than a bunch of fanatics; hence, though Nazi influence existed, its degree should not be overstated. He argued also that victory is neither the only nor even the most important yardstick for combat prowess. Indeed, an analysis of battlefield performance reveals that German tactical and operational performance was indeed exceptional, though not perfect.[66]

Many authors emphasized German strategic failures,[67] and one even criticized Wehrmacht performance on the operational level, though he praised its practice of mission command.[68] One author contended that Americans are as maneuver- and improvisation-oriented as was the Wehrmacht. Regardless, he argued, the concept and practice of maneuver denotes a style rather than an independent theory. He remarked cynically that

> Maneuverists act as if they are unaware of the American military heritage particularly in the area of leadership initiative. . . . They prefer to use the German term *Auftragstaktik*, and act like they have found another piece of the True (Iron) Cross . . . [while it actually] typified the American military since 1775. . . . Put a lieutenant in the jungle with a radio and he will ask forgiveness not permission. Try to micromanage him and he will find the off switch. . . . From the revolution to the gulf that has been the American method.[69]

Some felt that mission command could not transcend the cultural and historic context in which it was developed. There was little agreement concerning its comprising elements or their precise meaning.[70] Hence, it was unclear whether *Auftragstaktik* should be translated as mission-type orders, directive control, or mission command. Indeed, despite many efforts, the Americans have yet to reach universally accepted definitions of the various elements of mission command. According to one historian, while the 1993 FM demonstrated a deeper understanding of mission command, orders remained over-detailed.[71] Others drew attention to the fact that the latter manual advocated employing mission command primarily if direct communications fail.[72] To them, the overriding importance accorded to synchronization suggested that explicit coordination was required of commanders. Following the Gulf War (1991), some critiques argued that the emphasis on synchronization had eliminated mission command de facto.[73]

The authors of the revised 2001 FM edition attempted to improve and clarify mission command–related terminology and other German concepts.[74] Nevertheless, confusion abounded as indicated by the issuance of an FM devoted to command in general, and mission command in particular, merely two years later.[75] It was issued "because U.S. Army doctrine has been relatively sparse in its higher doctrinal literature," which led to "multiple versions of C2 doctrine."[76] The new publication also failed to achieve uniformity and additional literature has continued to appear. One such essay was written by Marine General (Ret.) Paul van Riper, who as the "red" commander defeated American planners during the famous millennium 2002 exercise.[77] Using simple terminology and many examples, Riper attempted to clarify the concept of "intent"—designating the higher purpose rather than the desired effect—the *why* of the mission. Commenting on prevailing confusion, Riper remarked that "The paragraph [of intent] often becomes an unfocused discussion of many unrelated items. . . . A mission statement tells subordinate commanders what the higher commander wants them to do, the task, and why they are to do it, the purpose or intent."[78] The difficulties in the comprehension and application of *Auftragstaktik* that arose led critiques to question its usefulness. However, most of them believed in its utility, disagreeing primarily about the best means of implementing it. They argued that popularization of the German concept and insufficient attention to its organizational and historic context had rendered it impotent.[79] It became a fashionable management concept, such as Total Quality Management (TQM) or Management by Objectives (MBO). Like these concepts, its life expectancy was rather short as its adapters failed to institute the necessary complimentary cultural transformation. One such critic, Daniel Hughes, remarked that adoption was hindered by "a careless and superficial application of German terms and concepts to current practices . . . [and] a general failure to place individual German methods and experiences in their proper historical context."[80] A full decade later he was still convinced that

> Wrenching the *Auftrag* principle from its broader context . . . might well be an undertaking of questionable validity. . . . As long as Western armies regard *Auftragstaktik* simply as a policy of short general orders, rather than a fundamental principle governing all requiring decisions and judgment, their officers will not understand what the principle entails, let alone implement it on the battlefield.[81]

Another soldier-scholar voiced his reservations:

> *Auftragstaktik* . . . reflected a deep tradition of encouraging initiative and allowing freedom of action to subordinate leaders. It was the tradition that came first. . . . To accomplish this, Army training manuals and publications must be congruent with the spirit of FM 100-5, and the use of the school or approved solution must be avoided.[82]

Despite these difficulties, scholars such as van Creveld opined, the adoption and adaptation of *Auftragstaktik* was feasible:

> Thus, although it is certainly true that the method of *Auftrag* and *Weisung* has deep roots in German military history, it is not necessarily true that a non German armed force has to traverse that history in its entirety, to understand and apply that method.[83]

Despite much opposition, mission command has endured the turmoil that followed the Cold War and the transformations of the American army. Considered well suited for the twenty-first century, it reflects democratic and individualistic values.[84] Also, it is congruent with the contemporary leadership theory that emphasizes empowerment, flat organizations, and the complexities of modern organization and battlefields.[85] Indeed, some even raised the concern that it had mutated from doctrine to dogma: "It is a religion. . . . There are no other forms of command or control. Detailed control is unmanly, sinful, and blasphemous. Best not to talk about it in polite society."[86] The consensus concerning the universal truism represented by mission command has signaled a shift in the focus of the debate, which will be discussed later on.

THE BRITISH ARMY

Adoption and Adaptation of Mission Command

A renaissance of British military thought began during the 1980s, a half decade later than in America; the written doctrine it bore included mission command. In contrast to the American experience, the British reforms are associated with the personality and actions of one individual, Field Marshal Sir Nigel Bagnall. Bagnall, commander of the First British Corps in 1981 and later of the Northern Army Group (NORTHAG) in 1983–1985, was convinced that the existing passive battle doctrine had to be replaced with a maneuver-based doctrine best suited to stop a Soviet invasion.[87] His ideas had begun to develop as a result of the adoption of the strategy of flexible response by NATO in 1967, which demanded a conventional rather than a nuclear response to a Soviet invasion.[88] He stated that "there is no alternative to us attempting to seize the initiative at an early stage" and that "[one] can not expect to win a war of attrition."[89]

Bagnall's strategic thinking and the changes he sought required adoption of mission command; British army command rigidity was an often lamented aspect of its tradition. He understood that the mobile operations he envisioned required a cultural transformation. This was the only way to achieve the necessary flexibility and responsiveness of command in a fast-paced battlefield. Bagnall desired rapid information-processing capabilities that would allow his army to impose itself on an opponent's command and control process. Seizing the initiative essentially denoted imposing oneself on an adversary's decision-making cycle and forcing it to react. He believed that mission command could allow subordinates to make independent decisions when changing circumstances required rapid reactions. Once its intricacies had been mastered by a generation of commanders, less information processing, central planning, or intervention would be required, and operations phases would be completed in an increasing speed. The system Bagnall envisioned resembled the Prussian-German original.[90] Contrary to the Americans, the British performed reforms under severe resource constraints; Bagnall's motto thus became to do more with less.[91] He promoted a transition to maneuver with an emphasis on speed in his corps, instituted small mobile headquarters (HQ), and introduced new SOPs. Bagnall believed that Her Majesty's officers had to learn how to make snap decisions, take the initiative, and comprehend the plans of superiors two levels up.[92] In addition:

> Wherever possible orders should be given as a single directive. . . . The mission should leave the subordinate commander as much freedom of execution as possible and should contain only those constraints, essential to cooperation with other units. . . . Dithering over the details, when these are not fundamental to the task, leads to delay and lost opportunities.[93]

As an army group commander, Bagnall instituted a maneuver-based deployment plan for the entire force, in place of the previous plan envisioning set-piece isolated battles. He further introduced a uniform doctrine for the army and established the army's operational-level course: the Higher Staff and Command Course. Both the doctrine and the course emphasized the operational level, mission command, and maneuver warfare approach.[94] However, the latter was fully incorporated into Army Command and Staff Course exercises only in 1994, after Bagnall's retirement. Then it was defined as a "warfighting philosophy which seeks to defeat the enemy by shattering his moral and physical cohesion . . . rather than to destroy him physically through attrition." It was also decided to favor the term "maneuverist approach" over the American "maneuver warfare."[95]

A practitioner rather than a theorist, Bagnall left little in writing.[96] The most prominent Briton to write on maneuver warfare and mission command at that period was Richard E. Simpkin.[97] He devoted a lengthy discussion to the concept of *Auftragstaktik*, which he translated as "directive control," rejecting the American term "mission command."[98] Simpkin argued that it better reflected the original idea, that is, controlling the process through general directives rather than detailed orders. He believed that due to unique officer training and education methodology, the Germans had practiced *Auftrags-*

taktik far better than the British ever had.[99] Above all he believed that the German system was able to realize mission command because it was based on professional trust. In order to further illuminate the issue, he discussed an analogy from the world of sports, where one sometimes finds self-directed competitive teams that require very little external guidance.[100] Simpkin's direct influence over Bagnall in particular and the maneuver reform in general is difficult to gauge as his style of writing severely restricted his readership.[101] Nevertheless, he was considered an important and original thinker, if often misunderstood, and it can be assumed that his work served to confirm and even inspire the winds of change in the British Army.[102]

The "Ginger" Group

Bagnall established the Tactical Doctrine Committee (TDC) when he commanded the First British Corps in Germany. An informal discussion group, its initial twelve members included representatives of various ranks and branches and even a Ministry of Defence (MOD) official. They were chosen because they understood the concepts he was promoting and could assist in developing a combined arms environment. Through the group, Bagnall hoped to develop ideas to improve the capabilities of his corps. The size and purview of the group expanded as Bagnall received command of NORTHAG and then again when he became chief of the general staff (CGS). By this time, the group numbered as many as thirty individuals and has become known as the Ginger Group.

It held heated debates and open discussions. Following these sessions, reports were made and disseminated to various officers within the military. Critics invited to share their opinion often left with a better understanding of the group's ideas; some were even converted.[103] The group served as a think tank, developing and testing these ideas. Bagnall's right hand in these events was Peter Inge, his corps chief of staff. Inge took over the group after Bagnall's retirement and maintained its momentum and focus.[104] Forces opposing the group within the British military establishment, including Field Marshal Craver and General Akehurst,[105] noted that its unorthodox methods circumvented the chain of command. This was a legitimate concern, as many junior officers were asked to join the group while various senior commanders were excluded from it. Moreover, it projected an image of elitism, and some believed they were creating a faction within the army.[106] Nevertheless, the group proved instrumental in establishing a consensus within the British military and implementing

Bagnall's reforms. More than a discussion group, it was a powerful tool for neutralizing opposition within the military and was more significant than Bagnall cared to admit.

The Bagnall Reforms

It took eighteen years (1971–1989) to bring Bagnall's reforms to fruition. The long journey began in 1971, when he first began to develop these ideas. It was continued in 1975, when as a divisional commander he demonstrated his novel operational concept through a series of exercises. But it was only when he became commander of the First Corps in 1981 that he began to systematically develop these ideas with the assistance of the TDC. By the time he became the commander of the BAOR in 1983, the reforms were in full swing.[107]

Bagnall's crowning achievement was the implementation of a new army group defense plan and an operational concept. These included an adoption of a joint land-air mobile warfare concept exploiting maneuver at the operational level: the "counter-stroke." In 1985 he was promoted to chief of the general staff, a position he held until his retirement in 1988, at which time the primary principles of the reforms became SOPs for the British Army. That year also saw the first class of the High Command Course, inspired and founded by Bagnall. The express purpose of the new program was to educate officers on the theory and conduct of the operational level. The new concept was endorsed by an official Statement on the Defence Estimates (1986), stating that "force improvements permit the adoption of a more mobile tactical concept. Static defence can lead only to a war of attrition, while the new concept would allow the defenders to seize the initiative."[108]

It would be safe to assume that some form of reforms in the British Army would have probably occurred without Bagnall, but they would have taken a different course if not for him, a flexible and shrewd individual who had the necessary patience and determination to see the process through. He provided the solid framework that enabled the army to exploit the potential of new weapons and equipment. In the absence of this framework, the reforms could have been mostly cosmetic and limited to minor tactical adaptations. He was often considered a cult leader due to the loyalty he commanded from his subordinates while he could be rather intolerant toward others. His success was due, as Bagnall himself believed, not to the development of radical new ideas but rather to the making of right decisions at the right place and at the right time.[109]

Defending Europe: British and American Concepts

The 1976 American FM 100-5 operations, *Active Defense*, advocated secur-ing operational initiative but in reality focused on firepower-oriented defense involving combined arms forces conducting lateral movements. Successive manuals issued in 1982 and 1986 presented the operational-level maneuver-oriented AirLand battle doctrine. Designed to meet the demands of the Euro-pean theater, the new doctrine afforded means of defeating an outnumbering foe through firepower, maneuver, and superior technique in a multidimen-sional battle.[110] In contrast, Bagnall proposed a combination of a positional and mobile defense, utilizing firepower to deny a rapid Soviet penetration and exploiting successes by means of a counterattack or counter-stroke.[111] His con-cept differed from the American concept in four major aspects: it was not heavily reliant on technology, it focused on army group interoperability, it did not rely on close air support (which the British lacked), and it did not culminate in a deep penetration (which the British could not support). Bagnall hoped to offset technology and resource disadvantages through development of the human element.[112]

Intellectual Origins

Bagnall's operational concepts were inspired by the Wehrmacht experience, particularly its mobile defense/counter-stroke operations on the Eastern Front. He derived his lessons from books such as von Mellenthin's *Panzer Battles*, Herman Balck's *On Tactics,* and Liddell-Hart's *The Rommel Papers.* Of similar importance were the conferences he held with individuals such as Generals Balck and von Mellenthin. It was Balck's and von Mellethin's counter-stroke operations that inspired his mobile defense concept. Bagnall hoped to adopt the means through which the outnumbered Wehrmacht had successfully held the Russian bear at bay.

The German experience was especially pertinent because the Soviets still utilized adapted versions of Marshal Mikhail Tukhachevsky's *Deep Battle* doctrine and the operational maneuver groups.[113] Bagnall found that the Ger-mans had secured surprise through offensive action and had dislocated the Soviet defense in depth by maintaining initiative and momentum. This was accomplished by deliberately targeting the enemy weaknesses rather than strengths—what his American colleague Lind defined as "surfaces and gaps" and *Schwerpunkt.* He believed that these high-tempo operations were enabled by a flexible command embodying the principles of mission command. They were able to maintain clarity of direction and purpose of attack—intent. Unlike other British officers, Bagnall did not rely on the British experience. He believed that though there had been successful instances wherein the proper principles had been used, they were too few and far apart to afford a comprehensive theoretical framework. Also, Bagnall paid scant attention to the Israeli experience. This may have been due to a belief that the Israeli and German experiences were essentially similar. His inclination toward the German experience may have stemmed from his fluency in German, which had enabled him to read German materials early on in his career. Nevertheless, his ideas evolved independently. The process was fueled by an individual searching for an alternative to an inadequate and insufficient attrition doctrine. He sought to strengthen NATO prowess through a doctrinal evolution and improved command performance. These, he believed, would facilitate operational maneuver-oriented warfare.[114]

Bagnall had to contend with shrinking resources, the regimental system, and a proclivity for set-piece battles; the defensive was based on attrition and delaying battles. Bagnall believed that conversion of tactical victories into a significant counter-stroke necessitated securing the initiative at the earliest possible moment. Put differently, his maneuverist approach relied on "opportunism—the calculated risk and the exploitation both of chance and circumstances . . . on winning the battle by surprise or failing this by speed and the aptness of response."[115] An operational-level design can facilitate exploitation of enemy weakness and avoidance of enemy strength. To ease the acceptance of the reforms, it was decided to retain existing terminology. The idea was to combine the best of the old and the new. Bagnall's operational philosophy was "you will adhere to the fundamentals of war. . . . You can't plan the next move without reading the current situation and planning in advance is not wise, you have to develop a skill to read the battlefield."[116] The process was difficult, for the British Army did not have the necessary cultural and traditional background or the understanding of maneuver warfare and mission command needed in order to ground the new concept in British warfare experience.[117]

Ironically, the Germans themselves opposed Bagnall's ideas, fearing that Germany would bear the brunt of these major engagements. Leopold Chalupa, the German commander in chief of the Allied Forces in Central Europe (1983–1987), felt that Bagnall's ideas relied on capabilities that the British forces lacked. Additionally, he did not appreciate being lectured to on the

German principles of the operational level and maneuver war by the British novice. He was surprised that the British could even contemplate a plan that the larger German army, defending its own land and boasting a tradition of operational and maneuver excellence, rejected as overambitious. Chalupa felt that Germans should decide how to defend Germany and that the British were actually motivated by a desire to gain more control over the alliance. Bagnall considered Chalupa an incompetent who failed to fully comprehend the new concept. Hans-Henning von Sandart (commander during the years 1987–1991), who replaced Chalupa, proved a more willing partner.[118] Due to Sandart's support, both the Bundeswehr and the Alliance adopted the new Operational Guideline (1987), which was based on Bagnall's ideas.

Accomplishments

The reforms led to the issuance of the first British operational doctrinal publication, *Design for Military Operations* (1989), and the establishment of the High Command and Staff Course (1987).[119] The course was Bagnall's brainchild; he began to develop it as commander of the First Corps and implemented it when he became chief of the general staff. Much of the preliminary work was carried out by Colonel M. McAfee while Lieutenant General Jeremy Mackenzie (both TDC members) prepared a detailed program for the course.[120] Its primary purpose was to provide higher staff education and training in mission command and operational-level principles for senior command and to promote interoperability. Each class had about twenty students from various services and arms, in order to enhance mutual understanding. A typical course was divided into nine segments dedicated to operational-level planning and conduct. The course themes included air power, technology and war, army and corps operations, counterinsurgency, peacekeeping, and the media. In the best German tradition, students participated in staff rides and war games. Their reading assignments included van Creveld's *On Command* and *Fighting Power* and Lind's *Maneuver Warfare*.[121] Ironically, by the time the British got around to establishing the High Command and Staff Course, it had become almost inconceivable that Britain would ever again field a mass army—the course's raison d'être.[122]

The course provided an elite education to select individuals, usually serving in G3 (operations) staff positions or as arm commanders and destined for senior command. It facilitated the intellectual leap Bagnall so desired and reflected the intellectual atmosphere and traditions of the TDC. Its students have made significant contributions to British military theory, and its ethos has been adopted by the Army Staff College, which now places a greater emphasis on the operational level. Bagnall believed that the military educational system should provide the structure and guidance for operational thinking. Also, it was to prepare students for independent actions within the framework of the commander's intent: mission command.[123] However, officer reeducation proved a slow process due to the influence of the traditions ingrained in the British Army.

Debates and Interpretations

The adoption of mission command in Britain triggered debates and interpretation, as it did in the United States. For instance, many Britons preferred Simpkin's translation of *Auftragstaktik*: directive control. The American translation, "mission command," was introduced into official terminology only with the publication of the 1995 Army Doctrine Publication (ADP).[124] Indeed, endless (and, probably, at least some pointless) semantic debates were held at the Staff College during the early 1990s during the development of the army's post–Cold War doctrine. They mirrored debates held at the American army's School of Advanced Military Studies (SAMS) and by the Marines at Quantico. The developers of the doctrine concluded that promoting cohesion while encouraging devolved authority action required channeling information through the three concepts: *end state* (our ultimate goal), *enemy center of gravity* (that which could stop us), and *main effort* (the focus of our energies).[125] The concepts of end state and center of gravity were regarded as analytical tools used in the formulation of campaign plans. They influence decisions concerning lines of operation, concurrent and sequential activities, decisive points, and so forth. Designation of a single main effort, both during the planning and execution phases, facilitates unity of effort. The point of main effort can and probably should be shifted during operations and campaigns; at such crossroads the primary consideration should be maintenance of momentum.[126] Following the debate regarding the concept of center of gravity central to both maneuver warfare and mission command, it was decided to break with Clausewitz's definition:

> Clausewitz (and contemporary Bundeswehr teaching) defined Centre of Gravity as that aspect of the enemy's capability which, if attacked and eliminated, will lead to the enemy's inevitable defeat or his wish to sue for peace through negotiations.[127]

Consequently, the center of gravity was confined to the operational art and only used down to the brigade level:

> Otherwise we would have had every section commander agonizing over his centre of gravity for an assault on a single machine gun, as started to happen. Centre of Gravity as a concept was seen primarily in the relation between strategic and operational levels.[128]

Subsequently, a distinction was made between center of gravity and main effort; the former alone was limited to operational-level command. The latter appeared in ADP *Command*, indicating that is was used in the exercise of (tactical) command rather than in the design of campaigns. According to the NATO definition adopted, it is "the activity which the commander considers crucial to the success of his mission at that time." Hence, the main effort can be shifted in accordance with the concept of operations, thereby clearly defining supporting and supported roles within the framework of the commander's intent.[129] Colonel Richard Iron of the British Army Doctrine Department argued in 2001 that the definition of the center of gravity is "rather confusing." Contrary to popular opinion, Iron contended, the center of gravity is dynamic for it is relative and easily transformed by events.[130]

Mission command was finally incorporated into British doctrine in 1995 through a manual dedicated to command. In this manual, mission command was discussed at length and regarded as the primary style of command for the British Army.[131] It was described as an implicit style of command utilized by generals such as Wolf, Wellington, and Slim. The message was that the British Army had in effect strayed from the path during the Cold War.[132] However, despite these clarifications, the cognitive confusion abounds. Thus, asked to define the concept of *intent*, 104 commanders, from staff sergeants to brigadiers, provided 60 distinct interpretations. In order to clarify this confusion, the British Army issued the revised manual, *Land Operations* (2005), in which a chapter was devoted to command. Mission command was discussed in clearer terms than before; commanders are expected to define the effect they desire and allow subordinates the freedom to realize it.[133]

ISRAEL DEFENSE FORCES

Adoption and Adaptation of Mission Command

IDF performance during the First Lebanon War (1982) and the first popular Palestinian uprising, the Intifada (1987–1993), was severely criticized by circles within and outside the army.[134] Criticism focused primarily on its marked lack of professionalism and rigid command system. It was apparent that the IDF had abandoned the flexible and decentralized style of command that had characterized it during its first three decades.[135] These shortcomings become more pronounced when compared with the American AirLand battle doctrine and performance during Operation Desert Storm (1991). The IDF was forced to reassess its command and operational doctrine. The assessment that the Oslo process (1993–1996) would ignite a new conflict with the Palestinians reinforced the sense of urgency and determination to avoid past mistakes.[136]

During that time, the IDF attempted to reintroduce the principles of maintenance of objective and mission command, which had suffered from the vague low intensity conflict (LIC) environment of the Intifada. Consequently, mission command was formally incorporated into official doctrine in 1993, though the official adoption proved insufficient.[137] A staff and command graduate final paper revealed micromanagement, centralization tendencies, and a number of cultural characteristics negating mission command.[138] These included a focus on results rather than process, a lack of professionalism, punishment rather than constructive criticism, encroachment on subordinate responsibilities, and frequent inspections. Moreover, mistakes often resulted in the introduction of new restrictive and detailed procedures instead of a thorough analysis of the origins of the problem.[139] Change, when it came, did not occur overnight, nor was it implemented through a top-down process. The IDF never held a comprehensive debate concerning the advantages and disadvantages of adopting mission command.[140] The process was initiated by a number of dedicated individuals who succeeded in steering the system in that direction. Among them were commander of the doctrine branch Brigadier Doron Rubin; the doctrine branch's Beni Amidror, a retired officer described as a "walking encyclopaedia" of military history;[141] and Colonel (Ret.) Hanan Shai.

Shai had served as a signal officer for the *Barak* Armored Brigade deployed at the first line of defense in the Golan Heights on 6 October 1973. Surprised and overwhelmed by the advance of the Syrian masses, the brigade was effectively annihilated, having lost most of its officers and many of its enlisted men. Following this traumatic experience, Shai vowed to dedicate his professional life to an investigation of this failure of the IDF. In 1982, he was assigned to develop a conceptual model for the next generation of command and control (C2) systems technology. On the basis of a series of studies, Shai concluded that IDF command and control difficulties ran deeper than the merely technical.[142] These studies included the Agranat Committee Report (1975) as well as internal historical monographs on the war.[143] The committee found that the IDF had come to disregard the amalgamation of British and German doctrines issued by the IDF during the 1950s and 1960s, as well as IDF field experience. The fact that they were not completely forgotten had enabled the IDF to quickly recover and achieve victory. However, the wrong lessons were learned from the war. The IDF concentrated on expanding the army at the expense of doctrine and professional development. These findings were later corroborated by Shai's own research.[144]

Shai argued that operations must be designed around a stratagem—"an outsmarting idea designed to dominate and unbalance your opponent."[145] Similar to the maneuverist approach, outsmarting requires identification of the enemy center of gravity and vital assets and the means of neutralizing them, through a professional process of a situational analysis. In this variant of mission command, the commander generates a concept of operations, his staff works out the details, and then he communicates his intent and the details necessary for its realization. Subordinate commanders then devise their own ideas and plans in order to play their part.[146] In accordance with these ideas, a section was added to the formal order format. In addition to "intent," the order included a "concept of operations," reflecting the belief that subordinates must know the objective and understand its purpose and the overall concept that led to it—that is, the principles of the outsmarting idea. For example, in the famous story of Troy, it was not enough that Agamemnon ordered the construction of the wooden horse: to the soldiers inside he would have had to explain the concept behind it, its purpose, and its relation to the operational goal of breaching the city walls. The outsmarting idea allows subordinates to make spontaneous independent decisions, understand the trade-offs, and adjust their own plans as the situation changes.[147]

According to Shai, mission command stands on four pillars that enable the generation and realization of a stratagem. The first pillar is a flexible doctrine responsive to the chaotic nature of war—principles rather than rules. The second is command and control procedures that afford the necessary latitude for subordinate initiative and creativity. The third pillar is a general staff organization in the form of the German model, which can support the commander effectively. The staff should include expert professionals capable of integrating and processing raw information into a comprehensive picture. The head of such a staff is either the operations officer, first among equals, or the chief of staff, who also function as the commander's "alter ego." He ensures the continuation of the command and control processes when the commander decides to leave the headquarters.[148]

The fourth and last pillar, perhaps the most important one, is the commander's intellectual ability and strength of character, which define him as a professional officer. The commander should be able to expect the unexpected and deal with uncertainty. He should possess significant intellectual and cognitive capabilities in order to "identify situations, create assumptions and hypothesis, and make decisions." Finally, he needs to "be able to work closely with his staff and convert his decisions into easily communicated plans and orders."[149] These capabilities can and should be developed through military education and training. The development process should include the study of theory, analysis of case studies, and extensive field practice. The final product, the ideal commander, is neither a pure intellectual nor a pure practitioner; he combines both.[150] This unique blend of qualities becomes even more important in command of larger formations, such as divisions or corps. On this level, the operational level, both the commander and his staff rely on abstract constructs. One of the primary purposes of the officer training process is the dissemination of unified professional terminology and methodology, which enable organizational integration and synergy. This shared understanding defines and characterizes the military profession in general and the purpose of command in particular.[151]

Shai and others concluded that one of the primary reasons for the decline in the practice of mission command was the absence of a proper military education and the poor state of the advanced military studies. While earlier generations had compensated for these shortcomings by independent study and wartime experience, later generations were more anti-intellectual and gained their experience mainly from on-going security and small-scale operations. The IDF is not an all-volunteer professional force; it relies on a small contingent of career officers, conscripts, and reserves. Professional standards are ensured through the efforts of that small contingent of career officers. They function as the "Brain of the Army" and are equipped with broad knowledge and an understanding of military theory and the military profession like their peers in western armies. However, they too failed to live up to expectations due primarily to a culture of *bitsuism* ("doing"),[152] which sanctifies field experience over the study of military theory. For example, doctrinal publications were few and far between, and those issued were rarely updated or read. The second problem was rooted in the Zionist ethos of the farmer-soldier, which rejected military professionalism. The military profession and its ethos was synonymous with the old European nobility and the social order it represented. Soldiering was regarded as an honorable pursuit only in times of serious crisis.

So, although the Israeli Staff and Command Course (*Pum*) was modeled after the British Staff College at Camberley, its achievements were, and continue to be, disappointing.[153] The disparity between the schools is due to a number of factors. First, as opposed to the Israeli program, Camberley students are graduates of a military academy (Sandhurst) that provides broader theoretical instruction.[154] In addition, the time spent in the Israeli program was also used in order to earn civilian undergraduate degrees, further restricting the time available to military studies.[155] Indeed, the dual-career policy instituted by Moshe Dayan has led many to pursue degrees relevant to civilian life, such as management or economics.[156] A third factor was the level of instruction and instructors. The culture of *bitsuism*, which favored field experience above theoretical studies, also affected the attitude toward instructing positions. Promotion, dependent as it was on field command, essentially guaranteed that few instructors could afford to be removed from the field for extended periods of time. Furthermore, those who took these positions did not represent the best and the brightest.[157] In addition, most instructors had little knowledge or appreciation of IDF or foreign doctrines and based their classes on their own field experience. Thus the knowledge passed on to new generations centered on current security, special, or small operations, which dominated the IDF experience after 1967.[158] These teachings were given an official doctrinal stamp and came to be regarded as official doctrine. Reflecting the emphasis on civilian studies, the program adopted civilian industrial management techniques. Detailed planning procedures replaced the chaos of war in the classroom and in field exercise.[159]

Consistent with IDF culture, and in contrast to the reforms in the United States, reformists concentrated on the officer training system rather than on written doctrine. This attitude stemmed from practical considerations and from a belief that better education would produce better commanders and that improvements to the rest would follow. With the backing of the head of the doctrine department, Major General Doron Rubin, reformists felt that they could indeed make a difference. A new Advanced Command and Staff course (*Pum Barak*) was added, and two other courses were established for higher and lower commands. The purpose was to equip a new generation of officers with the skills necessary for the practice of maneuver warfare and mission command.[160]

Debates and Interpretations

The various educational programs established during the 1990s taught mission command to midlevel officers (Majors before promotion to Lieutenant Colonel). Further development began to take place in 1998. It occurred mainly within the higher echelons of command and had an immediate impact on the conduct of the IDF during the Second Intifada (2000–2005). These newcomers sought to introduce radical ideas concerning what they believed should be the best way to face the new challenges posed by the contemporary LIC environment. This group, which was represented in the Operational Theory Research Institute (OTRI), included retired senior officers who earned PhD degrees in military studies, such as Zvi Lanir, Dov Tamari, and Shimon Naveh. The latter, who practically headed the institute, had the ear of General Bogi Ya'alon during his successive positions at Central Command, as deputy chief of staff and chief of staff (COS, which in the IDF is also the commander in chief). Ya'alon used the institute as a "think tank" in order to introduce new ideas for the operational level.[161] When he took over Central Command (1998), Ya'alon recognized that the existing doctrine and conceptual tools were inadequate in the face of the complicated conflict with the Palestinians.[162] Indeed,

> Already in 1992 as a division commander I felt that the *situation estimate . . .* didn't provide the relevant tools to deal with the situations we faced. . . . I felt that discussions, whether in headquarters or somewhere else, only scratched the surface, the symptoms and not the deep roots. . . . We dealt only with the tactical level and immediate causes and not with the entire complexities and intersections. . . . I felt we needed a new process of situation estimate.[163]

He decided to initiate the development of new methodologies and procedures for the preparation of situation assessments. Ya'alon was fascinated by Naveh's original ideas and began to work closely with the OTRI.[164] The basic conceptual framework the institute was developing was that operational events occur within the context of a wider system. The primary challenge in such cases is to define and redefine systems boundaries and the interrelationships of cause and effect within a system. This concept, labeled Systemic Operational Design (SOD), also included the use of software tools to enhance brainstorming processes. With a team from Central Command, Ya'alon began to break away from traditional military hierarchy and situation assessments. The output of this new methodology was three-phased: design, planning, and execution.[165] In order to assimilate the new approach, it was introduced in a series of seminars and workshops.

Mission command played a central role in Naveh's theory of SOD. In fact, Naveh argued that SOD methodology represents an advanced variant of mission command. Naveh had been heavily influenced by Moltke the Elder, whom he believed understood the limits of centralized command and sought a different way of command. Accordingly, Moltke believed that constant adaptation and continuous learning were a prerequisite for success. In order to create conditions for learning, the operational commander needs to define and provide a frame of reference. Tactical commanders perform what organizational theorist Chris Argyris has termed "reflection in action" as the situation unfolds. Commander and subordinate therefore engage in a continuous dialogue:

> By definition there will be gaps between your planning and the situation as it evolves. The operational commander develops an operational interpretation of the strategic idea which he then communicates to his subordinates. Next thing he does is to deploy them in the different tactical dimensions and assign them with missions and definitions. He expects each one of them to redefine and reinterpret again the mission in light of new patterns.[166]

According to Naveh, mission command represents a dialogue between the operational and tactical levels; admittedly, the two levels are not easily distinguished. On the operational level, it is most important to "have a deep system understanding and to create new designs, just like architects. . . . Look at things out of the box and out of the boundaries set by the physical world."[167] In effect, he asserted, *Auftrag* does not signify a mission, as missions change frequently; rather it signifies a logical frame that directs all actions.

Operational command exists and operates within the boundaries of a virtual world as the commander experiences the physical world of battle vicariously.

Nevertheless, the operational commander creates the mission, which then serves as a frame for the men who live and operate in the real world, the world of action, the tactical world. The operational commander must convert these ideas into actionable measures, so he provides subordinates with vectors and a primary frame. Then, using this frame, each subordinate develops his own small frame, that is, his mission plan. Yet, both commander and subordinates know that actual events will not conform to the plan. Therefore, Naveh explained, while the virtual commander creates the conditions and designs the frame through which his agent subordinates learn, he is dependent on their interpretations of the real world. The information a commander receives regarding the unfolding situation, and his consequent understanding of the "emerging logic," is filtered through the interpretation of subordinates. When he senses an increasing disparity between his frame and the emerging situation, he might reconsider and define a new frame that better represents the new situation.[168]

An inherent tension exists between the virtual world of the operational commander who constructs the frame and the physical world of the tactical commander who utilizes it. Both commanders maintain a constant dialogue regarding the emerging situation. The outcome is a continual process of reinterpretation and reframing. To support this process, Zvi Lanir developed a specific methodology, Systemic Reframing Thinking (SRT), the principles of which, representing a new paradigm, can be summarized as follows:[169]

- Holism versus reductionism: looking at the system as a whole, as something that is greater than the sum of its parts.
- Interpretation versus analysis: allowing different points of view to emerge, acknowledging that there is no one absolute truth.
- Design versus planning: working out the initial form using creativity versus applying rigorous procedures to devise future actions.
- Re-understanding versus re-engineering: looking at the basic assumptions versus trying to correct the process.
- Subjectivism versus objectivism: the understanding of various narratives.
- Contextualization versus universalizing: understanding the logic of events in the context of their own unique specific time and place.
- Critical reflection versus identification: the ability to look at past events from multiple dimensions and apply the principles above.

Mission command became more relevant than ever before. It was perceived as a central link between the tactical and operational levels, critical to the learning process. Naveh believed that the cultural roots of the IDF had facilitated the practice of mission command. He stated that "in contrast to the Anglos, we thrive in chaos; we have good foundations as a result of the legacy of Wingate and Sadeh." He was referring to the unique and unorthodox teachings of these two men who had emphasized initiative at all levels.[170] Naveh agreed that the IDF had lost much of its agility by the 1980s, becoming overly technocratic. However, contribution of both *Pum Barak* and the OTRI to the operational level dramatically altered IDF culture. Also, he perceived the Second Intifada as a positive learning experience:

> In a peculiar way it saved the IDF, because of the complex challenges it provided. This campaign produced the best tactical commanders who later developed into operational commanders. They are creative and aggressive and not only exploit opportunities but also constantly create and design new patterns of reality. Names such as Noam Tibon, Yair Golan, Aviv Cochavi, Moshe Tamir and many more. This generation is better than ever, it is the doctrine and the situation we are in (the *Intifada*). We are making something new here, that is why I believe it is alive so much, of course there are problems however despite what some may say it is a highly professional army, and on the combat level it is working magnificently.[171]

The key factor that enabled these theoretical and cultural developments was the leadership style of Bogi Ya'alon. According to Naveh, when Ya'alon served as head of Central Command, he redefined the relationship between himself and his brigade commanders. He expected them to make their own interpretations and arrive at solutions independently. His style of command served as an excellent example of mission command.[172] Indeed, as a lieutenant colonel, commander of the elite *Sayeret Matkal*, Ya'alon was praised by subordinates for his ability to delegate authority. According to one veteran:

> There were two types of commanders: those who used to provide ideas and then monitored closely the details in the planning process and those who just gave the people the latitude to work out their plans and then gave them positive reinforcements. . . . Bogi was the latter. . . . He was highly regarded as serious and professional. Another veteran officer said his creativity was based on his openness to hear others' suggestions.[173]

However, enthusiasm for the ideas developed by the OTRI was not universal. Some critiques have noted that the OTRI invented a jargon that could be understood only by a select few who had participated in the courses and discussions in which IDF doctrine was formalized and its behavior was shaped during the Second Intifada. These critiques asserted that this unique language has become the domain of, and an identifying mark for, this select group of officers who belonged to a specific social club, if not a cult. Critics of the OTRI included also Air Force general Dan Halutz, who succeeded Ya'alon as chief of staff and has spoken against this so-called sophisticated intellectual language.[174]

Others believe that the ideas developed by the OTRI have permeated throughout the army and senior command, inflicting serious damage. Their primary argument is that instead of seeking a traditional battlefield decision, the OTRI has advocated a containment approach. This stemmed from the overly sophisticated notion according to which the complicated nature of LIC requires military restraint combined with political measures. Eventually, when the Second Intifada escalated to such a degree that it spiraled out of control, the army had to intervene with force. Though eventually successful, victory was overshadowed by the high civilian casualty rate and a significant decline in its power of deterrence.[175] These critics believed the army had to resurrect the bold and aggressive ethos of 1950s reprisal raids. The newly elected prime minister, Ariel Sharon, who took office shortly after the hostilities began, proved a kindred spirit. Ya'alon was aware of the criticism against OTRI concepts but believed that the institute was designing the necessary means for converting an industrial age army into an information age army. Nevertheless, he too shared the general negative attitude toward the new terminology, arguing that "language should be understood and new words should not be invented to designate existing concepts."[176] However, he supported the OTRI because "Since I was the commander of Central Command . . . I understood I needed to encourage the independent thinking . . . [and that] the brigadier is the expert in his area[,] not the division commander or me."[177]

The OTRI had a profound impact on the IDF through the course it established for senior commanders and the heated intellectual debate on doctrine it inspired. Indeed, the new generation of commanders can be contrasted with that of the 1980s, which lacked, as one critique opined, "any interest or curiosity, what so ever, in the art of war in general and in strategy in particular and demonstrated hostility for any expression of intellectualism or capacity for military thinking."[178] One of the major debates between reformists from the OTRI and those of *Pum Barak* revolved around the usefulness and adaptability of mission command. They debated its interpretation, its effectiveness in the LIC environment of Gaza or the West Bank, how far down it should be applied, and the difference between mission command on the tactical and operational levels. For a while, the OTRI enjoyed the upper hand as its teachings held the appeal of modernity and language, its founder enjoyed world renown, and it had the ear of the chief of staff.[179] Career officers learned the new language and adjusted to the new conceptual framework. However, many failed to internalize or even comprehend the concepts developed by the OTRI. The sophisticated-sounding terminology was regurgitated by officers who sought to appear progressive.[180]

A few months after Dan Halutz replaced Ya'alon as chief of staff (2005), the OTRI was closed down amid charges of administrative mismanagement. Naveh and Tamari, the leading figures in the institute, resigned from the army in protest. Having lost *Pum Barak* and the OTRI, the two primary forces leading an intellectual revolution, the IDF was left with an intellectual void. Consequently, during the Second Lebanon War (2006), an overconfident general staff led by an Air Force general (Dan Halutz) attempted to implement borrowed American ideas of shock and awe and effect-based operations, hoping for a decisive outcome through the use of superior firepower and technology against a very different opponent.[181]

CONCLUSION

The adoption of mission command by the three armies resulted from a perceived need to improve military performance. For the U.S. Army, it was the traumatic experience of the Vietnam War and the understanding that existing doctrine would prove ineffective in case of a Soviet invasion. For the British, it was the experience of the Falklands War that demonstrated the capabilities of elite and special forces while revealing the shortcomings of the Continental British contingent facing the Soviets. The Israelis had begun to experience a decline in performance following the Yom Kippur War, and these deficiencies had only worsened during the First Lebanon War. Many sought a return to the glorious days of the 1956 and 1967 campaigns.

It is important to note that mission command was not adopted independently but rather within the context of a broader doctrinal transformation. The new framework, adopted in different variants, came to be known as maneuver warfare. In contrast to reliance on firepower and technology (attrition), it denoted the use of speed and surprise in order to paralyze the opponent system. In this new doctrine, mission command played a significant role.

The introduction and adoption of mission command in all three cases was facilitated by, if not dependent upon, the efforts of individuals within the army who were convinced of its necessity and adaptability. They became agents of change, educators, and mentors; their sphere of influence extended beyond their immediate official authority. In all three cases, the historical Prussian-German experience served as the role model, and its exploits were studied. Also, the IDF was considered a successor to the Wehrmacht during its early years, the feats of which were also studied. The process of adaptation and implementation of mission command in these cases involved resurrection of national figures who were practitioners of these principles: the Americans had Patton, the British had Slim, and the Israelis turned to Allon and Dayan. It could be said that in a way mission command was "nationalized." The process of adoption included the institution of new education and training programs for officers, which reflected the requirements of the new doctrine.

The process was not without challenges. These included the simple problem of translating German terminology and continued with understanding the cultural and historical context within which it was developed. It was soon evident that the armies were able to more easily adopt its mechanical procedures than imitate the German military's organizational and military culture. Misunderstandings and interarmy influences resulted in heated debates concerning the actual meaning of mission command and the continued relevance of its comprising elements. As will be demonstrated in the next chapter, these factors often exacerbated confusion and hindered the practice of mission command.

9 TESTING: MISSION COMMAND IN OPERATIONS

THIS CHAPTER EXAMINES the practice of mission command in recent operations by American, British, and Israeli armies, which officially adopted it into their doctrine and training.[1] The chapter investigates operational planning and conduct and relationships within the echelons of senior command. In order to determine the extent to which mission command had been practiced, the chapter relies upon two types of sources. The first is operational and battle analysis conducted by scholars or soldiers and the conclusions drawn from them. The second includes participant accounts of commanders and subordinates alike and their perception as to the degree to which mission command was exercised. It should be noted first that both mission and detailed command are essentially abstract models rarely pursued to their extreme. Rather, the exercise of command exists on a continuum. Secondly, the picture that will emerge in this chapter is a result of an integration of subjective impressions and battle analysis. The chapter begins with an examination of the American and British conduct during both Gulf Wars (1991 and 2003). It compares similar campaigns occurring within a decade of each other as well as between the armies that participated in them. The third part will be devoted to the Israeli experience during the Second Intifada (2001–2004) and the Second Lebanon War (2006). Both campaigns were unconventional and fought against non-state organizations: the Palestinian militia and Hezbollah fighters.[2] A short postscript will briefly review Operation Cast Lead in Gaza (2008), against Hamas.

THE U.S. APPLICATION OF MISSION COMMAND

Early Years

Following the official adoption of mission command into doctrine (1982), as discussed in the previous chapter, the U.S. Army was expected to utilize it in operational situations. This section will examine whether commanders were able to perform the required transition. The case studies include two major operations in which U.S. ground forces were heavily involved since the adoption of the doctrine: Desert Storm (1991) and Iraqi Freedom (2003).[3]

From the late 1970s through the 1980s, the U.S. Army was involved in a number of small operations and wars wherein it continued to suffer from Vietnam-era command deficiencies. These difficulties developed in part due to a lack of understanding and ignorance of mission command principles. For example, the various elements of the rescue force sent to Iran (1979) had never trained together;[4] the rescue plan itself had been overreliant on technology and had severely curtailed individual initiative.[5] American tactics in the invasion of Grenada (1983) still called on ground forces to fix targets for air strikes and artillery, rather than initiative-encouraging fire and maneuver tactics.[6] On the basis of his study of operations between 1970 and 1983, Richard Gabriel concluded that the American record had been one of "failure bordering on incompetence."[7] According to Gabriel, the officer education system was producing managers and bureaucrats, amateurs in the affairs of war.[8] Less than a decade later, the U.S. Army confronted a bigger challenge by an order of magnitude. Its performance convinced many that it had at last undergone a significant change.

Operation Desert Storm

Many who followed the American army's conduct in Desert Storm believed that it had executed a nearly perfect "AirLand battle" operation. Though confronting merely the Iraqi army rather than the feared Soviets, the Americans had successfully adapted to the new theater of operations. The swift 100-hour Blitzkrieg-like campaign demonstrated their adherence to the tenets of the AirLand battle doctrine, including mission command. The deep thrust into the desert, rapid envelopment of Iraqi forces, and relatively few casualties suggested excellent doctrine and execution. The Americans had demonstrated what the doctrine advocated: initiative, depth, agility, synchronization, and combined arms.[9] According to Shimon Naveh, Desert Storm exemplified this doctrine, marking it as the first battle in modern history where maneuver substituted the Western predisposition toward attrition.[10] He opined that the operation was a superb application of offensive maneuver relying on "depth, simultaneous operations and synergy, disruption and intellectual tension between tactical and operational poles of command, and synchronization."[11]

These elements, combined with the large-scale rapid maneuvers, led some to conclude that mission command had been practiced to its fullest potential, just as the Germans had done against France in 1940. Indeed, some accounts of the war have it that the large double envelopment had been accomplished through short orders issued on the move: mission-type orders.[12] Tacticians were described as having had the "remarkable ability to maneuver and to respond to changing situations."[13] In contrast, others noted the overwhelming coalition superiority in resources, management, organization, and technology; to them the disparity resembled a contest between an "elephant and a mouse."[14] Indeed, they argued, the Americans had overestimated Iraqi military capabilities.[15] However, it was not all about technological superiority; Stephen Biddle attributed the coalition's low casualty rate to a synergetic combination of superior technology and battlefield performance.[16] The Americans had greatly improved their technical and tactical skills and their ability to exploit what Lind termed "surfaces and gaps." Lind, a long-time critic of the U.S. Army and a devout proponent of mission command, agreed:

> In Desert Storm, the American ground forces, Army and Marine Corps, on the whole practiced maneuver warfare. There were certainly exceptions. . . . But the overall picture suggests this ship has come onto a new course, even if it had a long journey ahead before it was safe in the maneuver warfare harbor.[17]

Planning had revolved around the "Jedi Knights," officer graduates of the new Army School of Advanced Military Studies (SAMS). This two-year advanced program, modeled after the idea of the German General Staff academy, was to prepare a select few as expert operational-level planers. Their campaign plan was deemed a classic application of AirLand battle doctrine.[18] However, after the dust had settled, analysts began to question the actual extent to which maneuver and mission command had been applied in this conflict. Robert Leonhard opined that while some maneuver principles had been practiced, attrition had remained the dominant approach—thus the obsession with physical annihilation rather than defeat and surrender.[19] Moreover, he argued:

Operation Desert Storm was strictly controlled from the top down. There was no room for initiative, or even significant maneuver options, below corps level. Commanders at all levels were instructed where and when to move and were not permitted to find their own way to their objectives. In essence the coalition forces simply lined up and swept forward, careful to maintain contact with the friendly forces on their flanks, like rigidly disciplined Macedonian Phalanx, divisions and brigades had to march and stay dressed to the flanks throughout the advance, crashing through both strong and weak points in the enemy defenses.[20]

According to Leonhard, their success was due in part to the fact that mission command is not a prerequisite for maneuver warfare. In fact, he explains, as the Soviets had demonstrated during World War II, maneuver on the operational level is possible without using mission command.[21] That said, the curtailment of the freedoms afforded by mission command posed two primary problems: "One is our own perception of ourselves as a democratic and free society. . . . But even more dangerous is that if the US is engaged with a better rival . . . that is capable of showing initiative in every echelon of command, this might prove disastrous."[22] Similar criticism was offered by Steven Canby and Martin van Creveld, who argued that although U.S. forces were well trained and cohesive, Desert Storm had been:

> more a movement than *maneuver*. . . . Given the Iraqi passivity the notion of entering into the enemy's OODA loop never came into play. . . . At a critical junction VII corps was apparently more interested in synchronizing the moves of its own forces than vigorously exploiting battlefield success by sending spearheads forward.[23]

In practice, they argued, the system of command remained essentially centralized.[24] Robert Citino opined that mission command was a lost cause in the first place in this environment, that the complex communication and weapons systems actually increased dependency of action on all levels of command. He contended that centralized control of the American ground maneuver during Desert Storm allowed commanders no deviation from the plan.[25]

Another way to examine the role of mission command is to look at force organization and particularly at the role of headquarters. The Third Army's headquarters were located in Saudi Arabia, far removed from the actual battlefield. According to General Schwarzkopf, this arrangement had a negative impact on the tempo of operations. Senior command took little notice of subordinate reports detailing Iraqi weaknesses and failed to tailor the battle plan to battlefield developments. Unnecessary caution and risk aversion on the operational level hampered the ground offensive. Command centers functioned as information depots rather than as distribution points.[26]

Rupert Smith, who commanded the British First Armored division, likened the differences between the British and American headquarters to those between football and rugby. While the Americans fight set-piece, highly organized, well-rehearsed, and centralized wars, the British conduct a more dynamic and fluid operation wherein anyone can pick up the ball and lead.[27] These characteristics are reflected also in the headquarters' structure: the American headquarters is substantially larger than its British counterpart. The additional manpower in the American headquarters is used to plan and rehearse for every possible scenario, leaving little room for improvisation later on.[28] Smith noted that headquarters are often a reflection of commanders and are of two basic models.

In the first model, a small staff, headed by a chief of staff, is charged with developing and disseminating the course of action decided upon by the commander. They often issue short mission-type orders dictating the desired end result rather than the means of accomplishing it while subordinates are required to work out the details. This type of system requires a unifying doctrine.[29] In the second method, staffs prepare a number of alternate courses of action, from which the commander will later choose. The process is more formal and the planning detailed. During the 1990s, a single operational order emanating from division headquarters could run to 1,000 pages; supplementary plans of subordinate units totaled thousands more.[30] During Desert Storm, British headquarters was designed along the lines of the first model. It was smaller than its American counterpart, which was a

> function of national preference and philosophy. It took us some time to learn that the many plans emanating from the superior US Corps HQ were but contingencies. . . . I had one staff officer to deal with all this paper work where an equivalent US HQ had a branch of about five officers. . . . As a general rule responsibility and authority were found lower in the British HQ.[31]

The Americans' ability to practice mission command was hindered not only by these structural limitations but also by their commander. Schwarzkopf managed a complex coalition and a huge logistical tail. This complex system and the casualty aversion made him more of a Montgomery than a Patton or a Rommel (although one should also take into acount his role as theater commander and not field commander). Schwarzkopf has a dominant personality and was a dominant commander for better most times but in some occasions for worse. Due to frequent temper outbursts, his subordinates were disinclined to differ with him or raise problems. "No one over there," said Colin Powell, "was going to tell Schwarzkopf he made a mistake."[32] This is hardly an atmosphere conducive for mission command.

Despite their maneuver background, the "Jedi Knights" proposed a conservative frontal attack as they feared a negative force ratio and exposing their flanks. Mass and attrition substituted envelopment only as a result of pressure from Washington.[33] Friction, which mission command is designed to overcome, then prevented the destruction of the Republican Guard, the designated center of gravity.[34] Furthermore, despite the doctrinal emphasis, the Marine eastern pincer was not adequately synchronized with the multicorps western pincer. Due to the varying distances they had to cover and conflicting estimates of Iraqi military prowess, "the Army had prepared for a marathon while the Marines had planned for a sprint."[35] In addition, the Marines had incorporated lessons they had learned from fighting the Iraqis around Al-Khafji in late January 1991. In contrast, the VII Corps assumed that it was facing a Soviet variant toward which it directed massive air power and careful coordination. Obviously such an approach left little room for mission command–type operations. According to one historian, the one contingency the army had failed to anticipate was the speedy collapse of the Iraqis following the Marine attack.[36] Furthermore, despite Schwarzkopf's intent, VII Corps refrained from night operations primarily in order to minimize casualties.[37] Indeed, he later described the feeling "as if I were trying to drive a wagon pulled by racehorses and mules."[38]

A cognitive gap began to develop between the actual tactical situation and the operational understanding at Schwarzkopf's HQ. This gap was widened through imprecise reports.[39] There followed a physical gap compounded by adverse weather conditions and the unanticipated Iraqi preference for flight over fight. Consequently, the Republican Guard escaped nearly unscathed.[40] The constant emphasis on force alignment, driven perhaps by synchronization theory, prohibited the utilization of the "expanding torrent" or "surfaces and gaps." As one analyst concluded, "once again, the US did not know how to conduct a deep thrust into its enemy's rear."[41] The misguided attempt to control friction demonstrated a misunderstanding of both the concept and the utility of mission command. Thus, the First Gulf War experience revealed high performance in many areas of combat but exposed little of the Americans' decentralization capabilities.[42] The failure to destroy the Republican Guard secured Saddam Hussein's regime in Iraq and in the eyes of the Arab world. His continued defiance led to an American incursion in 1998 and a second full invasion in 2003.[43]

Operation Iraqi Freedom

The execution of Operation Iraqi Freedom (2003) satisfied some of the criticisms raised previously by proponents of maneuver warfare.[44] For instance, the unified ground and air command that had overwhelmed Schwarzkopf was now separated into two elements.[45] Also, a preference for speed over mass was revealed when the ground and air campaigns were begun simultaneously and directed toward the Republican Guard and the city of Baghdad. Undoubtedly, the march to Baghdad, which constituted the first phase of the campaign, validated the doctrine of speed and maneuver. According to Keegan, the disintegration of the Iraqi army should not diminish the American success.[46] The finest examples of mission command–based maneuvers were the two "thunder runs" (swift and unexpected, massive armored, deep penetrations designed to unbalance the enemy) directed toward Baghdad.[47] As one analyst has it, these were "the most important and decisive" actions of the war.[48] The army had taken a tactical risk that "paid off handsomely."[49] These penetrations constituted a change in the battle plan introduced as a result of battlefield developments.[50] The Third Division recognized the Iraqi inability to deal with attacks from unexpected directions and directed "thunder runs" toward the Iraqi rear. Consequently, Baghdad was taken earlier than anticipated and with fewer casualties.[51] David Zucchino's account of the "thunder runs" indicates a successful adoption of maneuver warfare and mission command during the decade following the First Gulf War.[52] To him, the evidence demonstrated a marked improvement in tactical command as well. Criticism was raised, however, regarding operational and strategic performance as well as the counterinsurgency phase that followed.

The 1990s' highly publicized Revolution in Military Affairs (RMA) coupled with Secretary of Defense Donald Rumsfeld's "transformation" spawned the doctrine of deploying small maneuvering forces relying on precision firepower and improved situational awareness capabilities. These forces were expected to affect the overall strategic situation.[53] However, plans for the aftermath and manpower allocations proved ineffective and insufficient.[54] Director of Operations General David McKienan complained that General Tommy Ray Franks, who led the 2003 U.S. invasion of Iraq, failed to issue concise and direct orders, preferring instead PowerPoint presentations first approved by Rumsfeld. Some felt this practice was amateurish, evidencing the degrading influence of the Office of the Secretary of Defense (OSD) and the RMA.[55] Especially severe criticism of the war plans was offered by Schwarzkopf, who felt that Pentagon officials were discarding the advice of senior commanders.[56] Retired Marine General Paul van Riper questioned the wisdom of the deployment plan itself.[57]

Others opined that General Franks failed to formulate his strategic intent, a cornerstone of mission command, and had therefore been unable to communicate it to his subordinates. A man of technology rather than strategy, Franks was accused of adopting the Blitzkrieg doctrine of "speed kills" with little consideration for the consequence or even of the real enemy in Iraq.[58] Franks should have questioned the incomplete nature of the task assigned to him. In an absence of a clear strategy for post–Saddam Hussein Iraq, the Americans would ultimately fight blindly. Despite aspiring to a Blitzkrieg campaign, American commanders often resorted to cautious set-piece battles at the first sign of trouble. Such was the case following the Battle of Karbala (April 2003). A massive Apache helicopter charge against the Medina Republican Guard division proved largely unsuccessful and costly. Though the fault had been doctrinal in nature,[59] massive helicopter attacks became as rare as World War II cavalry charges.[60] The debacle had led to an overestimation of Iraqi fighting power. Rumsfeld was persuaded to halt ground offensive operations until the Air Force bombed Iraq's meager ineffectual forces. Consequently, when Baghdad fell to the "thunder runs," the critical element of speed of attack had been lost.[61] Indeed, "By failing to press on and accept minimal risk to their flanks and rear . . . [they] missed the opportunity to enter the capital, and force the surrender of the Ba'athist leadership. . . . Gen. George C. Patton would have been deeply depressed by the whole affair."[62] The army's zest for overplanning was demonstrated when, following the fall of Baghdad, General Franks estimated it would take ten days to transfer an armored brigade to the vicinity of Tikrit. When Marine Task Force Tripoli received this assignment, it began rolling less than twelve hours later. Similarly, the first Battle of Fallujah (April 2004), initiated following the killing of the American Blackwater employees, was a slow, set-piece battle, which had allowed the enemy to escape. The battle was deliberate and conducted against the advice of the local commander, General Mattis.[63] Another example of micromanagement occurred when the commander of American forces in Iraq, Lieutenant General Sanchez (2003–2004), was ordered to present Washington with his plan to take the city of Najaf.[64]

An additional source of disappointment was the new digital system designed to increase tactical unit "situational awareness" by providing accurate real-time intelligence concerning the location of friendly and enemy forces. The "Blue Force Tracker," in both its designation and actual application,[65] provided senior command with an additional micromanagement tool.[66] Many complained that the system had created a "digital divide" as the significant intelligence it provided was, for all intents and purposes, restricted to senior command. Frustration soon ignited a controversy, transforming the digital divide into one of the primary criticisms of army performance during the invasion.[67]

The most serious flaws were uncovered in the aftermath of the invasion. Although the new RMA doctrines of effect-based operation (EBO), network-centric warfare (NCW), and shock and awe had proved somewhat effective in the regular phase of the war, they proved rather unsatisfactory in the counter-insurgency phase that followed. The army had been unprepared for either the lengthy counterinsurgency campaign or the nation-building measures.[68] Indeed, a report published in 2008 concluded that the army had relied on faulty planning assumptions; units were inadequately trained; headquarters were unprepared; and planners had failed to account for some fundamental contingencies.[69] Various agencies became involved in this stage, but their respective spheres of influence were insufficiently delineated. The principle of unity of command was violated, and the army knew not what or whose intent it was expected to realize. The rules of engagement (ROE) too were unclear; they led to incidents of fratricide and unduly harsh treatment of the local population.[70]

Lieutenant Colonel Isaiah Wilson, chief planning officer for the elite 101st Screaming Eagles during this stage, stated that although mission command had been applied during the regular fighting, a lack of doctrine for the second stage had negated further reliance on it. Thus, although a divisional study of the local dynamics in a certain region had resulted in an effective strategy of buying loyalty, the Pentagon bureaucrats eventually vetoed the plan. Other unauthorized initiatives even resulted in the freezing of promotions for the individuals involved. Similarly, while the 101st directed its efforts toward individual tribes, the American Occupation Administration preferred the notion of a unified Iraqi nation. Wilson was convinced that a more coherent doctrine for this "war and peace" situation could have enabled utilization of mission command.[71] Others added that mission command had been hindered by insufficient training and mental preparedness. British Brigadier Nigel Aylwin-Foster, attached to U.S. forces in Iraq, observed that

> Whilst the US army may espouse mission command, in Iraq it did not practice it.... Commanders ... rarely if ever questioned authority and were reluctant to deviate from precise instructions.... Each commander had his own style, but if there were a common trend it was for micromanagement.... Planning tended to be staff driven and focused on process rather than end effect. The net effect was highly centralized decision making ... [which] tended to discourage lower level initiative and adaptability.[72]

Aylwin-Foster also remarked that the Americans' strong "can-do" ethos[73] occasionally resulted in inaccurate reports calculated to ease pressure from above and satisfy superiors.[74] This tendency undermines the principle of trust critical to armies in general and to mission command in particular. U.S. officers dismissed these allegations. For instance, one officer responding to Aylwin-Foster stated that "his assessment is off target."[75] On the basis of testimonies of officers from the First Cavalry Division, he argued that mission command had indeed been practiced.[76] However, he added:

> One might argue that I only spoke with exceptional officers, and while this might be true, what is also true is that commanders will deal with subordinates according to their estimate of the subordinates' abilities. The best will be given maximum freedom of action; the others will get more guidance and control. This is not micromanagement; it is leadership.[77]

Though the ideal and actual state described here are not easily distinguished, and one must account for professional pride, the American and British accounts should be considered as similarly authoritative. TRADOC commander General William Wallace stated that although he disagreed with some of the Aylwin-Foster's criticism, most of it was "worthy of review." He pointed out that the British administration of Basra faced an inherently different situation than did the Americans in the Sunni triangle. Regarding mission command, he stated that Aylwin-Foster's notes were indeed "of concern." Nevertheless, "From my experience this is not indicative of the U.S. Army. To the contrary,

I have seen the remarkable ability of leaders and organizations to adapt and decentralize."[78] To a certain extent, then, Aylwin-Foster's observations are validated by the Americans.[79] Another commentator, a longtime red team analyst, found Aylwin-Foster's assessment a "enlightening, if somewhat painful, critique of U.S Army in Iraq." And further:

> It is much easier to dismiss Aylwin-Foster's assessment as limited or altogether wrong than it is to make changes in response to it. From an American perspective, it is difficult to see how our optimistic, action-oriented, technologically advanced, and command-centric military culture could have downsides. But Aylwin-Foster demonstrates that in a counterinsurgency, these attributes do not necessarily contribute to success.[80]

Indeed, many in the U.S. military analyst community voiced similar concerns to those raised by Aylwin-Foster.[81]

In fact, accusations of totalitarian micromanagement were raised against Secretary Rumsfeld and the Pentagon by a number of generals involved in the planning and execution of the war. When he first took office, Rumsfeld had been convinced that the Pentagon was in need of a "transformation." He initiated many reforms during his six-year tenure, some of which were embraced even by his detractors. These included restructuring the army's cumbersome fighting formations and the repositioning of American forces abroad. The army's military culture changed as well.[82] One senior officer declared that Secretary Rumsfeld had "shown himself incompetent strategically, operationally and tactically and is far more than anyone else responsible for what has happened to America's mission in Iraq. Rumsfeld must step down."[83] Another stated that "a fundamentally flawed plan was executed for an invented war, while pursuing the real enemy, al-Qaeda, became a secondary effort."[84] Moreover:

> Flaws in our civilians are one thing; the failure of the Pentagon's military leaders is quite another. Those are men who know the hard consequences of war. . . . When they knew the plan was flawed . . . many leaders who wore the uniform chose inaction. A few . . . actually supported the logic for war. Others were simply intimidated, while still others must have believed that the principle of obedience does not allow for respectful dissent.[85]

Retired Colonel Douglas Macgregor, whose *Breaking the Phalanx* is said to have inspired Rumsfeld's concept of deploying small forces in Iraq, blames the military rather than civilian leadership for the debacles in Iraq. He opined that "the high quality of American soldiers and marines at battalion level and below cannot compensate for inadequate senior leadership at the highest levels in war." Senior command was "overly bureaucratic, risk averse, professionally inadequate and, hence, unsuited to the complex military tasks entrusted to them." What's more, Macgregor argued, little had changed over the decade following the First Gulf War, as HQ remained improvised, uncoordinated, single-service organizations.[86]

To sum up, despite a doctrinal revolution and major reforms, mission command has only been partially implemented. During the Second Iraq War, there were several examples of successful reliance on mission command, such as the battalion and brigade "thunder runs" or the tactics developed by the 101st during the occupation phase. However, these were exceptions to the rule. Indeed, the twelve years that had elapsed since the First Iraq War and three successive field manuals espousing mission command had failed to bring about the desired result. A lack of trust and clear objectives coupled with a type of war the U.S. Army was unprepared for had come at the expense of mission command.

THE BRITISH APPLICATION OF MISSION COMMAND

Operation Granby

As in the American case, the Bagnall Reforms were first put to the test not against the Soviets in Europe but rather the Iraqis in Kuwait (1991). Then, the British First Armoured Brigade formed part of Franks's VII Corps. In addition, the Britons deployed a divisional headquarters commanding the Fourth and Seventh Armoured Brigades. The British force formed part of the great left hook that destroyed many a Republican Guard unit.

Conventional wisdom has it that the British traditionally perform well in small operations but are less successful in high-intensity conflicts. Indeed, the First Gulf War demonstrated certain shortcomings in the practice of combined arms and interservice warfare. General Rupert Smith's fine operational-level divisional plan and his reliance on mission command were sometimes hindered by subordinate inexperience with maneuver warfare.[87] Nevertheless, the British generally practiced the main tenets of the reforms, that is, operational-level maneuver warfare and mission command.[88] Smith had demonstrated flexibility and superior desert maneuver warfare skills. His field commanders, such as Patrick Cordingly and Ian Durie, were of a new breed and understood him completely. Smith had commanded the Higher

Command Staff Course (HCSC), and many of his subordinates were graduates of that institution and well versed in theory and practice of the operational level.[89] Smith claimed that the reforms, and the revised educational
system, had been largely responsible for the planning and execution skills
demonstrated during the campaign.[90] The question remains whether this success was due to the reforms or to the abilities of one of Britain's most capable
commanders in the post second world war era. Was he simply the right man
at the right place, like Nelson or Wellington at the time?

Like Smith, some have attributed wartime British prowess to the reforms,
and especially to the HCSC and the 1989 *Design for Military Operations*.[91] A
new breed of able and innovative officers had been reared. According to Colin
McInnes, Smith's daring, versatile, and refreshingly unorthodox ideas were
represented through his adaptability and creativity during the force build-up
stage.[92] Combined arms and interservice cooperation had been strengthened
through the personal ties established at the HCSC.[93] This experience further
demonstrated the importance of team building and shared doctrine for the
application of mission command. Commanders were issued mission directives
and granted great latitude in the pursuit of their objectives. Smith posited that
the increased tempo that resulted substituted for the shortage of real-time intelligence. Although the existence of a sixty-five-page SOP could have hindered British efforts, in effect it merely created a common understanding and
a basis for the short orders issued in practice.[94] In the spirit of the Bagnall Reforms, Smith's style of command facilitated subordinate initiative, ensuring
quick, decisive, and imaginative action.[95] Nevertheless, Smith also knew when
is the right time to switch and issue detailed orders.[96]

The disparity between British and American performance during the war
can be attributed to a number of factors: the size of their respective forces (one
division versus two corps); the impact of Bagnall and the Ginger Group; the
relatively small size of British HQ, as discussed earlier; and simpler and clearer
doctrinal concepts (lacking, for instance, the sophisticated but controversial
"synchronization").[97] Another contributing factor was the HCSC education
enjoyed by many of the British officers. Most significantly, one must credit
Rupert Smith's command style. As a paratrooper, he was accustomed to ex-
pecting the unexpected; his skills were honed further during his time in the
HCSC and through the intellectual efforts of the Ginger Group. The American general Franks described him as "bright, intensely focused and very much
at ease with himself. . . . Although he came from Special Forces, light infantry

background, he was not intimidated in the least from commanding an armored division and he was also quite willing to listen and to give subordinate commanders wide latitude."[98] According to a different critic: "Smith's emphasis upon seizing the initiative and maintaining a high tempo of operations was matched by his ability and willingness to act and react quickly moving formations to exploit opportunities . . . and changing his concept of operation when necessary."[99] The First Gulf War, then, essentially served as a case study in which the British Army was able to examine the applicability and advisability of the Bagnall Reforms. The experience demonstrated that the British Army had indeed been able to implement the basic tenets devised by Bagnall and his followers.

Between the Gulf Wars

Operational thinking in the British Army fostered confidence and boldness; it led to an expansion of the reforms. Wartime experiences proved that the reforms had encouraged flexibility and creativity, enabled independent judgment, and honed decision-making skills. These in turn allowed for the maintenance of tempo and speed even under adverse circumstances.[100] However, during the decade following the war, the British Army lost part of its hard-won edge, as one critic observed: "The British army appears to have forgotten about speed and tempo. This is the interesting case of the difference between espoused and enacted behavior. . . . [Although] achieving superior tempo relative to the enemy is endorsed in the doctrine . . . the British army immediately waters this down."[101] This development stemmed from seemingly rigid procedural training programs (including the Staff and Command College). According to Storr, it was also a result of a basic flaw in British doctrine, which no longer equated superior tempo with increased speed.[102] Shortly after this criticism was raised, the British Army faced its second major challenge.

Operation Telic

During Operation Telic (the Second Gulf War), the British deployed a division once again; this time it constituted nearly a third of the Coalition ground component. Similarly to the previous war, the British task force was designated First Armoured Division. However, the force was more improvised and consisted of only one maneuver element, the Seventh Armored Brigade. Due to diminished maneuver capabilities and their experience in pacification operations in Northern Ireland, the British Army was assigned the densely populated urban center of Basra, rife with armed gangs and militia. After a two-week siege used to conduct psychological warfare and gather intelligence, they took the city from multiple directions, primarily encountering irregular fedayeen fighters.[103]

Although the British had secured their objective, suffering few casualties and inflicting minimum collateral damage in the process, many Britons felt that the army had exhibited unsatisfactory decisiveness and failed to reach the best possible tempo of operations.[104] Additionally, a postwar study of the performance of British command revealed deficiencies in regard to HQ process and performance, which may have had an impact on the realization.[105] According to the authors of the report, the quality of individual British commanders and the poor quality of their adversaries were nearly undone by several factors. These included the mechanism by which the campaign plan was translated into tactical missions and orders; the length and timeliness of orders, resulting from the growth of headquarters; and a focus on contingency planning rather than coordination of subordinate actions.[106] It was found also that the existing method of generating a situation estimate actually impeded tactical decision making.[107] The report concluded that difficulties arose primarily as a result of structures and processes rather than individuals. For example, the divisional "base plan" dictating the mission, concept of operations, and subordinate assignments was thirteen pages long. Interestingly, the report revealed the existence of process difficulties only from the brigade level and higher. This may have been due to the fact that higher echelons are inherently dependent on processes; alternatively, it may simply reflect a lack of documentation from the lower echelons.

The lean British command system utilized and extolled by Rupert Smith in 1991 had transformed, for the worse, by 2003. Thus, while HQ functions remained essentially unaltered, the number of officers assigned to it had increased by 25 percent.[108] This increase, observed in several recent operations, is often attributed to the information overload resulting from the ever-increasing complexity of information-gathering and processing technologies.[109] This basic fact notwithstanding, operational analysis had demonstrated that as many as 40 percent of the officers in headquarters serve no concrete purpose. An additional 20 percent actually have a negative effect.[110] This deterioration was also revealed in a tendency toward excessive planning. For instance, one brigade HQ produced five different contingency plans within forty-eight hours. Such practices had the unfortunate effect of overburdening staff and delaying the issuance of orders. The aforementioned brigade kept four luckless officers working around the clock on plans that never materialized. This was due partially to the manner through which the campaign plan had been translated into missions and orders.[111] It also signified a strengthening of the American influence to the detriment of the system used so effectively by Rupert Smith.

In several cases, the orders—the process output—were excessively long.[112] Indeed, some units had (unjustifiably) reversed the common practice of issuing increasingly shorter orders during a campaign. In one (somewhat obfuscated) twenty-five-page-long operations order, the paragraph stipulating the "mission" appeared only on the tenth page. In another case, an inch-thick order was rendered meaningless not one hour into an operation,[113] thereby validating Moltke's dictum according to which "no plan survives the first contact with the enemy."[114] The lengthy order-issuing process meant that orders were often outdated. Thus, though the British had been discussing this very contingency for two months, neither the division nor the brigade had operational contingency plans when Basra fell two days earlier than expected (6 April). The orders that had been issued were either unnecessary or too late. Orders detailing peace-supporting operations were issued fully two weeks after the city fell, during which time the field units were essentially left to their own devices. Nor had the chain of command been adequately defined, as three different individuals were charged with military governance of the city.[115] In the final analysis, the report concluded, current British military education is leading toward "missions, and orders generally, that are excessively long, confusing and hard to understand . . . [and] inconsistent with the spirit and principles of Mission Command." In this context, the authors of the report recount various examples: a twenty-line mission statement and subunits receiving an average of eight tasks and as many as thirteen. Moreover, multitasked orders were often issued without a clarification of the commander's intent, thereby hindering the recipients' efforts at prioritization.[116]

Similarly, the concept of operation tended to be too long, obfuscated, and prone to obvious and inconsequential statements, such as "I intend to achieve my mission." Some commanders strove to inspire through the medium of the written word, in a manner better suited for oral presentation. The statement of intent was often either a simple reiteration of the mission or excessively complex: one such statement ran over seven lines and was followed by statements for each of the three phases of the campaign. In one case, the order had indeed contained a desired "end state"; however, it simply repeated the mission. In several cases, mission statements consisted of multiple contingent tasks (as in "be prepared to . . ."), which were either obvious tasks or coordination details. Consequently, the authors of the report noted the need to "clarify guidance for the content of orders, particularly missions and concepts of operations."[117] Nevertheless, they stated:

> In practice, there is considerable evidence that execution was generally decentralized during Operation TELIC. What appears to have happened is that missions were not phrased clearly and simply, which overshadowed the real flexibility that in practice appears to have been afforded. We must continue to stress the philosophy and principles of Mission Command, and reward their application.[118]

The authors of the report concluded that reliance on field commanders' initiative, professionalism, and tactical proficiency circumvented these highly detailed, restrictive, and obfuscated orders originating from intricate higher headquarters.[119] However, while the British officers enjoyed a solid professional background and common sense, a more capable enemy would have assuredly punished these shortcomings.

The success of the British contingent in the First Gulf War can perhaps be attributed to its having been a small professional force, commanded by able officers, supported by a small effective staff, and riding the successful doctrinal and educational reforms. The mission command variant practiced by its commanders held much promise for the future. However, its experience prior to and during the Second Gulf War had been less successful. The next chapter will investigate whether success had been largely due to unique individuals or to successful institutionalization of mission command.

THE ISRAELI APPLICATION OF MISSION COMMAND

The Second Intifada (2000–2004)

Toward the end of the Al-Aqsa Intifada, an Israeli daily ran a cover story on the commander of the Gaza Division, Brigadier General Shmoul Zakai. He was described as "innovative," which in IDF nomenclature "means offensive and aggressive. . . . An officer who is cautious in operations will never be described as creative."[120] This understanding reflected the conduct of the IDF as a whole during the Intifada.

Efforts to revive the IDF tradition of mission command during the 1990s proved more successful in large-scale offensive operations than in routine constabulary activities. As opposed to the civil unrest characterizing the First Intifada (1987–1993), the Second Intifada was characterized by gunmen equipped with firearms and explosives and the targeting of Israeli civilians by suicide bombers. The lethality of the terror campaign was perceived by many Israelis as an existential threat and the conflict itself as a full-blown war.[121] During the first phase (May–December 2000), the IDF sought to contain the situation and practiced self-restraint. During the second phase (2001), the IDF attempted to control events by pressuring the Palestinian Authority (PA). The objective of the third phase (January–March 2002) was the methodical dismantling of terror and armed resistance groups as well as of the PA.[122] During the fourth phase (June 2002–May 2003) Israel counterattacked, executing operations such as "Defensive Shield," while the fifth phase was dedicated to maintaining stability (March 2003 and onward).

It was during the latter two stages that brigade commanders were expected to demonstrate creativity and aggressiveness. Feeling under attack and endeavoring to defeat the terrorists, the political leadership unleashed the IDF. This was especially the case after a Passover night suicide bombing left 30 civilians dead and 140 injured (27 March 2002).[123] Under the leadership of Prime Minister Ariel Sharon, and Chief of Staff Shaul Mofaz, the IDF set out to "impress upon the Palestinian and Arab consciousness that terrorism and violence will not defeat us."[124] They knew that unequivocal victory would come neither immediately nor at a low price.[125] Shortly after his election to office in February 2001, Ariel Sharon attended a briefing at Southern Command concerning the situation with the Palestinians. The briefing officers assigned to plan and execute the campaign were primarily OTRI trained.[126] During the briefing, Sharon remarked: "In my time, I didn't know how to use a laptop or half of these fancy words, but I knew how to fight terror."[127] Sharon demanded action; he often stated: "I want to hear the officers stamping the ground, like horses that need to be restrained."[128] The elite infantry brigade and battalion commanders were encouraged to take the initiative. Like Sharon, the brigade commanders believed that the IDF should maintain the offensive; with his blessing they began to exercise initiative.[129]

The IDF had been wary of costly urban warfare and refrained from seizing Palestinian towns and refugee camps. The new generation of officers, however, often described as better educated and intellectually equipped than their predecessors,[130] pressed a hesitant IDF to reverse this policy.[131] And indeed, when the densely populated Nablus *Kasbah* (ancient quarter of a modern

Middle Eastern city) was captured, the IDF suffered only one fatality while inflicting seventy and taking hundreds into custody. The paratroopers penetrated the *Kasbah* from multiple directions, a maneuver that caused confusion and chaos among the Palestinians.[132] The same principles were later employed successfully when the IDF seized Tul Karem and Ramallah.

Their success was partially due to the fact that maintenance of objective followed immediately behind the understanding of the overall intent.[133] Missions were planned by subordinate commanders and were discussed openly in light of the higher intent. The IDF introduced the innovative concept of "swarming," denoting a multidirectional and highly synchronized deployment of many small groups against a single objective relying on mission command.[134] On the basis of the overall operational concept and commander's intent, individual forces were granted great latitude for independent planning and execution. Synchronization was maintained through a clear and concise communication of intent throughout the echelons of command.[135] Civilian casualties were usually lower than those inflicted when using other tactics, such as occurred in Jenin. Following these operations, Shimon Naveh reflected that:

> The war has produced the best tactical commanders. . . . They are creative and aggressive and not only exploit opportunities but also constantly create and design new patterns of reality. . . . I can say mission command is very much alive . . . [and] despite what some say it is a highly professional army, and on the combat level it is working superbly.[136]

As the Intifada continued, the frequency and aggressiveness of operations increased as units competed for credit and fame; the IDF tendency for *bitsuism* had resurfaced.[137] As in the 1950s, strategy was replaced by tactical objectives and opportunities.[138] Critics asserted that excessive force was actually contributing to the escalation of violence.[139] Nevertheless, commanders sought "special" missions in order to increase unit morale and combat readiness. Most units were conducting tedious and uninspiring routine constabulary operations, and commanders sought special operations in order to maintain combat motivation and readiness.[140] According to one company commander, "participation in operations sweetens the pill. . . . In their absence, one's actions seem meaningless."[141]

Thus, the call and drive for action often arose from the field units. Brigade and battalion commanders pressed for the offensive and took the initiative.[142] The increased number of raids conducted by large regular forces resulted in a comparative increase in collateral damage and civilian deaths.[143] Indeed, the IDF was criticized for employing excessive force during the highly publicized "Defensive Shield," "Rainbow," and "Days of Penitence" operations.[144] Furthermore, due to the spirit of *bitsuism*, units demonstrated excessive "enthusiasm" and disregard for the strategic implications of tactical actions. The first large-scale raids into Jenin and Tul Karem, for example, were initiated by local commanders without the "blessing" of senior command.[145] Operating without the benefit of clear intent or a desired "end state," IDF forces were left to devise "their own plans, methods and even objectives; they recognized only the need to act and act forcefully."[146] Initiative is a central part of mission command, but could become counterproductive without strategic intent to guide it, more so in counterinsurgency situations.

In late 2003, Ya'alon stated publicly that "in our tactical decisions, we are operating contrary to our strategic interests."[147] In another interview, Ya'alon reflected that "in LIC situations, tactical actions can have a strategic effect." In these situations, "every soldier manning a road block is a strategic soldier, if he doesn't understand the link to the bigger picture he can make a tactical mistake that will result in a strategic blunder."[148] However, despite these deficiencies and in contrast to its confusion during the First Intifada, this time the IDF was demonstrating initiative, determination, and unorthodox thinking. Targeted killings, destruction of weapons and bomb factories, and the mass arrests of suspected terrorists had struck a severe blow to the Palestinian terrorist and guerrilla infrastructure. In contrast, freedom of maneuver and initiative were curtailed during Palestinian attacks against the IDF. Then senior commanders were apt to intervene directly, thereby diminishing the authority and responsibility of local commanders. As one company commander described:

> As soon as commanders come to the scene of the incident, the brigade commander becomes a platoon commander, a division commander becomes a company commander, platoon and squad commanders get their orders straight from the battalion and brigade commanders while leapfrogging, and then the company commander has no control.[149]

The tendency to micromanage and intervene undermines the very fabric of mission command. These commanders followed the IDF ethos of "commanding from the front." While this practice is relatively harmless in small operations, it becomes positively devastating in larger operations that involved larger units. In the latter, commanders are forced to manage overwhelming volumes of information and make numerous decisions, they might choose to lead from the front but only after they have left trusted staff officers to ensure continuity of command and control. In a large battle scenario, they know most units are left to their own device. However, things are different in small scale operations that create conditions for micromanagement. This micromanagement tendency has aroused serious debate concerning the issues of trust, responsibility, and the proper conduct of commanders. Several senior officers were killed in the line of duty due to this practice over the years and as recently as November 2002, when a brigade commander was killed in Hebron leading a platoon against a Palestinian ambush.[150] Some argued that a brigade commander should never position himself as a squad leader that leads a charge against the gunmen. Others contested that this is exactly what is expected from the senior leader arriving at the scene: to lead by example and put his life on the line. While this debate is concerned more with leadership rather than mission command, it illustrates how the counterinsurgency environment impacts command and commanders. What would have been the natural job of a platoon sergeant in large wars, storming a gunmen position, becomes an issue for a brigade commander.

The Second Lebanon War

In some respects, many Israelis believe that the Second Lebanon War (2006) was unsuccessful. One of these aspects was the quality of command in general and the practice of mission command specifically.[151]

The war was singular in Israeli history in that both the prime minister (Ehud Olmert) and minister of defense (A'amir Peretz) had no substantial military experience. Due to their limited background, they were forced to rely heavily on their military advisors.[152] The general staff was dominated by air force generals who advocated reliance on the EBO doctrine. The war plans revolved around air force–delivered precison fire and additional ground stand-off fire and supported by limited ground incursions against Hezbollah strongholds along the border.[153] Chief of Staff Dan Halutz believed this would negate the need for a messy and costly ground invasion.[154] This approach suited the agenda of the political leadership, which feared repeating the sins of the fathers and foundering in the Lebanese quagmire. EBO thus promised a demonstration of air force prowess and a nearly casualty-free victory for the politicians.[155] Consequently, when the ground assault was finally authorized, it was ill prepared. The reserves were called up belatedly, and most units had poor combat readiness.[156] Those who were ready, such as the elite reserve paratroops, were used as simple infantry. Daring raids, for which they had practiced for years, were canceled in the hopes of minimizing risk and maximizing force protection.[157]

Toward the end, senior command realized that a massive ground incursion would be required in order to stop the rocket barrage directed at northern Israel. Once operations were begun, the fear of casualties led to micromanagement, and the four divisions assembled for the operations were used hesitantly.[158] Concurrently, a sense of crisis developed in the higher echelons. The deputy chief of staff, Major General Kaplinski, was sent to advise Northern Command; Gal Hirsch, commander of the largest division that bore the brunt of the fighting, issued unclear orders, which his subordinates could neither decipher nor translate into concrete plans; brigade commanders remained in the rear, developing their situation estimates based on information transmitted to plasma screens.[159] The "plasma screen" soon became an expression representing the overdependence of IDF commanders on the new digital systems. Tactical missions were altered frequently, hindering preparations and increasing the general feeling of a lack of direction.

Units encountering Hezbollah fighters proved unprepared, mentally and doctrinally. The tactics developed over the previous decade to fight poorly armed and trained Palestinian irregulars failed against the competent Hezbollah fighters.[160] The once successful practice of utilizing small units to conduct strikes in a semicontrolled environment now became an impediment to success. Conventional training had been neglected, basic fighting skills had been forgotten, and the army was no longer able to practice combined arms warfare in units larger than the company.[161] This neglect was felt more strongly by the reserves. When the RMA, EBO, and related doctrine was adopted years before the war, it gave rise to the notion that the reserves were losing their importance.[162] Once the backbone of the army and the heroes of the Six Days' and Yom Kippur Wars, the quantity and quality of the training they received diminished during the decade preceding the Second Lebanon War. When called upon to fight during that summer, their training, doctrine, and equipment were found lacking.[163] Commanders, especially from the brigade and above, lacked the experience, education, and training to lead large formations, as enjoyed by previous generations.[164] These deficiencies notwithstanding, the four divisions amassed by the border should have been enough to overwhelm Hezbollah. But in the final analysis, the IDF lacked the necessary resolve and "killer instinct."[165] Senior command consistently wavered; risk aversion led to cancellation or postponement of operations.[166] The atmosphere was obviously less than conducive for mission command.

After the war, the IDF commissioned some fifty studies, conducted primarily by retired generals, veterans of the 1973 and 1982 wars. Although they analyzed military performance in a variety of areas, most eventually remarked on the issue of command and control. The overriding conclusion was that control had taken precedence over command. Criticism centered on three themes: overdependence on plasma screens, lack of clarity in orders and written mission statements, and lack of trust between echelons.[167] Boaz Amidror, commander of a reserve paratrooper brigade and a graduate of *Pum Barak*,[168] testified that he quickly realized that mission command is the only way to command the battle. However, in a lessons-learned session conducted with his own company commanders, he found that they had understood their own missions but not the intent, the "in order to" section. He admitted then that this was a serious flaw. Amidror stated that commanders are duty-bound to understand the context of tasks allotted to them and, if need be, to harass their superiors until such an understanding is acquired. Thus, the purpose of occupying a certain village will impact the manner of its occupation. This knowledge affects different tactical choices.[169]

Internal studies revealed basic flaws in command, flaws that hindered mission command. For instance, the postwar account of the Ninety-first Division identified a clear preference for control over command. Orders lacked clear statements of purpose or critical constraints such as time. In general, initiative, once the hallmark of the IDF, was exercised only by the lowest echelons. Command from the front was rarely practiced, even in dire straits.[170] A different divisional report recorded complaints concerning the clarity of the assigned missions and their contribution to the overall situation.[171] Being left in the dark injured motivation and affected their ability to complete their missions.[172] Former Chief of Staff (1987–1991) and commander of the Entebbe raid (1976) Lieutenant General Dan Shomron conducted a study on doctrine and command decisions in General HQ. When explaining the deterioration in IDF performance, he chose a metaphor from the world of computer programming: "a virus had been injected into the operating system of the IDF," the virus being EBO doctrine. It constituted, according to Shomron, an extreme departure from the traditional IDF doctrine that called for rapid battle decision. The latter doctrine had allowed a surprised and disorganized IDF to turn the tables on the invading Arab armies in the war of 1973. Regrettably, the connection between brains and brawn, tactical and strategic, had been lost. The IDF, he concluded, must relearn time-honored doctrines and principles of war.[173]

The Vinograd commission, the politically sanctioned external investigative committee charged with examining every aspect of the war, reaffirmed these criticisms.[174] The committee concluded that these deficiencies reflected a "flawed organizational culture" and that the "the entire chain of command is responsible for the lack of clear orders and the lack of trust."[175] In an interview held on the first anniversary of the war, wartime Deputy Chief of Staff Moshe Kaplinski admitted that a deeply flawed situational assessment had led the general staff to issue confusing orders. Moreover, he added, senior command should have granted junior commanders "more latitude, to let them operate."[176] In the postwar period, and under the guidance of Chief of Staff Gabi Ashekanzi, the IDF has been attempting to regain its conventional capabilities and its old maneuver skills. For this purpose, intensive training regimes have been devised for regular and reserve units, and the officer educational system is undergoing revision.[177] Mission command, which had faded away (though was never formerly abandoned) as large ground operations appeared a thing of the past, is being reemphasized.[178] The success of these measures and the impact of mission command upon battlefield performance will be validated if and when the IDF is put to the test once again.

Postscript: Operation Cast Lead, Gaza (2008)

Following the unsuccessful campaign in Southern Lebanon, the IDF began a thorough examination of its failings and instituted sweeping changes. The opportunity to evaluate the degree to which these lessons were internalized came during Operation Cast Lead. Targeting the Hamas in Gaza the operation began on 27 December 2008 with a short but powerful airstrike followed by a ground assault deploying four brigade-size combat teams. To be sure, Hezbollah is better trained, organized, and equipped than Hamas, and the topography, terrain, and geostrategic circumstances of Southern Lebanon are more complex than those of Gaza.

Conversely, Hamas had been modeling itself on Hezbollah, and the densely populated urban Gaza Strip posed its own unique challenge. According to the Paratrooper Brigade commander, "there were IED's, tunnels and booby traps everywhere. Entire streets were covered with wires connected to IED's even I was surprised by the magnitude."[179]

By and large, the Gaza operation was well planned and well rehearsed. From a military perspective, the IDF had learned the lessons of the war and improved its performance on the battlefield in various issues, including command and control and particularly in regard to mission command. A central issue raised in the debriefings following the Second Lebanon War was the absence of mission command and subordinate independence and their adverse effect on combat effectiveness.[180] The IDF was determined to improve in this area.

On the strategic and operational level ,and in stark contrast to the relations between Chief of Staff Halutz and head of Northern Command Udi Adam during the war, Chief of Staff Ashkenazi gave the head of Southern Command Yoav Galanat full autonomy in running the show and was willing to back him up all the way.[181] The tasks and responsibilities of the general staff and those of Southern Command's staff were well defined and well synchronized. The process was facilitated by the professional respect both generals hold for each other.

In essence, the maneuver brigade served as the basic combat formation. Its commander was assigned additional resources as demanded by the nature of the brigade's missions, such as unmanned aerial vehicles (UAVs) and close air support from rotary and fixed-wing aircraft.[182] The transference of operational control and authority to the brigade allowed forward commanders to exercise initiative and creativity.[183]

Tactical command and leadership were strengthened as senior commanders and officers led their troops into the battlefield. All four brigade commanders fought alongside their units, rather than resort to the practice of commanding from operational headquarters in the rear as had been common in 2006.[184] In that war, operational commanders were accused of subscribing to the so-called plasma culture—that is, demonstrating excessive trust in digital command and control equipment, a command style that resulted in several operational blunders. This leadership style was stamped out by the incoming chief of staff, Lieutenant General Gabi Ashkenazi; the IDF would not repeat such command and control errors in Cast Lead. In an interview held after Operation Cast Lead, Ashkenazi stated: "We all remember the brigade commanders of the Second Lebanon War, sitting at their computers while their men were in the field. Now they led from the front."[185] In addition, and in contrast with occurrences in 2006, the orders issued and the missions assigned were clearly articulated and unambiguous.

Although the Gaza operation was not a classic, large, all-out maneuver operation, and Hamas did not pose a serious military challenge, it is still possible to conclude that the IDF has made considerable improvement in relation to mission command. Better training, clear missions, and a desire to redeem its reputation were all important ingredients to this success.

CONCLUSION

The battlefield experience of the three armies analyzed in this chapter revealed that the actual application of mission command has been only partially successful. Some units, such as the British First Armoured Division (1991), the American 101st Airborne (2003), and the Israeli Thirty-fifth Paratrooper Brigade (2002), have utilized mission command and demonstrated considerable battlefield capabilities. These experiences also bore a positive correlation between overall performance, mission command, and utilization of such principles as combined arms, maneuver, and tempo. However, it is important to note that such performance predates the adoption of mission command. Patton, Slim, and Sharon, to name a few, acted in this manner and encouraged their subordinates to follow suit long before the new doctrines had been devised.

Indeed, despite the lessons learned and reforms implemented between the various campaigns, the data suggest that the British and Israeli performance actually regressed. The Israeli adoption of American technology and air superiority–based doctrine came at the expense of ground forces' professionalism. When they faced complex combat situations in Lebanon, the ground forces achieved dismal results. Similarly, the British lost their agility and flexibility when they adopted the inflated U.S. model HQ. In a final analysis, despite espousing, educating, and training their armies to practice mission command principles, the Americans, British, and Israelis proved unable to escape their defining command traditions. The Israelis provide an interesting case study as they had originally practiced mission command but have hitherto been unable to recreate the experience due to changes in their social fabric and culture as well as their perception of the threats surrounding them.

10 THE PRAXIS GAP

THE PREVIOUS CHAPTER examined how mission command was employed in operations, the ultimate raison d'être of the armed forces. It demonstrated that the various armies had achieved mixed results, despite many efforts to incorporate mission command into the organizational fabric. Hence, the current chapter will attempt to identify other contributing factors that may have shaped the military culture and influenced the adoption process. These include current social, political, and technological trends that are impacting to various degrees all Western militaries and bear directly on their ability to execute mission command. Though external to the military organization, these trends have a significant influence over its conduct and culture.

The first of these changes that have occurred are in the area of civil-military relations, that is, changes in society that impact the role and conduct of the military. Charles Moskos described this change as a transformation from "modern" to "postmodern" armies.[1] He noted that one of the characteristics of the latter is increased interpretability of the civilian and military spheres.[2] This chapter will show how this process has altered different aspects of military organization and culture across all Western militaries and how it has impacted mission command. Postmodern armies are also increasingly involved in operations characterized by Rupert Smith as "war amongst the people." Armed conflicts are no longer fought on clearly delineated battlefields or between state actors:

> War amongst the people is both a graphic description of modern war-like situations, and also a conceptual framework: it reflects the hard fact that there is

no secluded battlefield upon which armies engage, nor are there necessary armies, definitely not on all sides.[3]

In this type of war, according to Smith, non–state organizations avoid an opponent's conventional arsenal. They concentrate on altering perceptions and intentions rather than securing a battlefield decision, consequently lengthening the duration of the conflict. Often, this strategy creates the "body-bag effect," whereby the public and the politicians are reluctant to incur endless casualties for distant and controversial campaigns.[4] All of the above affect the military's ability to practice mission command, which demands a degree of subordinate leeway and risk taking. Other factors internal to the organization and influencing the adoption of mission command include human resource policies (education, training, and personnel) and new information technologies. The former dictates promotions, placements, and training tenets and therefore shapes the behaviors of people in an organization. In the current chapter, I will attempt to investigate their effect on the practice of mission command. The latter, information technology (C2 digitization), has become central to command and control functions since the end of the Cold War. It has generated a range of behavioral options for commanders, and its impact can therefore not be ignored. The argument of this chapter is that these factors are shaping military culture in such a manner as to influence the practice of mission command.

THE U.S. ARMY

Civil-Military Relations

Toward the end of the Vietnam era, the U.S. Army was experiencing major crises. The attitude of American society toward the army was at an all-time low. Antiwar sentiments intertwined with the social upheavals of the 1960s and 1970s. The drugs and racial issues that divided America were reflected in the army as demonstrated by higher rates of desertion, insubordination, and violent attacks against military superiors (*fragging*) in Vietnam.[5] These difficulties quickly spread to the European theater as the best officers and NCOs were reassigned to Southeast Asia. Their hastily trained replacements only exacerbated existing difficulties. Discipline and unit cohesion deteriorated, and in some cases officers were physically attacked. The draft was terminated in 1973, leaving the army to rely on volunteers, most of whom left much to be desired.[6] The reforms of the 1970 and 1980s gradually improved the public image of the army and, consequently, the quality of recruits.[7]

However, since the end of the Cold War, the U.S. military has once again come under heavy scrutiny as evidenced by increased political intervention at every level.[8] These developments have ushered in what one analyst termed "Post Heroic Warfare," in which Western warfare is characterized by low casualty rates and reliance on technology and firepower.[9] In illustration, he cited the ill-fated 1993 Mogadishu operation, where the public outcry following the deaths of eighteen Rangers and Delta operators led to a complete withdrawal of U.S. forces from Somalia.[10] This trend is also reflected by increased litigation and enforcement of civilian values even when harmful to operational effectiveness. The latter refers to "political correctness," which dictates "postmodern" speech and behavioral patterns equating mainstream and minority narratives.[11] Many officers believe that the time allotted to sensitivity training would be better spent preparing for combat—indeed, that the military had been infiltrated by civilians emphasizing compassion, understanding, and friendship rather than courage, honor, sacrifice, and skill at arms. One critic quipped whether the military was training professional soldiers or social workers.[12] These foreign values have a destructive influence on the military in general and on mission command in particular. This occurs because they undermine the unique professional ethos, intervene directly with different affairs, and inhibit commanders from taking bold action for fear of casualties. By conforming to these trends, many officers exacerbate the problem.[13]

Public sensitivity to casualties, shared by Western democracies, forms an additional facet of postmodern heroism. The military is expected to deliver cheap and quick results, even in the aftermath of September 11th. This tremendous pressure has increased the tendency toward risk aversion and micromanagement.[14] Interestingly, studies have demonstrated that both military and civilian leaders underestimate the public's threshold for casualties. Indeed, if a conflict is perceived as just, the willingness for sacrifice remains similar to that in previous periods in history.[15] The complex relationship with the civilian world, however, can hardly be separated from another change: the character of conflict, which will be discussed in the next section.

War Amongst the People

Mission command has also suffered from the type of operations the U.S. military has been involved in. These included various forms of counterinsurgency and peacekeeping operations characterized by Rupert Smith as "war amongst the people." They typically involved lengthy deployment periods, an inability to gain a decisive victory, and mounting casualties. In addition, questions are raised about the pertinence of the situation to national security, as had been the case in Mogadishu, Afghanistan, and Iraq. These situations have introduced the "strategic corporal" phenomenon discussed by Marine General Charles Krulak.[16] In essence, the actions of the lowest ranking soldiers can have immediate strategic or even political consequences. Concurrently, the scarceness of operations in LICs leads to increased micromanagement, thereby hindering mission command. Nevertheless, there exists a general consensus that mission command remains relevant, as reflected by a recent joint army and marine field manual that reemphasizes the importance of mission command in LIC environments.[17]

In contrast to conventional operations, most "wars amongst the people" have no quick solution. In this context, low-level mistakes are likely to worsen a given situation while initiative on this level is less likely to achieve strategic resolutions.[18] Thus, tactical mistakes may occupy the national security echelons, including political leaders, international organizations, and even the courts. However, since the enemy thrives on manipulating public opinion, a corporal may be required to make snap decisions in situations where no proper course of action exists. Similarly, senior commanders are no longer expected to simply destroy the enemy, but they find themselves locked in a complicated situation, as described by Smith:

> Instead of only you and a gang of gladiators, there's at least one other producer and another gang of gladiators and you are all mixed up with the idiot who can't find the car park, the people who are late for tickets, the ice cream sellers and all the rest. At the same time, around the outside of the circus is this highly factional audience paying attention to what's going on in the pit. . . . Here the commander is actually writing and playing a story at the same time. His job is to produce the most compelling narrative and act it out, and every act he does is an act of sending information and causes an effect. The currency in these types of operation is not who has more effective firepower but who has more effective information. The type of information that will enable him to separate the enemy from the rest of the crowd.[19]

Senior commanders then attempt to control every event so as to maintain the narrative they wish to promote. Thus, Italian journalist Giuliana Sgrena was injured and her escort Major General Nicola Calipari (Italy's second highest-ranking military intelligence officer) killed by American fire following her release from captivity in Iraq.[20] Although the Pentagon cleared the troops, Italian prosecutors attempted to indict one of the men. This incident became a major source of tension between the Italian and U.S. governments.[21] Similarly, the infamous incident of prisoner mistreatment at Abu Ghraib prison, which represented a failure of the entire system and the chain of command, led to a political scandal that damaged the credibility of the United States and its allies in Iraq.[22] Although the administration argued that the incidents were isolated, critics said they represented an attitude of disrespect and violence toward Arabs.[23] According to the *New Yorker*:

> As the photographs from Abu Ghraib make clear, these detentions have had enormous consequences: for the imprisoned civilian Iraqis, many of whom had nothing to do with the growing insurgency; for the integrity of the Army; and for the United States' reputation in the world.[24]

The specter of altering the strategic balance so easily serves as a strong incentive for micromanagement. In contrast, mission command denotes a contract wherein superiors clearly define intent, mission, resources, and constraints while subordinates are free to act within these parameters. When the situation changes, subordinates are empowered to alter their plans while conforming to the original intent. However, only authority can be delegated; superiors remain responsible. This imbalance is felt strongly in wars among the people. Mistakes incur investigations and litigation designed to establish guilt and assign responsibility to individuals. Mission command then gives way to the "blame game" and career protection.[25]

Education, Training, and Human Resource Policies: Post-Vietnam Reforms

According to Suzanne Nielsen, the army began instituting reforms while still engaged in Vietnam under the leadership of Army Chief of Staff General William Westmoreland (1968–1972). These reforms included personnel management, training, and education, all of which are necessary for the practice of mission command. Due to the wartime expansion and the short-tour policy, the army experienced severe personnel turbulence. This led to a deterioration of unit cohesion, training, readiness, and morale as well as command. The issue was readdressed in 1971, when it was decided that company and brigade commanders would serve a minimum of twelve and eighteen months, respectively. Additionally, the army established the Officer Personnel Management System (OPMS). Fully implemented only in 1974, the new system transformed the procedures for officer placement, promotion, and selection for command. In order to improve the level of command officers, the evaluation system was redesigned to better reflect performance and potential.[26]

In 1971 Westmorland took steps to decentralize training, under the assumption that "the unit commander was the best judge of his unit's needs and training requirements."[27] Thus, Continental Army Command (CONARC) published mission-type training objectives rather than restrictive prescriptions for training individuals and units. These changes emphasized the need for a dynamic and innovative approach to training, including the reinstitution of the aggressor system, for training and strengthening the ties between units and service schools. The objective, in addition to training units rather than individual replacements, was to develop a professional NCO Corps. The third area of reform concerned the officer education system. From the military perspective, it included intensification of professionalism and leadership values; from the academic perspective, it improved the level of learning across the board. In order to further strengthen ties with the civilian educational community, Westmoreland approved the establishment of the Army Research Associates Program in 1971.[28] Training formed the basis for reform as reflected in the "train-fight-lead" trinity adopted by the U.S. Army. It culminated in the establishment of Fort Erwin's National Training Center (NTC) in 1981, which offered the best means of training, short of war. It provided large maneuver areas, fire ranges, and an Opposing Force (OPFOR) utilizing Soviet doctrine and equipment. Guest units were given objective After Action Reports (AAR) following two-sided exercises, which allowed self-criticism and lessons-learned sessions. The institutionalization of the self-criticism sessions in both training and officer education was evidence of how far the army's internal identity had changed.[29]

Contemporary Assessment of the Reforms

The reforms, though substantial, fell short as the existing personnel system still hindered the development of the agility General DePuy required for his active defense doctrine.[30] The number of officers was inadequate for the existing table of organization, and there was little or no unit cohesion.[31] Starry, upon assuming command on TRADOC in 1979, began examining substitutes for the existing personnel system. He settled on the British and Canadian regimental system, which reinforced unit cohesion through long periods of service. The American variant developed all-arms regiments, organized by state, to ensure a minimum recruiting base. However, the plan was rejected by army staff and personnel managers who felt that it would provide regiments with easily abused autonomy.[32] The challenges of the existing system to mission command were recognized when the AirLand battle doctrine was adopted.[33] Therefore, the army established educational programs such as SAMS in order to develop officers akin to those found among the German General Staff.[34]

A study conducted a decade after mission command was formally adopted demonstrated the difficulties inherent to the adoption process. Examining tactical-level mission orders doctrine, the study revealed great diversity as to the understanding of the term "mission," the comprising elements of "mission command," and experience in its application. It concluded that although the doctrine exists, "it was not commonly known nor, by inference, understood by those officers surveyed."[35] During the period of time that has elapsed since the publication of these findings, the U.S. Army has participated in two major wars and numerous operations. Evidence indicates that it is still plagued by personnel, education, and training deficiencies, hindering efforts to practice mission command. Donald Vandergriff maintained that whereas the Germans encouraged inventive solutions, American officers are confronted with checklists and scripted scenarios that have evolved little since the advent of active defense. Adherence to detailed processes is favored over the achievement of results. Indeed, though army education has come a long way since the 1960s, officers are still not taught to think holistically or to make decisions and pursue them in the face of adversary.[36] According to Vandergriff: "rather than encourage free thought the focus in the programs is on the confined use of template processes, pre-determined phases, matrixes, laundry lists, and pages of commander's guidance."[37]

In terms of training, the Laser Engagement System (MILES) enables more realistic training. Additionally, the two-sided exercises held at the NTC facilitate an adaptation of mission command. However, Vandergriff argued that due to the zero-defect mentality and inadequate resources, the two-sided exercises were limited to scripted duels from the 1980s through the 1990s. Thus, the blue (guest) force was assigned a large maneuvering zone of operations allowing it to flank the red team. And even then, most commanders failed to exploit this opportunity, and many who did were better equipped to synchro-nize their forces than to make rapid decisions. They issued detailed plans, in the spirit of the mission training plan (MTP) checklist, which was deemed more important than accomplishing the mission. Successful rotations are based on the question "did we follow doctrine and execute the process?" Fail-ures were often explained by pointing out the red team's home ground advan-tage or the lack of opportunity to exploit enemy weaknesses and vulnerabili-ties.[38] Douglas Macgregor, who fought in the First Gulf War, argued that these were merely excuses for dependency and lack of creativity. Executing bold and risky maneuver operations and relying on mission command, Macgregor had been able to beat the red force on more than one occasion.[39] Reports from the NTC and the Joint Readiness Center reveal that battalion and brigade commanders and staff continue to exhibit inadequate expertise and profes-sionalism.[40] They often pursue a safe course, including a slow advance, erec-tion of a hasty defense, and a prayer that the enemy falls into the obvious trap. Against a real enemy familiar with the American playbook, these weaknesses are likely to incur severe punishment.[41]

These deficiencies were exposed in the Pentagon's Millennium Challenge 2002 exercise. In the largest and most expensive war game in history, the U.S. military was pitted against a rogue Middle Eastern dictator. Utilizing decid-edly low-tech means, the red team was able to strike debilitating blows against the blue team. The latter's complex matrix analysis and the latest situational awareness technologies proved inadequate against human resourcefulness, cunning, and commitment.[42] Marine General Paul van Riper, who com-manded the red team, was a long-time Clausewitz and Moltke enthusiast who detested doctrinal fads such as NCW and EBO. His method of conducting bold and aggressive operations against his enemy's weaknesses while relying on mission command proved very effective against the cumbersome U.S. military.[43] Training is intimately linked with personnel policies, such as selec-tion and promotion. According to one officer, a proven mastery of battlefield tactics and tactical competence are not prerequisites for promotion to battal-ion and brigade command. This truth was demonstrated repeatedly in NTC exercises.[44] Previous experience for many battalion commanders included merely a year as company commanders and no operational deployments. In addition, most units are not given sufficient time to develop cohesion or all-arms training.[45] Macgregor identified three major problems with the selection and promotion process. First, the process is overseen by select individuals;

the lack of diversity ensures that similar thinking officers are chosen. Second, selection for promotion is decided upon within the various branches, consequently narrowing the fields of necessary experience and of the definition of warfare. Third, to a large extent selection is dependent on "who you know"; this system encourages nepotism and personal relationships rather than merit.[46]

The system rewards "efficiency and control in an artificial centralized decision making environment" rather than professional competence.[47] Control is substituted for results, and anything of significance is decided upon from above and executed from below. Army culture positively excludes the very notion that a subordinate will know more than his superior. In this culture, seniority ensures superior decision-making capabilities. Thus, "we talk about initiative and agility but we reward officers who follow a rigidly prescribed path to success. . . . We don't reward risk takers. . . . Officers are often told to do what they are told and not ask questions."[48] A recent RAND study confirmed these observations: individuals are promoted on the basis of position availability rather than on their ability to perform the necessary duties. In order to ascend the promotion ladder, officers must choose certain assignments—ticket punching. The authors of the report also concluded that the army's efforts to prepare future senior commanders have met with mixed results.[49]

Thus, despite reforms, the personnel system continues to present challenges to the institution of mission command. The "cultural legacy of bigger is better inspired by Henry Ford's assembly line" still persists.[50] And in spite of the post–Cold War reforms, the army's fundamental organization policies and training methods have remained practically unaltered. According to Staff and Command College students, command is practiced through intimidation rather than influence, and the army continues to promote micromanagement and a zero-defects mentality.[51]

As explained earlier, training and education are essential for mission command. The need to prepare for the both conventional state-on-state and war-amongst-the-people conflicts poses a serious difficulty for which the U.S. and other militaries are seeking a solution.[52] Although mission command is suited to both types of conflict, it requires well trained and highly confident troops. However, some critics believe that the proliferation of low-intensity operations has come at the expense of preparedness for conventional threats. Thus, the Iraqi experience has improved the U.S. Army's awareness, doctrine, training, and ability to practice mission command in low-intensity situations. Whether these new gains will be applicable against more conventional or sophisticated threats remains to be seen.

The Technological Factor

The impact of technology on mission command is largely related to the introduction of the Revolution in Military Affairs (RMA) theory in the 1990s. It was defined by Andrew Marshall as "a major change in the nature of warfare brought about by the innovative application of new technologies which, combined with dramatic changes in military doctrine, operational and organizational concepts, fundamentally alters the character and conduct of military operations."[53] Central to RMA theory is the understanding that technological advances invariably produce significant changes in force structure and operations, though the focus remains on technology.[54] Interestingly, though evidence does not support the theory, it continues to play a significant role in U.S. doctrine.[55] RMA technologies promise to significantly improve command information management capabilities and situation assessments.[56] Enthusiasts believe that these technologies can potentially negate the fog of war, chance, and friction and dramatically alter warfare.[57] Thus, the army's digital divisions are given direct access to information-gathering assets (e.g., UAVs and satellites), which provide commanders with accurate real-time intelligence regarding enemy and friendly positions. Information is superimposed on maps and disseminated throughout the ranks by way of computer terminals installed in all combat vehicles. The same system serves to upload essential logistical and personnel information back to headquarters. Ostensibly, the system shortens planning and execution cycles dramatically and allows commanders to communicate with all the comprising elements of their force.[58] The aim is to achieve "battlespace dominance," which means not only superior force but superior information as well.[59] The first of these divisions was deployed in 2000, the first corps in 2004.[60]

Advocates of the systems note that the unprecedented control over the battlefield yields "war-winning advantages."[61] By reducing chance and friction, the system affords commanders the clearest picture of developing battlefield situations and renders mission command superfluous.[62] According to Robert Bateman, C2 technology will signal the "Death of *Auftragstaktik*." He foresees that commanders will gain a level of battlefield intimacy previously reserved for the men in the trenches. Micromanagement will ensue, local initiative will fade away, and new officers will lack independence and decision-making abilities.[63]

Critics have pointed out that the new technologies can and have created information overloads and can deliver grossly inaccurate information.[64] The greater risk is that the elimination of the "fog of war" is but a smoke screen. In such a case, armies will pay a hefty price for suppressing initiative and for overcentralization.[65] Others reflect on the fundamental understanding that technology is designed by humans who can make certain choices, as, for example, how, what, and where information is distributed. As Martin van Creveld opined, "there does not exist, nor has there existed, a technological determinism that governs the method to be selected for coping with uncertainty."[66] According to Joseph McLamb, there are three battle characteristics that digital technology can never alter and therefore require independent action: improved information-gathering and dissemination capabilities cannot substitute for interpretation and decision making; growing battlefield complexities will distract commanders from tactical decisions; and technological limitations and the gap between perception and truth will continue to maintain friction and fog of war as part of the nature of warfare.[67]

Digitization, according to a third approach, can mitigate some of the difficulties hindering the implementation of mission command. By correctly designing the system and the accompanying doctrine, the army can "retain mission focused command and control with its inherent decentralization while moulding the Army's digital technology and tactical design to form a solid framework to support how we fight."[68] It is a challenging balancing act, one that "has been one of the most difficult issues facing the US military and it seems that no participant is completely satisfied."[69] However, digital systems reflect existing information flow structures and organizational mentalities.[70] In the American case, the system reflects a cultural bias toward solving complex human problems through technology and corporate centralized management practices.[71] A study of the development of U.S. Army digitization found a discrepancy between the original intentions and the current product. Thus, the army promised to create a "vertically integrated digital information system" for which it "would reform its doctrine and force structure to emphasize decentralized high-tempo manoeuvre and precision firepower."[72] However, the final product transfers information primarily to the higher echelons rather than to tactical commanders, thereby created the "digital divide."

The shift in the system objective was reflected also in the name chosen for it. The original Army Battle Command System (ABCS) was replaced in 1999 by Blue Force Tracker (BFT). As the new name suggests, the system no longer provides tactical tools but rather means by which senior command can track tactical units. Importantly, this digital divide had not been created by design but rather through a series of decisions about the character of the Force XXI initiative. Its true nature only emerged during the war in Iraq.[73] Alternately, the digital divide may have developed as a natural reflection of a military culture prizing centralization and control. As noted earlier, the design of technologies essentially echoes the basic assumptions and beliefs of a given society. Despite espoused declarations, it is the society's "theory in use" that will dominate the design.[74] If the "theory in use" tends toward centralization and control, it will be reflected in the design.

THE BRITISH ARMY

Civil-Military Relations

In the aftermath of the Cold War, the British Army began to redefine its objectives while undergoing a significant force reduction.[75] These led Max Hastings to issue the following warning concerning the widening civil-military gap in Britain: "I have argued for many years . . . to recognize the scale of political and public ignorance [regarding the military], and do something about it. In modern times, as bases have closed and barracks in city centres been sold off, the Services and the civilian community have grown disturbingly physically remote from each other."[76] The changes Hastings feared influenced core institutions and practices: the regiment structures, the legality of the use of force, and social changes in the composition of the army. The most important development is the transformation of Britain into a litigation society. The government supports this fundamental change in order to encourage public self-reliance and accountability. To this end, the government has also privatized many of its own services. The public has in turn become much more demanding and critical of the governmental agencies still providing services. The tentacles of litigation have also breached the once highly regarded and trusted military establishment. The principle of crown immunity is no longer applied to the armed services, which must now contend also with European

Parliament and European Commission legislation and administrative instruments. Military officers now fear malpractice suits much like other professionals.[77] No longer able to rely on tradition and patriotism, the military may become just another occupation or career.

The legitimacy of the military, that is, the belief that it is a "proper" state institution representing society at large, is central to civil-military relations. The British Army has been losing its legitimacy as critics argue that it has lost touch with the changing times.[78] While the army is forced to revise its policies regarding the integration of minorities, women, and homosexuals, its military prowess has deteriorated.[79] Though still a valued institution, the military is no longer considered an honorable and selfless pursuit rewarded by social status. Its perception as a commercial opportunity has affected the way the armed forces conduct themselves internally and externally.[80] In addition, in a manner similar to the Americans, the British Army is forced to deal with individual rights in the spirit of political correctness. Thus, MOD directives encourage racial and gender affirmative action.

Christopher Coker opined that the warrior ethos itself has given way to self-imposed limitations and risk aversion. The notion of the band of brothers is substituted by "contracted" relationships, and servicemen are discouraged from exercising independent judgment. Where risk-taking denoted bravery in the past, it is now a token of irresponsibility. War itself is considered a pathology, and feelings of vulnerability decrease readiness to accept risk. Soldiers commonly exclaim, "we weren't trained for this," as if war is predictable. Indeed, a 2002 study found that one in ten British soldiers was unfit for battle.[81] Many believe that the changes brought about by the "litigation society" hinder the application of mission command.[82] Incidents that had in past been dealt within the military establishment are now open to civilian inquiry. Thus, for example, Colonel Jorge Mendonca was tried for alleged abuses committed by his men against Iraqis suspected of terrorism. Though he was eventually cleared of all charges, his name had been removed from promotion lists for the duration of the two-year ordeal. Feeling betrayed and fearing new charges, Mendonca resigned his commission.[83] This social phenomenon has also begun to affect the attitude toward casualties. The British had traditionally tolerated light casualties in remote places for obscure reasons. However, the willingness to accept casualties is slowly transforming into what some officers have labeled "submission command."[84] These changes have affected the implementation of mission command:

Do we have a culture of risk avoidance and zero defects? The business management climate within which we now conduct our affairs, the mass of legislation which affects us and the constant and very clear risk of litigation all force us to operate only within the bounds of our specific authority. Thus the routine peacetime environment strongly discourages the use of initiative and the inclination to do anything that which does not follow normal procedures or the outcome of which we cannot predict.[85]

These observations were supported by a 2005 study that identified a proclivity for micromanagement stemming not from lack of trust but rather from risk aversion.[86] According to the report, politically induced strategic risk aversion, coupled with operational risk aversion, has led to tactical and individual risk aversion. Consequently, "there wasn't much room for that mission command stuff in barracks."[87] These findings, supported by other studies, reveal significant obstacles for the application of mission command.[88]

War Amongst the People

British forces in the post–Cold War period have proven better prepared than other militaries for peacekeeping and counterinsurgency operations. This expertise in LIC scenarios was borne of their experience in Northern Ireland. There, British commanders learned that they did not have to kill all the terrorists. Therefore, the experience did not politicize or brutalize the British Army. It did, however, affect authority and discipline throughout the British Army. Transforming necessity into virtue, the once formal officer-NCO relations became significantly informal, since Northern Ireland had been a series of "corporal wars." By the mid-1980s, informal subordinate-superior relations became the norm. Orders were routinely negotiated, and only sensible ones were "obeyed by spirit as in the letter . . . in accordance with . . . the German concept of *innere Führung*, the thinking fighting man."[89] In contrast to the Americans in Vietnam, British commanders usually refrained from micromanagement. Fortified by standardized drills and SOPs, the British coped successfully with hundreds of incidents annually. Short orders served as a code unleashing military force, unencumbered by long decision-making cycles. Essentially, the same modus operandi served the British well in Bosnia and continues to do so in Iraq.[90]

The experience gained through decolonization also influenced the British Army. Countering guerrilla tactics requires reliance on decentralized command of small units scattered over a large area of operations, to which conventional armies are less inclined. For the British Army, traditionally charged with policing the empire, internal security operations were the norm and conventional war the exception. The regimental system, too, facilitated decentralization, as small units were often deployed independently for extended periods, requiring them to develop close cooperation with local police and administrative authorities.[91] In effect, the colonial experience bore three operational principles: minimum force, civil-military cooperation, and tactical flexibility.[92]

These experiences prepared the British Army for the post–Cold War conflicts. Considered less proficient in mobile warfare by the Americans and the Israelis, the British Army is recognizably more comfortable with counterinsurgency than most. It was consequently able to utilize a more relaxed and decentralized system of command, fully appreciating the potential of the lowliest corporal.[93] Thus, a British observer during the 1980s was surprised at the degree of micromanagement employed by IDF senior commanders during military policing operations. Neither could he fathom how the same troops could demonstrate a high degree of initiative in conventional battles.[94]

This British variant of mission command is a fundamentally cautious philosophy of applying minimum force, avoiding escalation and stressing the relevance of both action and inaction. More compatible with British traditions than the aggressive German variant,[95] it has been referred to as "mission command—*Auftragstaktik* with Chobham armour."[96] While the German term was mostly associated with aggressive initiative and action, the British also preached inaction when appropriate.

Education, Training, and Human Resource Policies

In 1996, a British officer stated that "Ten years after General Bagnall first espoused mission command . . . there is evidence that we are failing. Unless we accept this the doctrinal movement of the 1990s will go down in history as one great wasted opportunity."[97] Following the Bagnall Reforms, the British Army instituted significant changes in education, training, and personnel policies. Thus, mission command is currently being taught in Sandhurst, the Joint Command and Staff Course (JCSC) enables the development of triservice cooperation, and the High Staff and Command Course emphasizes the operational level. Training has become more realistic, and the selection and promotion processes now include peer evaluation and feedback.

And yet some officers believe that all is not well. Though progress has been made, headquarters remain overly cumbersome, and staff work is not generated quickly enough. Additionally, although the new doctrinal vocabulary is well known, the army continues to practice in the old ways. The main challenge is therefore not to produce "more doctrine or better. . . . We need to change our practice."[98] An Israeli officer attending JCSC found the operational planning extremely detailed, slow, and procedure-oriented with little room left for originality.[99] Similarly, a British officer found his Israeli counterparts' planning less confined to procedures.[100] Other British officers remarked:

> At a unit level we think we have a manoeuvrist approach but our training emphasizes procedures over initiative. . . . In the Staff College new language is used in presentations but scratch the surface and little has changed. . . . Not a single exercise saw the enemy engaged at more than 90 degrees to his front. At CATAC any solution which suggested bypassing was viewed with suspicion.[101]

It is interesting to explore the contrasting perceptions of IDF and British officers. One British officer concerned with mission command and recognizing the basic flaws of the British Army wondered whether perhaps "[we should] swallow our pride and look to increasing the number of exchanges with the *Bundeswehr* or with the IDF?"[102] Some British officers perceive the IDF as an undisciplined, unprofessional militia bereft of military traditions and drills (such as salutes).[103] Others concentrate on the free spirit of the IDF, which encourages individuality, and reflect that although drill promotes self-confidence, alertness, and pride, it does not create leaders capable of making difficult decisions, independent judgment, or professional knowledge.[104]

The difficulties, critics believe, begin at Sandhurst. Thus, following a presentation on mission command, one instructor applauded the reliance on initiative but remarked that "we basically manage to get rid any initiative in the first 5 weeks of the officer training."[105] Sandhurst graduates, claims another officer, have no real idea what mission command is and have no feel for initiative. They cannot conduct a simple mission analysis, nor do they understand what their superiors wish to accomplish.[106] Mission command, like maneuver warfare, is taught as a discrete theme rather than serving as the underlying basis for the course itself.[107]

Many believe that the principle problem lies in the gap that exists between barracks and battlefield requirements.[108] The practice of mission command must, however, be continuous; it must be inculcated in peacetime training and include all levels of commands. Some contend that the army is better at writing than implementing doctrine and that while many understand the necessity of mission command, few actually practice it.[109] Indeed, "we have formally incorporated mission command in our doctrine, yet . . . the doctrine has barely penetrated the skin of the British Army."[110] Similarly, while training in British Army Training Unit Suffield (BATUS) has been described as realistic, barracks practice provides a different experience. Many instructors abuse or misrepresent the principles of mission command.[111] Additionally, safety regulations force them to focus on such things as cordoning inspection pits and the Health, Safety, and Welfare (HSAW) risk assessments.[112] Officers are concerned with following procedures, avoiding challenging the system or their superiors. Essentially the British Army is encouraging risk avoidance,[113] while honest mistakes are actually crucial to the training process. Suppressing them diminishes moral courage.[114]

As in the American case, the problem is partially rooted in the conviction that mission command is actually imbued in the British Army. Although the laissez-faire tradition resembles mission command,[115] it lacks the formal structure and methodology of *Auftragstaktik*. As one British officer noted:

> Anyone who asserts that the British Army has always been a mission command entity would be both almost correct and utterly wrong in the same sentence. Manoeuvre and mission command theories together offer just such framework but need to be taught both with more rigor and more understanding than is evident and should be implemented until it is part and parcel of the way we do our daily life.[116]

An additional difficulty stems from that of translating the doctrine into practical training guidelines, as they are either elementary or lengthy. The latter reflects a collective restrictive control mind-set, an attempt to detail mission command and maneuver thinking. Fundamentally then, it represents a contradiction in terms. The officer cadre can be divided into uninformed enthusiasts or covert opponents of mission command. The covert opponents, understanding that embracing mission command necessitates relinquishing control, fear the effect it may have on their own careers. They are unlikely to encourage the subordinate independence implicitly required for mission command.[117] Or as one battalion commander put it: "Of course I can receive mission command—*I've* been to the Staff College! But my company commanders are all a bunch of dimwits! I have to give them detailed orders."[118]

A third hindrance is that the educational system does not prepare commanders to assume the responsibilities of their superiors two levels up, as required for mission command. Thus, the Royal Military Academy Sandhurst (RMAS) Household Division devotes considerably more time to stylized Napoleonic absolute obedience battle drills than to modern tactics. Training for the former may be advantageous, but it hardly promotes mission command.[119]

The British Army has yet to develop autonomous junior commanders; it should therefore not expect them to simply emerge in war. Tactical Exercises without Troops (TEWT) should concentrate on alternate and dynamic scenarios rather than procedural competence.[120] Training should emphasize communicating intent and fostering mutual understanding, traditionally one of mission command's weakest links. Trust must also be developed in the barracks on the basis of a "trustworthy until proven otherwise" policy. Subordinates should be encouraged to accept risk and think freely rather than be penalized for what the army defines as "well intended mistakes."[121]

Nevertheless, conventional wisdom has it that the British are faring better than the Americans in the application of mission command.[122] For example, the Americans are believed to carry a stronger Vietnam-borne tendency toward force protection and risk avoidance.[123] However, it should be noted that as the counterinsurgency (COIN) campaign dragged on in Afghanistan and Iraq, critics within and outside of the British Army began to challenge the axiom of British superiority in this type of warfare. Overconfidence in their mastery of counterinsurgency theory and practice hindered their ability to adapt to the new circumstances. The Americans, conversely, who were eager to catch up, studied earnestly and constantly improved their performance in this environment. According to one critic, the British Army,

> has struggled with ongoing campaigns in Iraq and Afghanistan because, for reasons largely having to do with insufficient resources, it has not applied its own principles of counterinsurgency. Moreover the army today is a different force than the one that endured and ultimately "waited-out" the troubles in Northern Ireland; it is a much leaner "high-tech" force in structure, equipment and outlook. This makes it [a] formidable generator of combat power but compromises it in counterinsurgency.[124]

Another critic said that "by 2008 in face of mounting critics of British performance in Iraq . . . the transatlantic debate on small wars had been reverted. . . . It was now the Americans who seemed the masters of modern counterinsurgency and the British the students in need of instruction."[125]

The British officers, unsatisfied with the current state of affairs and feeling that the army should be faring better, may be right. However, according to Brigadier Mungo Melvin, it will take another generation before the British Army successfully adopts mission command.[126]

The Technological Factor

The British military has been influenced by the American transformations and the RMA.[127] It consciously adopted a variant of NCW: network-enabled capabilities (NEC).[128] The difference between the British and American variants is not only semantic but philosophical. While technology serves as a focal point for the Americans, Britons rely on it to facilitate. As one analyst wrote:

> A second cultural obstacle to the adoption of a full-blown network-centric approach is the scepticism inherent in the British military about what the technology can achieve. It is tempting here to draw a contrast with the techno centrism of US strategic culture. However, it would be a mistake to read technophobia in British military culture.[129]

In contrast to the Americans, the British prefer a network of networks, interlinked nodes carried by deployed operational assets, which should improve rapid decision making.[130] The British approach to technology is cautious for two reasons. The first is a preference for continuity and slow change:

> Revolutions from the contemporary British perspective . . . result in the likes of Robespierre, Lenin, Stalin, Mugabe and other such grotesque and unforeseen outcomes. It is therefore wholly consistent with British national and military culture that Liddell-Hart and Fuller's thoughts and writings on the potential armoured warfare would be slow to catch in the UK.[131]

The second reason is the necessity of doing more with less, as the defense budget has dwindled once again in the post–Cold War period.[132] Forced to rely on human rather than technological superiority, information technology is consider merely an enabler, as its designation suggests.[133] Having introduced the Industrial Revolution and pioneered such military technologies as the tank, radar, and computers, Britain can hardly be accused of fearing RMA or its derivative technologies. Indeed, a comparative report on the status of C2 technologies in Europe identified the British military as having the highest-level interoperability with the Americans. However, it also indicated that the Royal Air Force and Royal Navy had a higher level of interoperability than the army.[134] The British, then, embrace technological revolutions in an evolutionary process where "proven technologies are used to allow incremental change."[135]

Proponents therefore argue that these new technologies represent continuity rather than a revolution. According to Jim Storr, "the nomenclature jars somewhat and gives the concept to British ears, an air of improbability, but in essence this idea is not new." He stated that the American concept of self-synchronization actually involves broadening and deepening of mission command:

> As we introduce information-age command systems we should see an improved understanding of the higher commander's intent . . . [and] understanding of the operational situation and at all levels of command. . . . The move towards self synchronization . . . envisages commanders and even section teams . . . armed with commander's intent and highly developed situational understanding, doing what need to be done without traditional orders. . . . The . . . information age . . . actually creates conditions where such a command philosophy is the essential bedrock for success. We can therefore look forward to a *renaissance* of mission command.[136]

The British, confident in their ability to apply mission command, believe that this technology should facilitate their efforts.[137] According to Brigadier Melvin, the challenge will be to ensure that the technology reinforces existing doctrine rather than reshaping it. It is important, he warned, to maintain an appropriate stream of information to headquarters, as either extreme could prevent the practice of mission command.[138] Others have warned against the development of the "directed telescope" phenomenon,[139] which may lead senior command to influence tactical-level events while bypassing the chain of command:

> There is a very real danger that the principles on which mission command is based . . . are in danger of being shoehorned into the future procedures of digitization. The net result being that dogma will triumph over doctrine to the detriment of innovation. . . . Digitization is unlikely to respect our current tiered command structure.[140]

Seen as a whole, it appears that the British are more optimistic and less polar-ized than their American counterparts in regard to the effect of information technology on mission command. Indeed, "resource constraints and military culture have shaped the evolution of a very British approach to networking of the armed forces. The net effect is to make NEC less innovative than NCW, both in concept and in design."[141] However, while the Americans have been using digital systems and digital divisions for some years, the British have only just began to explore its operational possibilities in Iraq and Afghani-stan.[142] Time will tell how this experience will influence their views concern-ing the impact of technology on mission command.

THE IDF

Civil-Military Relations

In order to understand the circumstances that led to the development and later abandonment of mission command by the IDF, as well as the difficulties of reinstituting it, one must explore the "no alternative" (*ein brayra*) ethos that dominated Israeli society. During the first few decades of independence, Is-raelis believed that the very existence of their embryonic state remained pre-carious. Hence, so long as the military provided salvation, it was granted a special status in society, making it practically impervious to criticism. Addi-tionally, the army attracted the best and the brightest recruits, from among whom it picked NCOs and officers.[143] The special status the IDF enjoyed in Israeli society also facilitated the execution of daring missions, as it was prac-tically immune from public censure, open inquiries, and legal prosecution. The army was able to develop its doctrines through a process of trial and er-ror, and commanders could afford to grant subordinates significant discre-tionary powers. Mission command flourished during this period also due to a cultural emphasis on creativity, initiative, and improvisation,[144] which the IDF favored over "discipline, family background and formality."[145] These characteristics are developed already in basic training, where recruits are ex-pected to improvise, perform independently, and accomplish "impossible tasks."[146]

During the 1990s, the "no alternative" ethos was weakened. The Oslo Ac-cords and the signing of the peace treaty with Jordan coupled with the un-successful campaign in Lebanon led to a decline in motivation for enlist-ment.[147] Many felt that the war of 1982 had been unnecessary, one of choice rather than necessity. Public opinion shifted also as a result of the effects of globalization and privatization, which transformed the once collective-socialist society into an individualistic society.[148] Today, careers in security have been substituted by careers in high tech, as demonstrated by the growing impact of young IDF officers on the thriving Israeli high-tech and IT sectors. These bright young officers utilize leadership skills, initiative, and boldness acquired in the military and are able to thrive in the chaotic and uncertain nature of the high-tech industry.[149] For them, "no" simply represents a challenge to try again.[150] Awash with original ideas, many establish their own start-up companies. A former paratrooper officer and a CEO of an internet venture capital said that "The feeling around us was that we were part of an elite group and that the sky was the limit. . . . Therefore, you are allowed to make some mistakes. When I arrived at the Silicon Valley, I felt immediately at home. . . . There was room for bold actions, trial and error, just like in the unit I served in."[151] According to Aryeh Nusbacher, it is difficult to determine whether these characteristics are encouraged by civilian or military Israeli culture. Nevertheless, he stated, IDF culture is well adapted for chaos. Thus, training emphasizes surprises and unplanned situations, and the Israeli equivalent of the division (*Ugdah*) is more flexible and modular than the standard Western structure.[152] Others have noted that Israeli officers are taught that the fog of war is actually a protagonist of the battle and that the IDF operations often border on chaos.[153] This flexibility is also demonstrated through the approach to special units, which are formed and disbanded in accordance with circumstances. Decisions concerning operations or even personnel policies are influenced primarily by the task at hand rather than by units or military traditions.[154] However, although the IDF had struck a "proper balance between planning, discipline, and improvisation" during the Six Days' War, this was not always the case.[155] The IDF has been hindered by the absence of internal discipline, opportunism, and insufficient regard for long-term planning.[156] Indeed, IDF officers do not share the British or German propensity for meticulous long-term planning.[157] For better or for worse, this seems to be a general characteristic of Israeli officers.[158] The disregard for standard procedures and traditions has restricted the IDF's institutional memory and its capacity for learning.

The nature of the LICs in which Israel has been involved during the past decades has altered public expectations of the IDF.[159] Until the 1973 war, the IDF fought against stronger opponents, and therefore mistakes and casualties were expected. In these situations, military organizations often resort to mission command. But since that war, operations incurring even minor casualties have often resulted in the formation of investigative committees. This development, according to Martin van Creveld, has occurred because "If you fight someone weak long enough you too become weak. . . . The [1982] Lebanon campaign for example was brilliantly planned but poorly executed because of the fact that the IDF suffered from a lack of boldness for fear of casualties in a disputed war."[160] In effect, he explained, as armies become stronger, their tolerance for casualties diminishes. Risk aversion and centralization ensue, leading to the suppression of imagination, boldness, and creativity.[161] As perceptions play a significant role in this process, Chief of Staff Moshe Ya'alon repeatedly referred to the Second Intifada as a "Second War of Independence." Similarly, Prime Minister Sharon spoke of "defending our homes." Thus, the IDF recorded an increase in the number of volunteers for combat units, and reserve units enjoyed high turn-up levels.[162] Some officers have opined that the Second Intifada had saved the IDF in that public support rose and circumstances necessitated decentralization.[163] However, when it faced a better opponent during a war of choice in Lebanon in 2006, the IDF reverted back to risk-aversion behaviors, delaying and finally hesitantly executing unimaginative ground operations.[164] This behavior was somewhat corrected in the following operation in Gaza in 2008. Although it demonstrated better performance in all areas, including mission command, it used intensive firepower to secure its soldiers and minimize risk. The price paid was international legitimacy as manifested in the Goldstone report.

War Amongst the People

In addition to fighting frequent conventional wars, the IDF has continuously performed routine security operations (*Batash*). These include border patrols, raids, ambushes, and other border-securing operations. As various incidents flare up, the IDF rushes various reserves to the scene, primary among which are the various command-course cadets. Thus, over a period of eighteen months, between 2003 and 2004, every squad leader course was interrupted in such a manner.[165] *Batash* (ongoing security) on the Lebanese border has evolved into guerrilla warfare, while the Palestinians have employed everything from civilian demonstrations and rock throwing to full urban warfare.

Although IDF doctrine declares mission command as the system best suited to LIC situations,[166] operations in the territories and in the Southern Lebanese Security Zone were characterized by risk aversion, inclination toward force protection, and intervention of superiors.[167] As one officer put it, "incidents seem to draw the entire chain of command to the scene."[168] Another officer observed that the strategic corporal shoulders too heavy a burden as he is expected to consider political ramifications: "Mission command grows out of necessity—the limited span of control . . . but in LIC this is no longer the case."[169] The IDF seems more comfortable exercising initiative in conventional operations. The experience of recapturing urban Palestinian centers demonstrated that at least some elite units such as the Golani Brigade and the Thrity-fifth Paratroops Brigade have not lost the spirit of the 1950s and 1960s. Nevertheless, the events of the Second Lebanon War demonstrated the damage incurred by the experience of policing the territories. Accustomed to intelligence supremacy, abundant planning time, and familiarity with the operational zones, the IDF now lacked even clarity of purpose. Mission command was replaced with "confusion command" as commanders forgot the true meaning of friction in war.

Education, Training, and Human Resource Policies

The lack of proper military education and corresponding promotion system constitutes one of the IDF's primary weaknesses. Perceived and structured as a people's army, it developed a strong antiprofessionalism and anti-intellectual culture.[170] The Zionist pioneers who founded the state sought to create a new Hebraic archetype, forged in the fires of the new land. This *Sabre* endeavored to redeem the land through agricultural feats, only bearing arms in self-defense. Army service was necessitated by reality, the "no alternative" ethos, but was considered unworthy as a career.[171] The military was not regarded as a unique profession enjoying a "monopoly over unique theoretical and practical knowledge in a defined area of human activity."[172] Hence, the IDF rejected attempts to establish institutions for the research or study of the military profession and theory. For similar reasons, the retirement age was set at forty-five. Field experience overshadowed military educational and academic credentials in promotion considerations, one of the manifestations of the *bitsuism* ethos.[173] However, the lack of a professional ethos and military traditions hampers the IDF's ability to realize mission command:

We [in the IDF] have habits that have become ideology. Ideology is not a substitute for a doctrine. . . . Basically we are still a kind of *Palmach*. The typical
IDF officer knows less and less as he advances up the ladder. . . . The reason
foreign armies come to study from us is because we have a lot of practical experience. . . . But what they don't come to learn is the higher art of war-strategy
and operational level. They know it much better than we do. And I will tell you
that we forget our techniques and tactical lessons and then tend to rediscover
them, which means we are not a learning organization. . . . Mission command
is the official logo of the command in the IDF. However I can't tell you if it was
practically adopted.[174]

Others have described the IDF as an excellent fighting militia lacking some of
the fundamentals necessary for a professional army. The problems with the
education system begin with the fact that the officer candidate course (Bahad 1)
is essentially a platoon commanders' course. Instructors are merely company
commanders (captains) while West Point cadets are exposed to the brightest
military and civilian minds.[175] An additional problem is the increasing skill and
knowledge gap between regular and reserve officers. The former usually join the
ranks of the latter after approximately four to six years, following which their
actual experience, training, and formal education decline steadily.[176] Efforts are
ongoing to rectify this situation lest the utility of the reserves vanishes completely. These include courses offered by the army for reserve officers and a dedicated master's program at Bar Ilan University.[177]

These educational deficiencies notwithstanding, junior officers have gained
much battlefield experience, which strengthens the levels of trust and respect conferred to them by senior command.[178] In addition, and as opposed to
West Pointers, IDF officers are highly capable and motivated soldiers who
rose through the ranks. However, the performance-oriented mentality, which
monopolizes the career structure, continues to value practical experience over
all else. Indeed, if an officer becomes an instructor, it is for him "the end of the
road."[179] In an attempt to change the system, Chief of Staff Dan Halutz decided to raise the minimal age and length of service period requirements for
promotion.[180]

Others have been calling for reforms of the educational system. According
to one critic, the military profession is distinct because it is practiced in a
highly uncertain environment, mastery of which requires reliance on mission
command. This system is based on shared knowledge, skills, experience, and

ethics, that is, professionalism.[181] However, this critic argues, although many IDF officers have sufficient tactical-level knowledge, the system does not provide adequate training above that level. Additionally, the IDF is "results" rather than "process" oriented, thereby depriving personnel of the feedback crucial for the learning process. Finally, the overreliance on field experiences denies the army the benefits of a universally based theory.[182] These issues are discussed also in one officer's account of his own experiences in Southern Lebanon. He remarked that "our inadequate knowledge . . . regarding the theory of counter guerrilla warfare . . . severely slowed our learning curve and the army's adaptation to the conflict with Hezbollah."[183] In an effort to address these issues, the army has established a Tactical Command College for captains and is requiring all future lieutenant colonels to attend the Staff and Command Course.[184]

Reforming the IDF Education System

The IDF revised the Staff and Command Course in the 1980s, designating the new program *Pum Barak*.[185] It was launched in 1988, and a 1991 audit concluded that "the program is vital . . . [and] if it hadn't existed, it should have been invented."[186] The curriculum featured increased military studies of doctrine, general staff procedures, and mission command.[187] Instructors included renowned security experts and military historians, such as Yehoshafat Harkabi, Yoav Gelber, and Martin van Creveld. Simulations and case studies instead of rigidly planned field exercises emphasized the dynamic planning process.[188] *Barak* was endorsed by then Chief Of Staff Dan Shomron, who sought to recreate a small and smart IDF. Opposition to the *Barak* was raised primarily by instructors from the old program who felt marginalized and by officers who rejected the emphasis on mission command.[189] Overall, the program proved a great success. It influenced prevailing attitudes toward the role and significance of staff work and developed a generation of independently minded officers who would leave their mark during the next conflict with the Palestinians.[190]

Its success was followed by further changes. It was decided that candidates would have to first earn a BA and that the program would offer MA-level courses. For this express purpose, the Tactical Command College for company commanders was established in 1999.[191] Until that time, the preparatory course for company command had lasted only twelve weeks devoted primarily to field exercises. In contrast, the new two-year program offers a BA in military studies. The college also instituted staff rides in historical battlefields abroad and meetings with foreign cadets. Originally, it was meant to replace the six-month Officer Candidate Course (Bahad 1), but various considerations proved this goal both unattainable and undesirable. Some feel that having the two schools allows officers to enjoy the benefits of both worlds.[192] Most officers attending the college up until 2005 had already gained experience in the Intifada. What they lacked was an understanding of the bigger picture:

> We dedicate 50 hours entirely to command and control, 15 of which solely to mission command. . . . It's a lot about understanding higher intent in the most profound way, not only technical. . . . They must understand that mission command is not only about freedom of action but about understanding how they best serve the intentions of superiors.[193]

Or, put differently:

> When a day after graduation, a commander is ordered to recapture Abu Snen (Palestinian village), he'll do it better because he knows the Prime Minister's intent as it was communicated in his previous speech to the nation. He also has a better understanding of the ramifications of exercising force through his company's actions. The College is a true revolution in that regard.[194]

As stated above, the constraints of LIC pose unique challenges—therefore, the program also prepares cadets for its complexity; thus, for example, cadets receive training on how to speak with reporters. As opposed to the traditional ethos represented by the field exercise–oriented Bahad 1, the college emphasizes a broader military education. As former COS Amnon Shachak stated: "Soldiering is a profession . . . and in the IDF we did not treat it in all seriousness."[195]

In 2002, the college established a research center for the tactical level. It affords officers an opportunity to reflect on their own experiences and develop theoretical principles for dealing with them in the future. The center set out to create a previously foreign culture in the IDF: an intellectually friendly environment for officers between assignments.[196] While the research papers written at the institute are academically accredited, the primary purpose is to accumulate and institutionalize the organizational knowledge acquired by individuals and to derive lessons for future generations. In 2003, the center began to initiate research and publish two periodicals, the title of one (not surprisingly) of which is loosely translated *The Wisdom Behind Action*. The center also organized a conference on tactical issues, in order to maintain a close dialogue with leading experts in the field.[197] Currently, there is talk of integrating the various educational programs into a military university specializing in security and military studies.[198] Advocates argue that these fragmented programs represent ad hoc solutions to certain issues, in the best tradition of improvisation, but would benefit from a more systematic approach. An additional program was established in 2004 granting an MA in military studies to reserve battalion commanders, in effect creating a "professional militia."[199] All these measures were taken as part of an attempt to balance the typical IDF *bitsuist* officer, taught to act rather than to reflect on consequences. The LIC environment, coupled with the lack of significant field experience in high-intensity conflicts (HICs) as in the past, has demonstrated the importance of these qualities.[200]

The IDF is forced to oscillate between two modes of behavior (and probably more than two, as there are great differences in various fronts—Hamas versus Hezbollah, for example) nearly on a daily basis. The challenge of operating effectively in both low- and high-intensity conflict scenarios simultaneously, a difficult assignment for any army, is exacerbated by the IDF's inclination toward decisiveness. Thus, although it was thought that actual experience could substitute for training in the decade preceding the Second Lebanon War, the events of the war demonstrated the falsity of this idea. In the aftermath of the war, the IDF has been focusing on reacquiring conventional warfare skills. The training itself, usually conducted in the *Tzeelim* training center, is designed to encourage application of mission command. Training officers ensure that commanders remain focused on the issues crucial for the realization of their operational objectives. Debriefing sessions focus on whether various actions contributed (or failed to contribute) to the realization of the operational concept. In these sessions, participants are encouraged to discuss communication difficulties and misunderstandings that led to misinterpretation of the operational concept. At the conclusion of the exercise, the training officer and the commander analyze the training evolution on the basis of radio communications and the force tracking system. In the following lessons-learned session, which now includes all subordinate commanders, the commander may begin by saying, "I failed today." The analysis that ensues will thus be professional rather than personal.[201]

The doctrinal changes introduced through *Pum Barak* were gradually incorporated into training routines. For example, the operational concept was added to the situation estimate, thereby facilitating understanding of the commander's intent.[202] Similarly, the plans confirmation phase of the pre-battle procedure was replaced by the less controlled plan presentation phase. The change signifies the understanding that a commander needs to know not how his subordinates intend to realize his intent but merely the details necessary for the complicated coordination that is so crucial in today's battlefield.[203]

Failings Exposed in Lebanon

During the Second Lebanon War, tactical-level commanders had practiced the traditional principles of "maintenance of objective" and "commanders first" and had avoided significant failures. Conversely, the experience had exposed the professional weaknesses of IDF senior command, which many observers had been clamoring about since the mid-1980s. A parliamentary commission charged with investigating the education and qualifications of senior command concluded the following: training requirements for promotion to brigade and division command, though short and narrowly focused, were not strictly enforced.[204] Moreover, the more comprehensive programs provided by the Operational Theory Research Institute (OTRI) or the National Security College were never made a requirement. Indeed, once the OTRI ceased the operational course in 2003, the subject was not taught by any other institution in the IDF.[205] Hence, the commission suggested strengthening the institute and the concurrent establishment of a military academy that could create relevant bodies of knowledge.[206] The committee also found that the instructors replacing the original cadre do not possess the necessary skills and capabilities. Last, the committee recommended that professional criteria and measures replace the existing personnel-review section and promotion process. Some of these recommendations were efficiently implemented after the Lebanon War, but the IDF is still waiting for its own military academy.

The Technological Factor

One of the major obstacles to the application of mission command is an Israeli obsession and fascination with technology.[207] The traditionally dominant agricultural ethos of the 1920s through the 1950s was replaced first by industry (1960s–1970s) and then by high tech. High-tech entrepreneurs and the founders of start-up companies are today's equivalent of the pioneers who erected kibbutzim on the frontier.[208] There are over 100 Israeli high-tech companies traded on the NASDAQ, and most high-tech industry giants, such as Intel and Microsoft, operate large research and development departments in the country.[209] The influx of qualified manpower from the former Soviet Bloc countries to Israel has strengthened this trend significantly.[210] Israelis are among the world's leaders as consumers and developers of this technology.[211] The IDF has always claimed that its qualitative human superiority had been the one factor that had given it an edge over its Arab enemies. Yet, this claim represented by the armored corps slogan "it's not the steel but the person operating it" had lost some of its validity as Israel began to rely on advanced technologies, such as the *Merkava* (chariot) main battle tank. Indeed, in the aftermath of the Yom Kippur War, Israel sought to increase its technological superiority; the backing of the United States facilitated the addiction to technology. Concomitantly, Israel began developing a high-end RMA military industry.[212]

In the aftermath of the First Gulf War, the Israeli security establishment recognized the need for change.[213] Obviously it fitted well with the changes of Israeli society and the change in ethos discussed earlier. By the Second Gulf War, it was decided that developmental and acquisition efforts should be directed toward RMA technologies. The focus was gradually directed toward technologies that were part of the information revolution.[214] One of the negative outcomes of this process was that "when asked about the poor state of the reserve combat readiness, the defence establishment's automatic reply is technology. It's the new idol everyone worships."[215] The most prominent project was the *Tzayad* digital ground force system.[216] Similar to the British and American variants, the *Tzayad* is designed to dramatically enhance situational awareness as well as mission planning and execution.[217] By freeing approximately 40 percent of HQ manpower from the task of information collection and analysis, the system increases decision-making capabilities. However, in a manner similar to the experience of the Americans and the British, the system facilitates micromanagement. The system designers are hoping to address this issue through appropriate doctrinal adjustments.[218]

Its advantages notwithstanding, the system reinforces the belief that technology offers the ultimate solution to all battlefield problems. Thus, when the IDF announces it has yet to find a solution to Hezbollah or Hamas rockets, it is referring to a technological solution.[219] In other words, these technologies inadvertently discourage the innovation, independence, and preference for preemption that had characterized the IDF.[220] When Chief of Staff Ya'alon described his vision to Tactical College cadets, it was focused on advanced information and communication systems.[221] In that vision, the future soldier was closely monitored and controlled by his superiors, leaving very little latitude for autonomy. It was during Ya'alon's tenure that the new operational manual was issued, suggesting that due to technology, stand-off munitions have tipped the balance between maneuver and fire in favor of the latter. Consequently, while battalion commanders have more accurate information than ever before, their tank commanders have much less training and experience.[222]

The system designers are well aware that technology can facilitate processes but cannot substitute for human creativity nor make judgment calls. However, the risk of mission command "disappearing in ten years," as one officer prophesied, remains.[223] Avoiding this risk entails the introduction of a cultural emphasis on commander independence, which will be difficult to achieve in an environment believing in the superiority of technology above all else. The IDF attraction to technology stems from three primary sources: the "Americanization" of Israeli society; increased sensitivity to casualties and the anticipation minimizing them through stand-off munitions; and the fact that leaving one's mark in the rapid rotation environment of the IDF is accomplished more easily through the introduction of highly visible technologies than through education or training. Leading Israeli military thinkers, such as Itzik Ben Israel, equate technology with quality and believe it will afford the IDF a much needed advantage over its enemies.[224]

The trend of examining the battlefield through the technological prism reached a zenith during the Second Lebanon War. Under the leadership of Air Force General Dan Halutz, the IDF adopted American doctrines such as EBO and shock and awe.[225] The failure in Lebanon and the designation of former Golani commander General Avi Ashkenazi as chief of staff may signify an attempt to reshift the balance back toward the human element.

CONCLUSION

This chapter focused on factors that have impacted the American, British, and Israeli armies' ability to integrate and implement mission command. First among these were the force reductions of the post–Cold War era and the changes in the character of conflicts. These in turn gave rise to a culture of risk aversion and micromanagement. In the American and British cases, this was demonstrated through the debate over the wars in Iraq and Afghanistan. In the Israeli case, it became evident through the designation of the Second

Intifada as a war for survival. The changes in civil-military relations also led to the insertion of civilian values into military culture, such as litigation culture, individuality, media intervention, and political correctness. Consequently, commanders have become more reluctant to delegate authority.

In addition, despite their involvement in large land campaigns, these armies primarily have fought "wars amongst the people" and found it difficult to practice mission command. As tactical mistakes made in this environment often had strategic and even political ramifications, micromanagement abounded. Over the past two decades, all three armies embraced the information revolution and adopted a similar command and control digital system. Although its full impact is not yet known, all three armies have discovered its potential to "kill mission command." Thus, Americans criticized the "digital divide" revealed during the Second Gulf War; and Israeli commanders led from behind plasma screens rather than from the front.

In reaction to the trends discussed above, the three armies established institutions dedicated to developing and introducing professionalism, operational-level theory, and mission command (SAMS, the High Command Course, and the OTRI/Dado Center). However, these institutions have yet to achieve the status and influence enjoyed by the Prussian-German *Kriegsakademie*. Human resource policies, which were adapted to encourage mission command, succumbed to "zero-defects" and other business-related efficiency-focused practices. Consequently, a gap developed between "espoused theory" and "theory in use"—the behavioral patterns necessary for success.

Various differences were observed in the armies' manner of coping with these factors, stemming from their respective traditions and historical cultures. Thus, the U.S. Army remains culturally inclined toward conventional operations, mass, technology, and efficiency, though it has made significant progress over the past few years toward developing counterinsurgency capabilities and changing its doctrine and culture. The risk is that, similar to the IDF before 2006, the U.S. Army shift of balance will cause a neglect of conventional fighting capabilities. The British Army has maintained a more cautious attitude toward technology and a perception of its officers as gentlemen rather than professional soldiers. Its attempt to implement mission command has been supported by its long tradition of fighting small wars but hampered by its tradition of doing things "by the book." The IDF had actually practiced in its first decades a form of mission command but had failed to institutionalize it or develop an educational system in support of it. Hence, changes in society and in the types of military challenges since the 1980s have led to a decline in the practice of mission command. An attempt to formally adopt mission command and establish a supporting educational system has yet to prove effective in total elimination of counter–mission command behaviors although it has made serious positive contribution.

CONCLUSIONS AND IMPLICATIONS   # Part IV

"OLD HABITS DIE HARD"

This study has examined the American, British, and Israeli armies' adoption of mission command, first developed by the Prussian-German army during the nineteenth and twentieth centuries. The specific historical-strategic cultural context within which it was conceived favored swift, decisive land operations and encouraged delegation and decentralization. Since modern armies perceived mission command as a "force multiplier" that strengthened German military effectiveness, they sought to emulate it.

The main argument of this work is that a successful adoption of mission command requires profound cultural change and a process of adaptation because it relies on specific supporting cultural characteristics. The desire to adopt a successful practice is often hindered by the inherent organizational aversion to change. The final part of the book consists of two chapters. Chapter 11 briefly summarizes the case of mission command and then offers a more general discussion of the process involved in borrowing a "best practice" from a different military organization. Chapter 12 assesses the overall success and benefits associated with the long journey toward adopting mission command.

11 SUMMARY REMARKS AND WIDER IMPLICATIONS

THE IMPACT OF EARLY TRADITIONS OF COMMAND

The development of particular national ways of war, military culture, and approaches to command is influenced by factors such as national history, geostrategic position, and socioeconomic conditions.

The Americans resisted military professionalism throughout the nineteenth century, primarily for ideological reasons. The absence of a direct threat on the continental United States led to a reliance on, and even glorification of, the militia system. Contempt for military professionalism was evident in the country's premier military academy, West Point. During this period, West Pointers were trained primarily as engineers rather than as practitioners of war. The inherent limitations of the militia system were revealed during the Civil War; it was the superior resources, technology, and firepower of the North, rather than superior tactics and command, that won the day.

In many respects, as this book has demonstrated, this belief continues to influence the U.S. Army.[1] Following the Spanish-American War, some reforms were introduced, but their effect was offset by the adoption of the French centralized headquarters model during World War I. It was also influenced by French élan, which emphasized brave frontal attacks and abhorred tactical subtlety. By World War II, the U.S. army had embraced corporate ideas, such as quantitative models, efficiency, and resource management. These had enabled the army to face the trials of expansion as well as the challenge of maintaining a force of eight million soldiers. The war, many felt, had demonstrated the superiority of American firepower and knowledge of mobilizing national resources over German tactical and operational prowess. In the Vietnam War, corporate ideas and technology were used to manage not only logistics but the war itself. The failure of these methods resulted in a deep sense of crisis and much soul searching.

In the case of Britain, the security of the British Isles had traditionally been entrusted to the Royal Navy while a small ground component was maintained for the purpose of policing the empire. When diplomacy failed and a continental conflict became unavoidable, as in the Napoleonic Wars, Britain would field an army of foreigners under British command, a practice perfected in the colonies. Two other characteristics have typified the British way of war and have endured over the centuries: the regimental system and great captains. The former provided clanlike, independent, and cohesive forces, which facilitated policing in colonies far and apart. Although this system created capable and independent commanders, decentralization in this case took on an extreme nature, as the units were practically autonomous (Umpiring).[2] Interestingly, the Americans underwent a similar experience during the last quarter of the nineteenth century, fighting the Indian Wars on the Great Plains.

The phenomenon of the great captains denotes the appearance of excellent commanders "in the nick of time." Typically descendents of aristocratic families, they felt duty bound to perform military service. Naturally, the British had their fair share of incompetent commanders but had nevertheless averted a debilitating Jena-like defeat. By the First World War, they had modeled many doctrines and practices after the Prussian-German example, yet chose to increase centralization through the new communications technology. In the Second World War, the British gradually began to execute mission command–based mobile operations, though the primary pattern remained one of centralization. Throughout the Cold War, the bulk of the army was deployed on the Continent in anticipation of a Soviet invasion. Training, maneuvers, and operational plans continued to favor firepower and centralization. The experience of the Falklands War demonstrated the deficiencies of this practice.[3] It was argued that implementation of the counterstroke doctrine in Europe would require a cultural transformation and the adoption of mission command.[4]

The Israelis face geostrategic constraints fairly similar to those of Prussia in the nineteenth century. Similar, too, are its offensive national security doctrine and basic force structure. Indeed, German literature served as the basis for much of the instructional material written for command courses during the pre-state period. This offensive spirit was born in the late 1930s through the efforts of commanders and military educators, such as Wingate and Sadeh. The unconventional thinking and methods they preached endured through such commanders as Allon and Sharon, who executed mobile operations, relying on flexibility and subordinate initiative. Officers were encouraged to take risks and could usually expect the support of superiors in case of failure. The successful campaigns of 1956 and 1967 and the remarkable recovery in 1973 had been largely due to subordinate initiative and independence in the context of a general plan of operations.

However, as a result of the trauma of 1973 and the newly gained access to the U.S. arsenal, the IDF gradually increased its reliance on firepower and technology.[5] The difficulty of maintaining a dual strategic focus (Northern and Southern Commands) during the 1973 war led the IDF to double the number of its combat units, consequently diminishing its ability to practice mission command. Moreover, in contrast to the Prussians, the IDF failed to incorporate mission command into its doctrine and education system. Indeed, the primary source of knowledge for most efforts was actual experience. As regular conventional battles gave way to asymmetric warfare, the old ways were slowly forgotten. The ambiguity regarding operational objectives from 1982 onward led to confusion and further restriction of initiative. In addition, commanders were forced to contend with media and legal scrutiny, resulting in increased centralization and risk aversion.

THE DRIVE TO TRANSFORM

Past performance of the army in all three case studies was deemed unsatisfactory, and it was felt that none of them were prepared to face upcoming challenges. To address these deficiencies, doctrine and praxis were transformed and mission command was adopted.

The most obvious case was that of the U.S. Army. The new course set following the trauma of Vietnam was essentially tailored around the primary challenge of the day, a Soviet attack against Western Europe. For the first time in over a century, American army resources were significantly inferior to those of its potential opponent, and it was forced to seek alternate means of increasing its military prowess. And so, an initial surge of reforms leading to the publication of the 1976 *Active Defense* was followed by a comprehensive intellectual investigation. This exploration landed the Americans at the door of the historic Prussian-German army, which had benefited greatly from the institution of mission command. As a result, the Americans devised the 1982 AirLand battle doctrine and adopted mission command. However, the process of adoption was marked by intense debate regarding the necessity, applicability, and even the correct understanding of *Auftragstaktik* and other related concepts. Implementing this approach to command required that adjustments be made in the education and training system. Notable among the changes instituted was the establishment of SAMS for the training of *Generalstab*-like officers. Ironically, by the time the transformation had been completed, the Cold War had ended. The new doctrine was implemented in the Iraqi desert rather than on a European battlefield.

The British were spared a traumatic battlefield experience during the second half of the twentieth century but nevertheless recognized the inadequacy of their countermeasures against a Soviet threat. The war over the Falkland Islands, though successful, revealed that an able opponent could inflict considerable damage on British forces. That conflict also revealed a gap between the elite infantry and special forces regiments and the heavy divisions in Europe in regard to initiative, improvisation, and resolve. As a result, the British instituted reforms, which though influenced by the Americans were an independent creation. This process culminated in the issuance of a doctrine tailored to the British Army and its unique way of war.[6]

The individual most responsible for these reforms was Sir Nigel Bagnall. A student of German military history and theory, his conviction and determination led the British Army to adopt mission command. Bagnall and his disciples succeeded in revising training procedures, transforming the Staff and Command Course and establishing the Higher Command Course. These efforts also led to the issuance of an official British doctrine emphasizing mission command. One of Bagnall's most talented students was General Rupert Smith, who led the First Armoured Division in the 1991 Gulf War. His performance in that campaign is considered by many to be a masterful example of mission command. The British Army continues to advocate reliance on mission command in its counterinsurgency campaigns so prevalent in the post–Cold War era.

The loss of flexibility and agility by the IDF during the 1970s, some observers noted, was partially due to its unrestricted expansion and an overreliance on resources and technology. The situation continued to deteriorate in the 1980s as conscripts and reservists began to question the legitimacy of fighting the First Lebanon War or the Palestinian Intifada. Concurrently, the IDF came under unprecedented levels of civilian scrutiny and criticism. During the late 1980s, it began instituting reforms, which included the establishment of a new Staff and Command Course (*Pum Barak*) and the Operational Research Theory Institute (OTRI) during the late 1990s. Reform efforts culminated in the issuance of a 1993 basic doctrinal publication embracing the principles of mission command.

VARIANTS OF MISSION COMMAND

Despite efforts to institutionalize mission command, there remains a gap between the espoused intent and actual practice (in operations, garrison, and training). The degree to which this gap exists varies and is dependent on the extent of commonality between a particular culture of command and mission command.

The Americans probably conducted the most profound intellectual foray into the intricacies of the German system and launched the most sweeping changes in their educational system in support of mission command. However, the development of RMA theory in the 1990s, precision munitions, and command and control technologies have served to reinforce the traditional reliance on firepower and technology. Yet the parallel efforts to introduce mission command have been fruitful and did improve American military prowess.

The British Army has probably been most successful in implementing mission command. A small professional force charged with a wide range of missions, it enjoys the advantages of agility and a tradition of professionalism. In addition, its policy regarding military action in the empire had granted subordinates considerable independence and freedom to act. Original and independent minds, such as Lawrence of Arabia and Wingate, also constituted an element of this tradition. Conversely, the British Army lacked experience in the conduct of large operational-level mobile maneuvers for which *Auftragstaktik* was originally designed. Additionally, during both world wars, the Imperial Army was expanded into a large conscript force. These hastily trained, mediocre armies were unqualified for the tempo and aggressiveness of mission command,[7] though their performance did improve gradually.

In contrast, they were better prepared for the LIC or counterinsurgency situations typifying the post–Cold War era. Due partially to conservative tendencies and partially to the vast experience garnered in the colonies and in Northern Ireland, the British focused their energies on LIC while the Americans were absorbed by the RMA.[8] Consequently, according to some pundits, the British developed a more subtle variant of mission command, better suited to LIC and counterinsurgency than to maneuver warfare. Accordingly, the British alone emphasize the importance of "knowing when *not* to act," which is so important in counterinsurgency, in contrast to the Israeli *bitsuism* or the American "can do" attitudes.[9]

Echoing the historic Prussians, Israel's doctrinal response to its geostrategic predicament was the development of a strong ground element, quick and decisive wars transferred as early as possible to enemy territory, and a reliance on subordinate initiative and aggressiveness. The mythological status the IDF enjoyed in Israeli society allowed greater latitude for mistakes, and commanders could therefore unleash their subordinates more freely. In contrast to the Germans, the Israelis failed to balance theory and praxis; the IDF rewards "hands-on" experience rather than a military education. Its "people's army" ethos and the Zionist delegitimization of the military career and rejection of anything that has to do with what they considered as militarism prohibited the development of true military professionalism. The decline of its status in Israeli society coupled with the challenges of LIC led the IDF to increase centralization.

The attempt to reintroduce mission command during the 1990s through doctrine and education was only partially successful. The nature of the conflict in the Palestinian Territories combined with a fascination with American technology and doctrine led the IDF to neglect the maneuvering elements of ground forces and mission command. The occupation of Nablus during Operation Defensive Shield demonstrated that well-trained and -led units could utilize mission command in LIC operations to a great effect. In contrast, the untrained units led by inadequately educated and trained officers during the Second Lebanon War were unable to realize mission command and failed to achieve their objectives.

As Israeli society produces commanders that are by and large aggressive, creative, good improvisers and initiative takers, mission command could conceivably flourish in the IDF once again. It would necessitate setting clear objectives, better training, and a broader military education. In addition, senior command would have to restore the element of trust lost in the latest Lebanese debacle between commanders on the operational and tactical levels. This potential was proved to a large extent during the 2008 Operation Cast Lead, in which IDF units were better prepared and better led. General (Ret.) Giora Eiland opined that the IDF has made great strides toward rectifying the failings revealed in the Second Lebanon War.[10] However, he raised an important issue facing all three armies examined in this book:

> To what degree should the army be ready and is it ready to pay the price of preparing the field officer to take more initiative and responsibility? For example, is it correct or even possible to allow lower-grade officers to plan and lead current security operations with less control from above only in order to prepare them better for the conventional war?[11]

Eiland also expressed reservations concerning the ability of senior IDF generals to restore a culture of debate fostering independent thinking and challenging superiors, clearly absent during the war in Lebanon.[12]

ADOPTING FOREIGN CONCEPTS: WIDER IMPLICATIONS

The three case studies examined in this book demonstrate that good intentions and the diversion of considerable resources in order to adopt a foreign concept may not be sufficient to overcome the "imperfect imitability." As discussed in Chapter 2, this concept refers to the difficulty of identifying the factors that contribute to the success of a certain practice or the tacit infrastructure that supports it. Whereas much of the literature on military innovation has been devoted to dimensions such as top-down/bottom-up innovation or the impact of external/internal groups on the organization,[13] there has been little discussion of emulating a "best practice."[14] In contrast, the discussion of this phenomenon in the corporate world has advanced sufficiently to warrant the coining of the term "benchmarking," which signifies the systematic comparison of successful organizational practices and the adoption of the best of them.[15]

Alan Wilkins, the organizational theorist, stated that organizations usually attempt to effect cultural change through one of the following methods: a piecemeal imitation of a successful organization, importation of a new culture, or fostering of a revolution. In the first case, a particularly worthy idea or practice is adopted, along with the skills, habits, institutional memory, and individual commitment of another organization. Wilkins warns, however, that the execution of that concept requires adaptation through trial and error and cannot be rushed by applying quick fixes or blind imitation.[16] Indeed, such a process often entails a transformation of the organization's basic assumptions. Using the second method, the army imports a culture by merging units or appointing commanders from different branches or services.

The third and most radical way of instituting cultural change is through a revolution.

Mission command has both procedural and cultural dimensions. The former is relatively easy to emulate, as armies often adopted foreign tactics. In contrast, the latter is more difficult to transfer as these dimensions stem from national characteristics and organizational traditions. Efforts to adapt the necessary cultural dimensions often result in the creation of the cognitive and praxis gaps. Hence, the adoption of mission command calls for the third approach. A crisis must occur that shakes the faith in the methods of the "old guard." Then new leaders can introduce new ideas and practices. The organization must then attribute its successes to the new methods. This condition was met, in varying degrees, by the three armies. Finally, the change is institutionalized through a revised reward system, including selection and promotion. If the process is not completed, as was often the case with mission command, people tend to learn "how to resist the new ways while appearing to support them,"[17] a phenomenon encountered in all the case studies. In order to overcome these difficulties, Wilkins recommended that the organization not limit its focus to embedding the new culture. Rather, it should seek inspiration, instruction, and the enduring principles from its own history; "promote hybrids"; and find the "current success examples within the organization."[18] And indeed, attempts were made to "nationalize" mission command by conjuring the memory of great national commanders who had utilized it intuitively and successfully. By invoking Patton, Slim, or Dayan, the armies sought to demonstrate the existence of a natural link between mission command and their particular culture of command. These attempts were successful to a certain degree as larger forces, internal—and more importantly external—shifts in international relations, society at large and technology, worked against the full internalization of mission command.

12 FINAL VERDICT: HAS MISSION COMMAND BEEN ADOPTED SUCCESSFULLY?

THIS STUDY EXAMINED both actual operations and the testimonies of individuals intimately acquainted with the three organizations. The evidence presented in the previous chapters suggests that the adoption of mission command and attempts to emulate the German system and procedures have achieved mixed results. Generally speaking, while the process encouraged the armies to reform doctrine, education, and training as well as to reexamine their command approach, mission command was realized only in some places some of the time. The Americans only partially practiced mission command in their operations, and the few budding applications were smothered by the prolonged counterinsurgency campaign following the invasions of Iraq and Afghanistan. The Israelis used mission command intermittently during Operation Defensive Shield (during the second intifada, 2002) but ceased to do so by the Second Lebanon War. Following reforms and lessons learned, the practice somewhat recovered during Operation Cast Lead in Gaza (2008). Though some gaps remain, the British have enjoyed considerable success with mission command during the first and to a lesser extent the second Gulf wars. Moreover, having established common doctrine and terminology (a prerequisite for mission command) for counterinsurgency, they have enjoyed somewhat greater success in the stability phase that followed the ground offensive; however, a note should be made that the American military quickly caught up in a learning effort led by Generals Petraeus and Mattis.[1]

Chapter 1 suggested that adaptation difficulties often stem from two gaps. The first, a cognitive gap, occurs as a result of misunderstandings and misinterpretations of the foreign concepts. The second, a praxis gap, develops as a result of internal and external organizational factors, which restrict the latitude of leaders and limit their ability to fully embrace the borrowed doctrine. These difficulties, observed in all three case studies, beg the question: does mission command warrant the effort? According to Robert Citino, the historic concept is incompatible with the social and technological complexities of battlefields today.[2] In contrast, I believe that, if nothing else, mission command has been a cultivator of military reform. It has weathered the Cold War and the RMA and remains valid in LIC and counterinsurgency situations. Thus, though it has been only partially implemented, the process of implementation has forced militaries to reexamine their doctrine of command and has triggered changes that resulted in positive outcomes in most dimensions of military organization and culture. If only for these reasons, the process of adopting and adapting mission command has proved a valuable investment.

In the final analysis, this book has demonstrated the following points: mission command is a complex, elusive, and multifaceted phenomenon, not easily quantified, measured, or institutionalized. Therefore, any conclusions regarding its implementation must be taken with a grain of salt. That said, evidence suggests that the three military establishments discussed in the book have yet to fully institutionalize mission command.

On the positive side, the efforts to institute mission command proved to be a trigger for doctrinal development and improved officer training and education and battlefield performance. Also, as mission command holds the promise of enhancing operational effectiveness, it is likely to maintain its allure. Additionally, its inherent emphasis on maximizing the potential of every individual is congruent with our modern Western values.

These points were recently illustrated by a directive issued by General James Mattis, commander of the United States Joint Forces Command. In a memo dated 14 August 2008, he declared that doctrines such as EBO, operational net assessment, and system of systems analysis have failed to deliver "their advertised benefits."[3] Consequently, he called for a return to "to time honored principles such as mission type orders."[4] Mattis recognized the enduring nature of mission command and conceded that the search for new and exciting concepts over the past two decades may have hindered its proper adoption by the U.S. Army. This memo is an acknowledgment that the journey toward the realization of mission command has not been completed. The findings of this book, that the forces inhibiting the practice of mission command outweigh the forces supporting it, confirm Mattis's analysis. An even more recent acknowledgment of the centrality of mission command is the latest version of the Army's Capstone Concept which mentions mission command fifteen times in different contexts.[5] These documents serve as strong indication of the commitment to the idea of mission command. Nevertheless, at the same time, the promise of realizing mission command will galvanize Western military organizations to relentlessly continue their journey of adopting and adapting mission command for the foreseeable future.

REFERENCE MATTER

NOTES

Foreword

1. *The Army Capstone Concept: Operational Adaptability*, 21 December 2009, available at http://www.tradoc.army.mil/pao/2009armycapstoneconcept.pdf.

2. Field Manual 1, *The Army*, Headquarters, Department of the Army, Washington, DC, 14 June 2001, available from http://www.army.mil/features/FMI+FM2/FMIFM2. htm. Although these unrealistic assumptions were removed from the subsequent version of the manual, this thinking pervaded many army documents written between the late 1990s and 2004.

3. Michael Howard, "The Use and Abuse of Military History," *Journal of the Royal United Services Institution* 107 (February 1962), 4–8.

1. Setting the Stage

1. Of the translations offered for *Auftragstaktik*, "mission command" is the most common and is the one used in American field manuals.

2. See, for example, Richard Lock-Pullen, *U.S. Army Innovation and American Strategic Culture after Vietnam* (Oxford: Routledge, 2006); Rodler F. Morris et al., *Initial Impressions Report: Changing the Army* (Fort Leavenworth: Center for Army Lessons Learned, 1996). Concerning the British, see Sangho Lee, *Deterrence and the Defence of Central Europe: The British Role from the Early 1980s to the End of the Gulf War* (PhD diss., King's College London, 1994).

3. Antullio J. Echevarria II, *After Clausewitz: German Military Thinkers before the Great War* (Lawrence: University Press of Kansas, 2000), 38.

4. For a discussion of Blitzkrieg, see Chapter 3, 48–52.

5. Trevor N. Dupuy, *A Genius for War: The German Army and General Staff, 1807–1945* (Englewood Cliffs, NJ: Prentice-Hall, 1977), 268, 307.

6. Joint Warfare Publication 0-01, *British Defence Doctrine* (2001), 3–5.

7. Department of the Army, Field Manual 3-24/MCWP 3-33.5, *Counterinsurgency* (Washington, DC: Department of the Army, 2006), 1–26, 7-4; Army Doctrine Publication, *Land Operations,* Army Code 71819 (2005), 115.

8. Jim Storr, "A Command Philosophy for the Information Age," in *The Big Issue: Command and Combat in the Information Age,* ed. David Potts (Washington, DC: Command and Control Research Program, 2003), 77–94.

9. Daniel Hughes warns against such a superficial view in "Auftragstaktik," in *International Military Defence Encyclopedia,* vol. 1A–B, ed. Trevor N. Dupuy (London: Macmillan, 1993), 332.

10. On the adoption of corporate practices by the U.S. Army, see Francis Fukuyama and Abram N. Shulsky, *The "Virtual Corporation" and Army Organization* (Santa Monica, CA: RAND, 1997).

11. Oliver J. Daddow, "British Military Doctrine in the 1980s and 1990s," *Defence Studies* 3:3 (Autumn 2003), 103–113.

2. Command and Military Culture

1. Army Doctrine Publication, *Land Operations,* Army Code 71819 (2005), 114.

2. Army Doctrine Publication, *Command,* vol. 2, Army Code 71564 (1995), 4.

3. Department of the Army, Field Manual 6-0, *Mission Command: Command and Control of Army Forces* (Washington, DC: Department of the Army, 2003), 1–6.

4. Ibid., 1–11.

5. Ibid., 1–15.

6. Ross Pigeau and Carol McCann, "Re-Conceptualizing Command and Control," *Canadian Military Journal* 3:1 (Spring 2002), 53–64.

7. Gregory D. Foster, "Contemporary C2 Theory and Research: The Failed Quest for a Philosophy of Command," *Defence Analysis* 4:3 (September 1988), 213.

8. Martin van Creveld, *Command in War* (Cambridge, MA: Harvard University Press, 1985), 11.

9. Jim Storr, *The Nature of Military Thought* (PhD diss., Cranfield University, 2001), 5. Also, see his discussion of Lind's OODA (Observe, Orient, Decide, Act) Loop and the definitions of command and control. Ibid., 6–9.

10. For instance, see John Keegan, *The Mask of Command* (New York: Penguin, 1987).

11. For example, most command and control research program (CCRP) conferences focus on technology. Available at http://www.dodccrp.org (accessed 15 February 2005).

12. Eliot A. Cohen and John Gooch, *Military Misfortunes* (New York: Free Press, 1990), 231–232.

13. G. D. Sheffield, ed., *Leadership and Command: The Anglo-American Military Experience Since 1861* (London: Brassey's, 1997), 1–2.

14. Carl von Clausewitz, *On War*, trans. Michael E. Howard and Peter Paret (Princeton, NJ: Princeton University Press, 1984), bk. 1, chap. 3, 101.

15. Richard Simpkin, *Race to the Swift: Thoughts on Twenty-First Century Warfare* (London: Brassey's, 1985), 106.

16. Barry D. Watts, "Clausewitzian Friction and Future War," *McNair Paper 52* (Washington, DC: Institute for National Strategic Studies, 1996), 13.

17. Alan D. Beyerchen, "Clausewitz, Non Linearity and the Unpredictability of War," *International Security* 17:3 (Winter 1992), 9.

18. Clausewitz, bk. 1, chap. 7, 119.

19. Ibid.

20. Ibid., 119–120.

21. Watts, 32.

22. Beatrice Heuser, *Reading Clausewitz* (London: Random House, 2002), 53.

23. Clausewitz, bk. 1, chap. 1, 78.

24. Ibid., 120.

25. Watts, 27.

26. At least one journalist used it to describe the difficulties inherent to an open information policy during the American war in Afghanistan (2001). Quoted in Heuser, 89.

27. Eugenia C. Kiesling, "On War Without the Fog," *Military Review* 81:5 (September–October 2001), 85–87.

28. Watts, 49–51.

29. The incident was recounted by Dodge Billingsley in a graduate lecture at King's College London, October 2005. A journalist in the war, Billingsley later made a documentary on the theme of friction in that war.

30. Beyerchen, 2–4.

31. Watts, 137.

32. Ibid., 125.

33. Bill Owens, *Lifting the Fog of War* (New York: Farrar, Straus and Giroux, 2000), 15.

34. Jacob W. Kipp and Lester W. Grau, "The Fog and Friction of Technology," *Military Review* 81:5 (September–October 2001), 89.

35. David Betz, "The More You Know the Less you Understand," *Journal of Strategic Studies* 29:3 (June 2006), 505–533.

36. Amos Harel and Avi Isacharoff, *The Seventh War* (Tel Aviv: Miscal-Chemed, 2004), 196–197 [Heb.].

37. The history of mission command is discussed in greater detail in Chapter 3.

38. Werner Widder, "*Auftragstaktik* and Innere Führung: Trademarks of German Leadership," *Military Review* 82:5 (September–October), 4.

39. Hanan (Schwartz) Shai, *The Command and Control Method in the Modern Military Organization: An Examination of Its Essence and Validity* (Master's thesis, University of Haifa, 1993), 82–84; Jim Storr, "A Command Philosophy for the Information Age: The Continuing Relevance of Mission Command," in *The Big Issue: Command and Combat in the Information Age*, ed. David Potts (Washington, DC: Command and Control Research Program, 2003), 77–94.

40. Judith A. Gordon, *A Diagnostic Approach to Organizational Behavior* (Boston: Allyn & Bacon, 1991), 510.

41. Creveld, 234–235.

42. Gordon, *A Diagnostic Approach,* 514.

43. Gareth Morgan, *Images of Organizations* (Thousand Oaks, CA: Sage, 1998), 103.

44. Gordon, *A Diagnostic Approach*, 510–518.

45. Jay A. Conger, "Leadership: The Art of Empowering Others," in *A Diagnostic Approach to Organizational Behavior,* ed. Judith A. Gordon (Boston: Allyn & Bacon, 1991), 433.

46. Albert Bandura, "Self-Efficiency: Toward a Unifying Theory of Behavioral Change," *Psychological Review* 84:2 (1977), 191–215.

47. On Theories X and Y, see Douglas McGregor, *The Human Side of Enterprise* (New York: Penguin, 1987). On the Pygmalion effect, see Micha Poper, *On Managers as Leaders* (Tel Aviv: Ramot, 1994), 75–77 [Heb.]; R. Rosenthal and L. Jacobson, *Pygmalion in the Classroom* (New York: Reinhart & Winston, 1968).

48. Conger, "Leadership," 434–437.

49. On the military as a bureaucracy, see Charles A. Beitz and John R. Hook, *The Culture of Military Organizations: A Participant Observer Case Study of Cultural Diversity,* available at http://www.pamij.com/beitz.html (accessed 6 March 2003); James Q. Wilson, *Bureaucracy: What Government Agencies Do and Why They Do It* (New York: BasicBooks, 1989), 27–28.

50. Peter Block, *The Empowered Manager* (San Francisco: Jossey-Bass, 1987).

51. Rosabeth Moss-Kanter, *The Change Masters* (New York: Simon & Schuster, 1983); Robert Simons, "Control in the Age of Empowerment," *Harvard Business Review* (March–April, 1995), 80–88.

52. Gordon, *A Diagnostic Approach*, 438.

53. Morgan, 226–227; Margaret Wheatley, "Goodbye, Command and Control," *Leader to Leader* 5 (Summer 1997), available at http://www.pfdf.org/leaderbooks/l2l/summer97/wheatley.html (accessed 19 November 2005).

54. Morgan, 229.

55. Daniel J. Hughes, ed. and trans., *Moltke on the Art of War: Selected Writings* (California: Presidio, 1993), 47.

56. For a summary of these approaches, see Edgar H. Schein, *Organizational Culture and Leadership* (San Francisco: Jossey-Bass, 2004), 12. For a comprehensive review of literature concerning military culture, see Terry Terriff, "Innovate or Die: Organizational Culture and the Origins of Maneuver Warfare in the United States Marines Corps," *Journal of Strategic Studies* 29:3 (June 2006), 477–480.

57. To cite a few, see J. Collins and J. Porras, *Build to Last* (New York: HarperBusiness, 1994); Ralph H. Kilman, Mary J. Sexton, Roy Serpa, and associates, *Gaining Control of the Corporate Culture* (San Francisco: Jossey-Bass, 1985), 4; Tom J. Peters and Robert H. Waterman, *In Search of Excellence: Lessons from America's Best Run Companies* (New York: HarperCollins, 1982). In the military context, see James S. Corum, "A Clash of Military Cultures: German and French Approaches to Technology Between the World Wars," paper presented at a USAF Academy Symposium (September 1994); Theo Farrell and Terry Terriff, eds., *The Sources of Military Change: Culture, Politics, Technology* (Boulder, CO: Lynne Rienner, 2002); Walter F. Ulmer Jr. et al., *American Military Culture in the Twenty-First Century* (Washington, DC: Center for Strategic and International Studies, 2000), xv.

58. From a business perspective, see Jay W. Lorsch, "Strategic Myopia: Culture as an Invisible Barrier to Change," in *Gaining Control on Corporate Culture,* ed. Ralph H. Kilman et al. (San Francisco: Jossey-Bass, 1985), 84–102. A number of works explored the relationship between national strategy and culture: Steve Attridge, *Nationalism, Imperialism, and Identity in Late Victorian Culture: Civil and Military Worlds* (New York: Palgrave, 2003); Beatrice Heuser, *Nuclear Mentalities? Strategies and Belief Systems in Britain, France and the FRG* (London: Macmillan, 1998); Elizabeth Kier, *Imagining War: French and British Military Doctrine Between the War* (Princeton, NJ: Princeton University Press, 1997).

59. Some of the more famous works in this category include James C. Colins and Jerry I. Porras, *Build to Last: Successful Habits of Visionary Companies* (New York: HarperCollins, 1994); W. G. Ouchi, *Theory Z* (Reading, MA: Addison-Wesley, 1981); Peters and Waterman.

60. Farrell and Terriff, 7.

61. Terriff, 477–478.

62. Corum.

63. On strategic culture, see Colin S. Gray, "Comparative Strategic Culture," *Parameters* 14:4 (Winter 1984), 26–33; Colin S. Gray, *Nuclear Strategy and National Style* (Lanham, MD: University Press of America, 1986); Jack Snyder, *The Soviet Strategic Culture: Implications for Limited Nuclear Operations* (Santa Monica, CA: RAND, 1977); Alistair Iain Johnston, "Thinking About Strategic Culture," *International Security* 19:4 (Spring 1995), 33–64.

64. Colin S. Gray, *Modern Strategy* (New York: Oxford University Press, 1999), 130.

65. Ibid., 135.

66. Ibid.; Thomas Donnelly, "Countering Aggressive Rising Powers: A Clash of Strategic Cultures," *Orbis* (Summer 2006), 413–428.

67. Kier, 28–30.

68. Terriff, 475–503. See also Shmuel L. Gordon, *Air Leadership* (Tel Aviv: Ma'arachot, 2003), 238–245 [Heb.].

69. John Nagl, *Learning to Eat Soup with a Knife: Counterinsurgency Lessons from Malaya and Vietnam* (Chicago: University of Chicago Press, 2002), 6.

70. Farrell and Terriff, 7.

71. Schein, 17.

72. Ibid., 13.

73. Adapted from ibid., 25–37.

74. Corum.

75. Chris Argyris, *Learning and Action: Individual and Organizational* (San Francisco: Jossey-Bass, 1982), 50–56.

76. Ibid., 2, 3.

77. Chris Argyris and Don A. Schön, *Organizational Learning* (Reading, MA: Addison-Wesley, 1978).

78. Schein, 245–271.

79. Terriff, 480.

80. Farrell and Terriff, 8–9.

81. Alan L. Wilkins, *Developing Corporate Character: How to Successfully Change an Organization Without Destroying It* (San Francisco: Jossey-Bass, 1989), 1.

82. Ibid., 7–19.

83. For a more detailed discussion, see Chapter 6, 88–89.

84. Amir Oren, "Who Needs All These Soldiers," *Ha'aretz*, 3 June 2005 [Heb.].

85. Wilkins, 17.

86. Ibid., 24–31.

87. Ibid., 52.

88. Daniel Hughes, "Auftragstaktik," in *International Military Defence Encyclopedia*, v. 1A–B, ed. Trevor N. Dupuy (London: Macmillan, 1993), 332.

89. David Schmidtchen, "Developing Creativity and Innovation Through the Practice of Mission Command," *Australian Defence Force Journal* 146 (January–February 2001), 7–11.

90. Ad L. W. Vogelaar and Eric-Hans Kramer, "Mission Command in Dutch Peace Support Missions," *Armed Forces & Society* 30:3 (Spring 2004), 409–431.

91. Walter von Lossow, "Mission-Type Tactics Versus Order-Type Tactics," *Military Review* 57:6 (June 1977), 87–81.

92. Antulio J. Echevarria, "Auftragstaktik: In Its Proper Perspective," *Military Review* 66:10 (October 1986), 50–56.

93. This summary was derived from the sources discussed above and from following Ronald J. Bashita, "Auftragstaktik: It's More Than Just a Word," *Armor* 103:6 (November–December 1994), 19; David M. Keithly and Stephen P. Ferris, "*Auftragstaktik* or Directive Control in Joint and Combined Operations," *Parameters* 89:3 (Autumn 1999), 118–133; John Silva, "Auftragstaktik: Its Origin and Development," *Infantry* 79:5 (September–October 1989), 6–9.

3. The Origins of Mission Command

1. For a discussion of this translation, see Chapter 1, note 1.

2. Martin van Creveld, *Command in War* (Cambridge, MA: Harvard University Press, 1985), 261.

3. Azar Gat, *A History of Military Thought: From the Enlightenment to the Cold War* (New York: Oxford University Press, 2001), 28–29; John A. Lynn, *Battle: A History of Combat and Culture, from Ancient Greece to Modern America* (Boulder, CO: Westview, 2003), 125–126.

4. Martin van Creveld, *Technology and War: From 2000 B.C. to the Present* (London: Macmillan, 1991), 119.

5. Gat, 30.

6. Gareth Morgan, *Images of Organizations* (Thousand Oaks, CA: Sage, 1998), 31. Concerning the continuing relevance of parade drills, see Patrick Mileham, "Military Metaphysics: In Praise of Drill," *British Army Review* 130 (Autumn 2002), 62–69.

7. Ibid., 40.

8. Peter Paret, *Yorck and the Era of Prussian Reform, 1807-1815* (Princeton, NJ: Princeton University Press, 1966), 16.

9. Martin van Creveld, *The Art of War: War and Military Thought* (London: Cassell, 2002), 84.

10. Christopher Duffy, *The Army of Frederick the Great* (New York: Hippocrene, 1974), 62.

11. Creveld, *Art of War*, 85.

12. Morgan, 20.

13. Creveld, *Command*, 55.

14. Larry H. Addington, *The Patterns of War Since the Eighteenth Century* (Bloomington: Indiana University Press, 1984), 4–5.

15. Ibid., 3.

16. Concerning the origins of drill in European armies, see John A. Lynn, "Forging the Western Army in Seventeenth Century France," in *The Dynamics of Military Revolution, 1300-2050,* ed. MacGregor Knox and Williamson Murray (Cambridge: Cambridge University Press, 2001), 48–50.

17. Michael E. Howard, *War in European History* (New York: Oxford University Press, 1976), 90–91.

18. Macgregor Knox, "Mass Politics and Nationalism as Military Revolution: The French Revolution and After," in *The Dynamics of Military Revolution*, 62.

19. However, it should be noted that relative to the period, the German commanders showed compassion for their troops; for example, the surrendering commander of the Hessian troops at Trenton died asking Washington to look after his troops. Also, an argument can be made that it was Fredrick himself that contributed to the decay of the Prussian army as he becomes rigid and suspicious of anyone who manifests the capacity of independent thought in his old age.

20. W. O'Conner Morris, *Moltke: A Biographical and Critical Study* (London: Ward and Downey, 1894), 30.

21. Howard, *War*, 60–61.

22. Ibid., 65–66.

23. Peter Paret, "Napoleon and the Revolution in War," in *Makers of Modern Strategy: From Machiavelli to the Nuclear Age*, ed. Peter Paret (Princeton, NJ: Princeton University Press, 1986), 138.

24. Ibid., 131.

25. Knox, "Mass," 67.

26. Paret, "Napoleon," 137.

27. Ibid., 137.

28. Creveld, *Command*, 95.

29. Paret, "Napoleon," 132–133.

30. It is important to note that although the term "decentralization" is used to describe both the Napoleonic and Prussian-German systems of command, it denotes different practices. In the Napoleonic example, the independence was born of necessity—marching units were out of Napoleon's control. Nevertheless, their routes and tactical objectives were prescribed in advance. In the Prussian-German examples, field commanders were actually granted freedom of choice as regards to the routes chosen and so forth.

31. Creveld, *Command*, 96–99; Gunther E. Rothenberg, *The Napoleonic Wars* (London: Cassell, 2001), 216–217.

32. Gat, 142–143; Lynn, *Battle*, 192–200; Hew Strachan, *European Armies and the Conduct of War* (London: Allen & Unwin, 1983), 91.

33. Lynn, *Battle*, 192; Gat, 144.

34. Gat, 141. Georg Heinrich von Berenhorst (1733–1814), adjutant to Prince Heinrich of Prussia and later to Frederick the Great, is best known as the author of *Observations on the Art of War, Its Progress, Its Contradictions and Its Reliability* (1796–1799).

35. Gerhard Johann David von Scharnhorst (1755–1813) was chief of the Prussian General Staff until his death.

36. Gat, 162.

37. It is interesting to note that Scharnhorst was not a Prussian but Hanoverian and a product of the middle class—not an aristocrat or a Junker. He understood the link between society and the military and therefore sought to exploit national anti-French sentiment and wanted to channel it into a formation of a more liberal Prussian state and a more effective army based on meritocracy. Both Gneisenau and Clausewitz, who were Prussians, were more hesitant to unleash this social revolution but were persuaded to support him as they understood the necessity.

38. Gat, 169.

39. Gat, 178, argues that Clausewitz was influenced primarily by Kant. Peter Paret, *Clausewitz and the State* (Oxford: Clarendon, 1976), 84, emphasizes the influence of Schiller and Goethe. Beatrice Heuser, *Reading Clausewitz* (London: Pimlico, 2002), 6, rejects both assumptions.

40. Gat, 179.

41. Ibid., 187.

42. Carl von Clausewitz, *On War*, trans. Michael E. Howard and Peter Paret (Princeton, NJ: Princeton University Press, 1984), bk. 1, chap. 7, 119–121.

43. Peter Paret, "Clausewitz," in *Makers of Modern Strategy*, 202.

44. Barry D. Watts, "Clausewitzian Friction and Future War," *McNair Paper 52* (Washington, DC: Institute for National Strategic Studies, 1996), 25.

45. Paret, "Clausewitz," 205.

46. Donald D. Chipman, "Clausewitz and the Concept of Command Leadership," *Military Review* 68:8 (August 1987), 34.

47. Clausewitz, bk. 1, chap. 3, 101–102.

48. Paret, "Clausewitz," 212. The second concept was the battle of annihilation.

49. Martin Kitchen, *A Military History of Germany from the Eighteenth Century to the Present Day* (London: Weidenfeld and Nicolson, 1975), 40.

50. Michael E. Howard, *The Franco-Prussian War: The German Invasion of France, 1870–1871* (Oxford: Routledge, 1981), 11.

51. Arden Bucholz, *Moltke and the German Wars, 1864–1871* (London: Palgrave, 2001), 17–18.

52. Martin van Creveld, *The Training of Officers* (New York: Free Press, 1990), 22–24.

53. Paret, *Yorck*, 182.

54. Kitchen, 49.

55. Paret, *Yorck*, 186.

56. Charles E. White, *The Enlightened Soldier Scharnhorst and the Militärische Gesellschaft in Berlin, 1801–1805* (New York: Praeger, 1989), 139.

57. Paret, *Yorck*, 190. Hans Ludwig von Yorck (1759–1830) was instrumental in the institution of the extensive Prussian military reforms.

58. Kitchen, 49.

59. Paret, *Yorck*, 158.

60. Ibid., 166.

61. Ibid., 215–216.

62. Kitchen, 57.

63. Walter Görlitz, *The German General Staff*, trans. Brian Battershaw (London: Hollis & Carter, 1953), 41.

64. Kitchen, 42–45.

65. Like Scharnhorst, Moltke was not Prussian but was of Danish descent and was born in Mecklenburg-Schwerin. He served in the Danish army but could not express his full range of intellect in the Danish military environment and therefore moved to the Prussian General Staff, the only military institution at the time that was also a truly intellectual hub.

66. Stephen Bungay, "The Road to Mission Command," *British Army Review* 137 (Summer 2005), 22–29.

67. Cyril Falls, "Introduction," in Walter Görlitz, *The German General Staff*, trans. Brian Battershaw (London: Hollis & Carter, 1953), vi.

68. Antulio J. Echevarria, "Moltke and the German Military Tradition: His Theories and Legacies," *Parameters* 26:1 (Spring 1996), 91–99.

69. Martin Samuels, *Command or Control: Command, Training and Tactics in the British and German Armies, 1888–1918* (London: Frank Cass, 1995), 11.

70. Kitchen, 103.

71. Concerning the telegraph and *Auftragstaktik*, see Shimon Naveh, *In Pursuit of Military Excellence: The Evolution of Operational Theory* (London: Franc Cass, 1997), 57–58.

72. Samuels, 15.

73. Daniel J. Hughes, ed. and trans., *Moltke on the Art of War: Selected Writings* (Novato, California: Presidio, 1993), 5; Strachan, 98–99.

74. For a detailed analysis of Moltkean strategy, see Hajo Holborn, "The Prussian-German School—Moltke and the Rise of the General Staff," in *Makers of Modern Strategy*, 288–290; Gunther E. Rothenberg, "Moltke, Schlieffen and the Doctrine of Strategic Envelopment," in *Makers of Modern Strategy*, 296–302.

75. Hughes, *Moltke*, 47.

76. Ibid., 92.

77. Ibid., 131.

78. Ibid., 133.

79. Samuels, 11.

80. Kitchen, 129.

81. Ibid., 133; Howard, *Franco-Prussian War*, 22. As will be demonstrated later, this tradition proved a mixed blessing.

82. Samuels, 61–69; Dennis E. Showalter, "The Prussian-German RMA, 1840–1871," in *The Dynamics of Military Revolution*, 100–111.

83. Howard, *Franco-Prussian War*, 29.

84. Concerning the limitations of Moltke's general staff, see Creveld, *Command*, 112; Samuels, 12–13. Regarding his personal influence, see Bucholtz, *Moltke*, 52–53; Howard, *Franco-Prussian War*, 25–29.

85. Samuels, 16–17, discusses these relationships.

86. Ibid., 18.

87. Creveld, *Command*, 143.

88. Creveld, *Training*, 26.

89. Ibid., 28.

90. Ibid., 29.

91. Hughes, *Moltke*, 228.

92. Bucholtz, *Moltke*, 58, 121.

93. Creveld, *Command*, 144.

94. Hughes, *Moltke*, 132.

95. Ibid., 157.

96. Bucholtz, *Moltke*, 61–63.

97. Trevor N. Dupuy, *A Genius for War: The German Army and General Staff, 1807–1945* (Englewood Cliffs, NJ: Prentice, 1977), 116.

98. Howard, *Franco-Prussian War*, 25.

99. J. F. C. Fuller, *A Military History of the Western World*, vol. 3 (New York: Frank and Wagnall, 1956), 134.

100. Ibid.

101. Samuels, 77–79.

102. Robert T. Foley, "Institutionalized Innovation: The German Army and the Changing Nature of War, 1871–1914," *RUSI* 147:2 (April 2002), 84–90.

103. Ibid., 81.

104. Ibid., 88.

105. Graham Lumley, "On the Training of Prussian Officers, Their Promotion and How Their Capabilities Are Tested," *RUSI Journal* 25:113 (1881), 747.

106. Ibid., 748.

107. Ibid., 749.

108. Ibid., 754.

109. Ibid., 755.

110. Ibid., 756.

111. Ibid., 760–761, 763.

112. Geoffrey Wawro, *The Franco-Prussian War: The German Conquest of France in 1870–1871* (Cambridge: Cambridge University Press, 2003), 62.

113. Antulio J. Echevarria II, *After Clausewitz: German Military Thinkers Before the Great War* (Lawrence: University Press of Kansas, 2000), 32.

114. Eric D. Brose, *The Kaiser's Army: The Politics of Military Technology in Germany During the Machine Age, 1870–1918* (New York: Oxford University Press, 2001), 18.

115. Echevarria, *After Clausewitz*, 33, argues that the differences between the proponents of *Normaltaktik* and *Auftragstaktik* were less pronounced than is commonly assumed.

116. Ibid., 39.

117. Brose, 20–23.

118. Ibid., 58.

119. Bruce I. Gudmundsson, *Stormtroop Tactics: Innovation in the German Army, 1914–1918* (New York: Praeger, 1989), 9; Samuels, 73, 77.

120. Brose, 90.

121. Ibid., 94–97.

122. Ibid., 88.

123. Ibid., 153.

124. Ibid., 77, 188–189.

125. Strachan, 132.

126. Naveh, 58.

127. Echevarria, *After Clausewitz*, 197, 279.

128. Robert T. Foley, ed. and trans., *Schlieffen's Military Writings* (London: Frank Cass, 2002), 192.

129. Ibid., 10.

130. See Robert Citino, *The German Way of War* (Lawrence: University Press of Kansas, 2005), 227.

131. Creveld, *Command*, 169.

132. Ibid., 169; Allan R. Millet and Williamson Murray, eds., *Military Effectiveness*, vol. 1, *The First World War* (Boston: Allen & Unwin, 1989), 97.

133. Adam Grissom, "The Future of Military Innovation Studies," *Journal of Strategic Studies* 29:5 (October 2006), 923–924; Samuels, 91–93.

134. Gudmundsson, 172–175.

135. Samuels, 93.

136. Creveld, *Command*, 188; Gudmundsson, 177–178; Jonathan M. House, *Combined Arms Warfare in the Twentieth Century* (Lawrence: University of Kansas Press, 2001), 55–56; Samuels, 271–275.

137. For the origins of the term *Blitzkrieg*, see Michael P. Sinesi, *Modern Bewegungskrieg: German Battle Doctrine, 1920–1940* (Master's thesis, George Washington University, 2001), 1.

138. Larry H. Addington, *The Blitzkrieg Era and the German General Staff, 1865–1941* (New Brunswick, NJ: Rutgers University Press, 1971), 33–40; Addington, *Patterns*, 179; Matthew Cooper, *The German Army, 1933–1945: Its Political and Military Failure* (London: Macdonald and Jane's, 1978), 143–158; Len Deighton, *Blitzkrieg* (London: Cape, 1979), 116–121; B. H. Liddell-Hart, *The Other Side of the Hill* (London: Hamilton, 1956), 48–64.

139. Christon I. Archer et al., *World History of Warfare* (Lincoln: University of Nebraska Press, 2002), 528; Barry Posen, *The Sources of Military Doctrine: France, Britain and Germany Between the World Wars* (Ithaca, NY: Cornell University Press, 1984), 87, 206.

140. Robert M. Citino, *Blitzkrieg to Desert Storm: The Evolution of Operational Warfare* (Lawrence: University Press of Kansas, 2004), 19.

141. James S. Corum, *The Roots of Blitzkrieg: Hans von Seeckt and German Military Reform* (Lawrence: University Press of Kansas, 1992), 136–142; Williamson Murray, "May 1940: Contingency and Fragility of the German RMA," in *The Dynamics of Military Revolution*, 155–174; Naveh, 105–163; Sinesi, 34–36, 65–67.

142. Corum, 40, 43

143. Ibid., 76–77.

144. James Corum, "Foreword," in *On the German Art of War: Truppenführung*, ed. and trans. Bruce Condell and David T. Zabecki (Boulder, CO: Lynne Rienner, 2001), x.

145. Ibid., 5.

146. Eric Von Manstien, *Lost Victories* (Chicago: H. Regnery, 1958), 382–383.

147. William DePuy, *Generals Balck and Von Mellenthin, on Tactics: Implications for NATO Military Doctrine* (Munich: Bundeswehr University, 2004), 17.

148. Martin van Creveld, *Fighting Power: German and U.S. Army Performance, 1939–1945* (London: Arms and Armour, 1983), 166. In contrast, Omer Bar Tov, *Hitler's Army: Soldiers, Nazis, and War in the Third Reich* (New York: Oxford University Press, 1991), 38–67, contends that on the Eastern Front, due to severe casualty rates, the primary-group basis of combat motivation was replaced by ideology. He does not explain how the Germans sustained unit cohesion in the Western Front. See Max Hastings, *Armageddon: The Battle for Germany, 1944–1945* (London: Macmillan, 2004), 105, 169–170, 233.

149. Creveld, *Command*, 191.

150. Ibid., 193.

151. House, 111.

152. Naveh, 129–135, 143.

153. Richard E. Simpkin, *Race to Swift: Thoughts on Twenty-First Century Warfare* (London: Brassey's, 1985), 289–290.

154. Stephen Bungay, *Alamein* (London: Aurum, 2002), 31–33.

155. Strachan, 174.

156. Robert M. Citino, *The German Way of War: From the Thirty Years' War to the Third Reich* (Kansas: University Press of Kansas, 2005), 300.

157. Ibid., 301.

158. House, 162.

159. Concerning this remarkable quality, see Dupuy, 1–4; Michael E. Howard, "Leadership in the British Army in the Second World War: Some Personal Observation," in *Leadership and Command: The Anglo-American Experience Since 1861,* ed. G. D. Sheffield (London: Brassey's, 2002), 123.

160. Walter von Lossow, "Mission-Type Versus Order-Type Tactics," *Military Review* 57:6 (June 1977), 87, suggests that the practice was introduced in Germany by Hessian mercenaries returning from the American Revolutionary War. However, Paret, *Yorck,* 40, demonstrates it was not common practice in America.

161. Daniel H. Hughes, "Auftragstaktik," in *International Military Defence Encyclopedia*, vol. 1A–B, ed. Trevor N. Dupuy (London: Macmillan, 1993), 332.

4. Inspired by Corporate Practices: American Army Command Traditions

1. David E. Johnson, *Commanding War: The Western Origins of American Military Hierarchy* (Santa Monica, California: RAND, 2004), 157–158.

2. Ibid., 157.

3. Benjamin Amidror, "Forward," in Bruce Catton, *The American Civil War*, trans. Shimshon Inbal (Ma'arachot: Tel-Aviv, 1979), 12 [Heb.].

4. Ibid., 14, 18–19.

5. Johnson, *Commanding War*, 161.

6. Jehuda L. Wallach, *Called to the Coloures: The Creation of a Citizen Army in War Time, the American Civil War and the Israel War of Independence—A Comparative Study* (Tel Aviv: Ma'arachot, 1997), 17 [Heb].

7. Johnson, *Commanding War*, 162.

8. Stephen E. Ambrose, *Crazy Horse and Custer: The Parallel Lives of Two American Warriors* (New York: Simon & Schuster, 1975), 106.

9. Wallach, *Called to the Colures*, 139.

10. Ibid., 15.

11. Johnson, *Commanding War*, 178.

12. Ibid., 182–184.

13. Ibid., 189.

14. Ibid., 170–171, 177.

15. John Nagl, *Learning to Eat Soup with a Knife: Counterinsurgency Lessons from Malaya and Vietnam* (Chicago: University of Chicago Press, 2002), 45.

16. T. R. Fehrenbach, *Comanches: The History of a People* (New York: Anchorbooks, 1975), 482–483.

17. Ronald Barr, "High Command in the United States: The Emergence of a Modern System, 1898–1920," in *Leadership and Command: The Anglo-American Experience Since 1861*, ed. G. D. Sheffield (London: Brassey's, 2002), 57.

18. Ibid., 58.

19. J. D. Hittle, *The Military Staff: Its Origin and Development* (Westport, CT: Greenwood, 1975), 196–204.

20. Barr, 65.

21. Ibid., 66.

22. Ibid., 72.

23. Martin van Creveld, *The Training of Officers* (New York: Free Press, 1990), 61.

24. Ibid., 62.

25. Ibid., 62–63, 66.

26. Johnson, *Commanding War*, 218, 299.

27. "Report of the Superior Board on Organization and Tactics" (1919). See David E. Johnson, *Fast Tanks and Heavy Bombers: Innovation in the U.S. Army, 1917–1945* (Ithaca, NY: Cornell University Press, 1998), 26.

28. "Report of the Superior Board on Organization and Tactics"; see David E. Johnson, "From Frontier Constabulary to Modern Army," in *The Challenge of Change: Military Institution and New Realities, 1918–1941*, ed. Harold Winton and David Mets (Lincoln: University of Nebraska Press, 2000), 167.

29. Ibid., 181.

30. Hittle, 210 (G-1 Administrative; G-2 Intelligence; G-3 Operations; G-4 Supply; G-5 Training).

31. Martin van Creveld, *Fighting Power: German and U.S. Army Performance, 1939–1945* (London: Arms and Armour, 1983), 51.

32. Johnson, *Commanding War*, 186.

33. Ibid., 185.

34. Richard A. Gabriel and Paul L. Savage, *Crises in Command: Mismanagement in the Army* (New York: Hill and Wang, 1979), 18.

35. Frederick Winslow Taylor (1856–1915) was an American mechanical engineer who sought to improve industrial efficiency. A management consultant in his later years, he is considered "the father of scientific management." An intellectual leader of the Efficiency Movement, his ideas, broadly conceived, were highly influential in the Progressive Era.

36. Creveld, *Fighting*, 31–33.

37. Ibid., 40.

38. Ibid., 38.

39. Ibid., 63, 73; Donald Vandergriff, *The Path to Victory: America's Army and the Revolution of Human Affairs* (Novato, California: Presidio, 2002), 56–63.

40. Creveld, *Fighting*, 127–146.

41. Edward N. Luttwak and S. L. Canby, *Mindset: National Styles in Warfare and the Operational Level of Planning, Conduct and Analysis* (Washington, DC: Pentagon Reports, 1980), 4–5.

42. Creveld, *Fighting*, 168.

43. Max Hastings, *Armageddon: The Battle for Germany, 1944–1945* (London: Macmillan, 2005), 32–33.

44. Ibid., 392.

45. Martin Blumenson, "General George S. Patton," in *The War Lords*, ed. Michael Carver (Boston: Little, Brown, 1976), 383–384.

46. Hastings, *Armageddon*, 587.

47. Creveld, *Fighting*, 37; Martin van Creveld, *Supplying War: Logistics from Wallenstein to Patton* (Cambridge: Cambridge University Press, 1977), 214–215.

48. Robert M. Doughty, "The Evolution of U.S. Tactical Doctrine, 1946–1976," *Leavenworth Papers* 1 (Fort Leavenworth, TX: Combat Studies Institute, 1979), 7. Concerning the Korean War, see Clay Blair, *The Forgotten War: America in Korea, 1950–1953* (New York: Times Books, 1987); David Halberstam, *The Coldest Winter: America and the Korean War* (New York: Hyperion, 2007); Max Hastings, *The Korean War* (New York: Simon & Schuster, 1987).

49. D. Clayton James, *Refighting the Last War: Command and Crisis in Korea, 1950–1953* (New York: Free Press, 1993), xii, 1.

50. Ibid., 3–7.

51. Gabriel and Savage, 17–22; Vandergriff, 95–105.

52. Michael Goodspeed, *When Reason Fails: Portraits of Armies at War: America, Britain, Israel, and the Future* (Westport, CT: Praeger, 2002), 15–16.

53. Martin van Creveld, *Command in War* (Cambridge, MA: Harvard University Press, 1985), 238–251.

54. Ibid., 256.

55. Ibid., 259.

56. John English and Bruce I. Gudmundsson, *On Infantry* (Westport, CT: Praeger, 1994), 156–160.

57. Gabriel and Savage, 18, 176–177.

58. Martin van Creveld, *Moshe Dayan* (London: Weidenfeld & Nicholson, 2004), 119.

59. Roger Beaumout, "Perspectives on Command and Control," in *Principles of Command and Control*, ed. Jon L. Boyes and S. Andride (Washington, DC: AFCEA International Press, 1987), 4.

60. Gabriel and Savage, 33.

61. Ibid., 20.

62. The phrase was introduced by Russell Weigley, *The American Way of War: A History of United States Military Strategy and Policy* (Bloomington: Indiana University Press, 1973).

63. Max Boot, "The New American Way of War," *Foreign Affairs* 82:4 (July–August, 2003), 41–58.

64. Martin van Creveld, Kenneth S. Brower, and Steven L. Canby, *Air Power and Maneuver Warfare* (Alabama: Air University Press, 1994), 8.

5. Caught Between Extremes

1. Normally a small force, the army was expanded drastically during the World Wars.

2. Ian Knight, *Go to Your God Like a Soldier: The British Soldier Fighting for Empire, 1837–1902* (London: Green Hill, 1996), 13.

3. Rod Thornton, "The British Army and the Origins of Its Minimum Force Philosophy," *Small Wars and Insurgencies* 15:1 (Spring 2004), 83–106.

4. J. D. Hittle, *The Military Staff: Its Origin and Development* (Westport, CT: Greenwood, 1975), 140.

5. Army Doctrine Publication (ADP), *Command*, vol. 2, Army Code 71564 (1995), 2-A2.

6. Examples include the nineteenth-century Afghan campaigns, the Boer War, Gallipoli, and Dunkirk.

7. Richard Holmes, *Redcoat: The British Soldier in the Age of Horse and Musket* (London: HarperCollins, 2001), 41.

8. Hittle, 134.

9. Hew Strachan, *European Armies and the Conduct of War* (London: Allen & Unwin, 1983), 18.

10. Ibid., 140.

11. Hittle, 138–139.

12. Michael E. Howard, "Leadership in the British Army in the Second World War: Some Personal Observations," in *Leadership and Command: The Anglo-American Military Experience Since 1861,* ed. G. D. Sheffield (London: Brassey's, 2002), 119.

13. John Keegan, *Mask of Command* (New York: Penguin, 1988), 98.

14. Ibid., 154.

15. Ibid., 100.

16. Hittle, 141–147.

17. Keegan, 127.

18. Ibid., 129.

19. Ibid.

20. Knight, 12.

21. Ibid., 21–24.

22. Holmes, 393.

23. Knight, 13–14.

24. Ian F. W. Beckett, "Command in the Late Victorian Army," in *Leadership and Command*, 39.

25. Knight, 14.

26. War Office, *Field Service Regulations: Part—Operations* (London: His Majesty's Printing Office, 1912), 27. However, one must not discount other rules, such as that stipulating that commanders should only rarely disclose their intent, which would then require the recipient to alter his plans in accordance with battlefield developments. Ibid., 26. Thus, the British model was not synonymous with mission command.

27. Martin Samuels, *Command or Control? Command, Training, and Tactics in the British and German Armies, 1888–1918* (London: Frank Cass, 1995), 49.

28. Martin van Creveld, *Command in War* (Cambridge, MA: Harvard University Press, 1985), 151.

29. Samuels, 103.

30. Ibid., 116–118.

31. Creveld, *Command*, 156.

32. Ibid., 157.

33. Ibid., 159.

34. Ibid., 162–163.

35. ADP, *Command*, 2-A-7.

36. Hew Strachan, *The First World War* (London: Simon & Schuster, 2003), 169.

37. Samuels, 49. Within the regiment system, battalions too were granted an independent identity.

38. Ibid., 53.

39. Ibid., 55.

40. J. M. Bourne, "British Generals in the First World War," *Leadership and Command*, 94–95.

41. Samuels, 51, 57.

42. Bourne, 98.

43. Hew Strachan, "The British Army, General Staff and the Continental Commitment: 1904–1914," in *The British General Staff Reform and Innovation,* ed. Brian Holden Reid and David French (London: Frank Cass, 2002), 90.

44. Samuels, 58.

45. Andrew A. Wiest, *Haig: The Evolution of a Commander* (Washington, DC: Potomac, 2005), 64.

46. Bourne, 111.

47. Ibid., 105.

48. Wiest, 101.

49. Ibid.

50. Bourne, 112.

51. Hittle, 149–150.

52. Ibid., 151.

53. Martin van Creveld, *The Training of Officers* (New York: Free Press, 1990), 49.

54. Hittle, 151.

55. Spencer Wilkinson was a British military theorist (1853–1937) and the first professor of military history at Oxford.

56. Hittle, 154.

57. Ian F. W. Beckett, "Selection by Disparagement: Lord Esher, the General Staff and the Politics of Command, 1904-1914," in *The British General Staff Reform and Innovation*, 41–42.

58. Strachan, "The British Army," 80. Walther Franz Georg Bronsart von Schellendorff (1833–1914) was a senior *Generalstab* officer and secretary of war.

59. Hittle, 154.

60. Ibid., 157.

61. Creveld, *Training*, 48.

62. Ibid., 49. Sir William Robertson served as chief of the Imperial General Staff (1915–1918).

63. Samuels, 42–43.

64. Henry Seymour Rawlinson (1864–1925) was a general during the First World War.

65. Strachan, "The British Army," 89.

66. Samuels, 123.

67. Ibid., 40.

68. Strachan, "The British Army," 91.

69. Samuels, 48.

70. Concerning the relationship between Blitzkrieg and mission command, see Chapter 3, 49–50.

71. Strachan, *European Armies*, 152.

72. Ibid., 155.

73. Brian Holden Reid, *Studies in British Military Thought: Debates with Fuller and Liddell Hart* (Lincoln: University of Nebraska, 1998), 19.

74. Ibid., 65.

75. Ibid., 89. In that respect, see Fuller's comments on Moltke in Chapter 3.

76. Howard, 91.

77. Stephen Bungay, *Alamein* (London: Aurum Press, 2002), 32.

78. Ibid., 33.

79. Ibid.

80. Howard, 120.

81. General (Ret.) Sir Rupert Smith, Commander of First British Armoured Division (First Gulf War), GOC Northern Ireland (1996–1999), Deputy Supreme NATO Allied Commander (DSACEUR). Interview with author, 1 September 2006, Brussels.

82. Max Hastings, *Armageddon: The Battle for Germany, 1944–1945* (London: Macmillan, 2005), 93.

83. Howard, 119.

84. Ibid., 122.

85. Bungay, 33–34.

86. Howard, 124.

87. Hastings, 32–33.

88. Karl Rudolf Gerd von Rundstedt (1875–1953) rose to the rank of *Generalfeldmarschall* during World War II.

89. Hastings, 90–92.

90. ADP, *Command*, 2-A-11; Howard, 124.

91. Stephen Hart, "Montgomery, Morale, Casualty Conservation and 'Colossal Cracks': 21st Army Group's Operational Technique in North-West Europe 1944–45," *Journal of Strategic Studies* 19:4 (December 1996), 132–135.

92. Howard, 125–126.

93. Bungay, 207.

94. Hastings, 33.

95. ADP, *Command*, 2-A-12

96. Bungay, 208–209.

97. For a list of these small wars, see http://www.britains-smallwars.com (accessed 10 November 2006).

98. Colonel David Benest, Director of Security Studies and Resilience, Defence Academy. Served with 2 PARA during the Falklands War. Interview with author, 13 December 2005, London; Smith, Interview. Brigadier General Stephen White, Military Assistant to Chief of the General Staff Sir Nigel Bagnall (1988–1989), Lieutenant Colonel SO1 Doctrine in Army Staff College (1990–1993). Interview with author, 17 January 2006, London.

99. Brigadier General (Ret.) Matty Harary, Commander of 35 Paratroopers Brigade; participated in the Entebbe Raid. Interview with author, 28 February 2006, Amsterdam.

100. Thomas R. Mockaitis, *British Counterinsurgency, 1919–1960* (London: Palgrave, 1990), 100–111.

101. For a detailed account of the Battle for Wireless Ridge, see Max Hastings and Simon Jenkins, *The Battle for the Falklands* (New York: Pan, 1997), 343–346. Lieutenant Colonel Dr. Jim Storr, General Staff Northern Ireland Study Team, Principal Author of Land Operations Doctrine. Interview with author, 31 March 2006, London.

102. Spencer Fitz-Gibbon, *Not Mentioned in Dispatches: The History and Mythology of the Battle of Goose Green* (Cambridge: Lutterworth, 1995), 183–184.

103. Smith, interview; Storr, interview; White, interview.

6. Molded by Necessity

1. Julian Thompson, "Foreword," in Martin van Creveld, *Moshe Dayan* (London: Weidenfeld & Nicholson, 2004), 11.

2. Robert M. Citino, *Blitzkrieg to Desert Storm: The Evolution of Operational Warfare* (Lawrence: University Press of Kansas, 2004), 6.

3. For more on these striking similarities in their operational conduct, see Martin van Creveld, *The Sword and the Olive: A Critical History of the Israeli Defense Force* (New York: Public Affairs, 1998), 106, 114.

4. On the contribution of British army veterans and the rivalry with the Haganah, see Yoav Gelber, *A Nucleus for a Hebrew Army: The Contribution of Veterans of British Army to the IDF* (Jerusalem: Yad ben Zvi, 1986), 33–36 [Heb.].

5. Creveld, *The Sword*, 50.

6. Edward Luttwak and Dan Horowitz, *The Israeli Army* (London: Allen Lane, 1975), 12.

7. See in: *Palmach*, available at: http://he.wikipedia.org/wiki/ [Heb.] (accessed October, 2008).

8. Reuven Gal, *A Portrait of the Israeli Soldier* (Westport, CT: Greenwood Press, 1986), 5.

9. Luttwak and Horowitz, 39, 40.

10. Ibid., 48.

11. Concerning Palmach values, see Motti Shalem, *Searching for Meaning in the Creation of a Jewish Fighting Force* (Tel Aviv: Ma'arachot, 2004), 55 [Heb.].

12. Luttwak and Horowitz, 21; Shalem, 46, 55.

13. Luttwak and Horowitz, 61.

14. For the IDF order of battle during the war, see Gunther Rothenberg, *The Anatomy of the Israeli Army* (London: Redwood Burn, 1979), 58.

15. The Palmach was affiliated with Ben Gurion's political rivals, the Kibbutzim party.

16. Creveld, *The Sword*, 51.

17. Luttwak and Horowitz, 54, 81.

18. Yigal Sheffy, *Officer's Badge: Training and Education of the Haganah Officers* (Tel Aviv: Ma'arachot, 1991), 32 [Heb.].

19. Ibid., 32.

20. Ibid., 57.

21. Anita Shapira, *Yigal Allon: Spring of His Life* (Tel Aviv: HaKibbutz HaMeuchad, 2004), 141 [Heb.].

22. Ibid., 193–196.

23. Ibid., 177–179. Dayan was injured in that operation and consequently lost one eye.

24. Rothenberg, 87.

25. Luttwak and Horowitz, 54.

26. Ibid., 55.

27. David Tal, "Between Intuition and Professionalism: Israeli Military Leadership During the 1948 Palestine War," *Journal of Military History* 68:3 (July 2004), 885–909.

28. Yehuda Vagman, "What in Fact Was the Mission?" *Ma'arachot* 403–404 (December 2005), 60 [Heb.].

29. Creveld, *Dayan*, 60–62. Dayan's cavalry-like charge through the city of Ramla was typical of his approach. He believed such tactics were sufficient against the Arabs.

30. Zahava Ostfeld, *An Army Is Born: Main Stages in the Buildup of the Army and the Ministry of Defence under the Leadership of Ben-Gurion* (Tel Aviv: Ma'arachot, 1994), 220–230 [Heb.].

31. Creveld, *The Sword*, 101; Luttwak and Horowitz, 59.

32. Luttwak and Horowitz, 128.

33. Creveld, *The Sword*, 65; Ostfeld, 200.

34. Jehuda L. Wallach, *Called to the Colures: The Creation of a Citizen Army in War Time, the American Civil War and the Israel War of Independence—A Comparative Study* (Tel-Aviv: Ma'arachot, 1997), 50.

35. Ibid., 70.

36. Creveld, *Dayan*, 97.

37. Concerning IDF anti-intellectualism, see Avi Kober, "The Intellectual and Modern Focus in Israeli Military Thinking as Reflected in *Ma'arachot* Articles, 1948–2000," *Armed Forces & Society* 30:1 (Fall 2003), 141–142.

38. Zeev Drory, *Israel's Reprisal Policy, 1953–1956: The Dynamics of Military Retaliation* (London: Frank Cass, 2005), 101.

39. Luttwak and Horowitz, 108; Meir Pa'il, *Humane Military Leadership* (Tel Aviv: Ma'arachot, 2003), 163 [Heb.].

40. Drory, 182–183; Luttwak and Horowitz, 116–167.

41. Rothenberg, 93.

42. On the tactical innovativeness of the 101, see Luttwak and Horowitz, 113.

43. Luttwak and Horowitz, 116; Rothenberg, 93.

44. Drory, 31.

45. Ibid., 184.

46. Creveld, *The Sword*, 150.

47. Luttwak and Horowitz, 160.

48. Yaakov Hasdai, "Doers and Thinkers in the IDF," *Jerusalem Quarterly* 24 (Summer 1982), 16–18.

49. Quoted in Chaim Lapid and Haggai Ben Zvi, "Leadership Concepts and Training of Commanders: The Development of Bahad-1 Commanders," in *On Leadership: Theory of Leadership in the IDF*, ed. Micha Poper and Avihu Ronen (Tel Aviv: Ma'arachot, 2001), 159 [Heb.].

50. Luttwak and Horowitz, 142–144, 162–163.

51. Ariel Sharon, *Warrior* (New York: Simon & Schuster, 1989), 160–161.

52. Ibid., 172–173.

53. Chaim Laskov, *Military Leadership* (Tel Aviv: Ma'arachot, 1997), 108.

54. Creveld, *The Sword*, 169; Luttwak and Horowitz, 181.

55. Efraim Inbar, *Rabin and Israel's National Security* (Washington, DC: Wilson Center and Johns Hopkins University Press, 1999), 88–90.

56. Ibid., 94.

57. Creveld, *The Sword*, 170.

58. Martin van Creveld, *Command in War* (Cambridge, MA: Harvard University Press, 1985), 200.

59. Luttwak and Horowitz, 288.

60. Ibid., 241.

61. Creveld, *Command*, 194–202; Creveld, *The Sword*, 169–170; Eric Hammel, *Six Days of War in June: How Israel Won the 1967 Arab Israeli War* (New York: ibooks, 1992), 104–114; Patrick Wright, *Tank* (New York: Penguin, 2000), 338.

62. Creveld, *The Sword*, 173–174.

63. Ibid., 169.

64. S. L. A. Marshal, *Swift Sword: The Historical Record of Israel's Victory, June 1967* (New York: American Heritage, 1967), 133.

65. Creveld, *The Sword*, 203.

66. Gunther E. Ruthenberg, "Israeli Defence Forces and Low Intensity Operations," in *Armies in Low-Intensity Conflict: A Comparative Analysis*, ed. David A. Charts and Maurice Tugwell (London: Brassey's, 1989), 67.

67. Avrhahm Adan, quoted in Wright, *Tank*, 354.

68. Creveld, *The Sword*, 232.

69. Creveld, *Command*, 203–226.

70. Concerning small-unit leadership in the Northern Front, see Oakland McCulloch, *The Decisiveness of Israeli Small-Unit Leadership on the Golan Heights in the 1973 Yom Kippur War* (Master's thesis, Command and General Staff College, Fort Leavenworth, 2003).

71. The division in question, 187, was commanded by Major General Arik Sharon. The episode is a classic example of mission command. Ron Ben Ishay, "The Gap That Changed the War," *Yedioth Ahronot*, 12 October 2005 [Heb.].

72. Elyashiv Shimshi, *By Virtue of Stratagem* (Tel Aviv: Ma'arachot, 1995), 203–209 [Heb.].

73. Vagman, 63.

74. "Final Report of the Agranat National Inquiry Commission into the Yom Kippur War" (1975), 1347 [Heb.].

75. Ibid., 1339.

76. Emanuel Wald, *The Wald Report: The Decline of Israeli National Security Since 1967* (Boulder, CO: Westview, 1992), chap. 4.

77. Creveld, *The Sword*, 253.

78. Wald, chap. 5.

79. Martin van Creveld, Professor of Military History, Hebrew University. Interview with author, 15 February 2005, Jerusalem. Colonel (Ret.) Hanan (Schwartz) Shai, Founder and Director, Staff and Command College (1989–1994). Interview with author, 23 February 2005, Hertzelia, Israel.

80. Wald, 72–79. For example, the Thirty-fifth Paratrooper Brigade under the command of Colonel Yoram Yair performed well and demonstrated mission command approach in his conduct during the campaign.

81. George C. Solley, *The Israeli Experience in Lebanon, 1982–1985* (Quantico, VA: Marine Corps Command and Staff College, 1987), 131.

82. Hanan (Schwartz) Shai, *Training Generals* (PhD diss., Hebrew University, Jerusalem, 1996), 14–23, 39 [Heb.]; Vagman, 63–64; Wald, 72.

83. Moshe Tamir, *Undeclared War* (Tel Aviv: Ma'arachot, 2006), 16, 23 [Heb.].

84. Ibid., 276.

85. Lieutenant Colonel David Kanizo, Head of Doctrine Section Ground Forces Command (MAZI). Interview with author, 10 February 2005, Tel Aviv.

86. Charles C. Krulak, "The Strategic Corporal: Leadership in the Three Block War," *Marine Corps Gazette* 83:1 (January 1999), 18–22.

87. Ze'ev Schiff and Ehud Ya'ari, *Intifada* (Tel Aviv: Schocken, 1990), 165 [Heb.].

88. Ibid., 135, 142.

89. Ibid., 149.

90. Between 1987 and 1994, there were "300 officers and men who [were] investigated, subjected to disciplinary action or put on trial." Creveld, *The Sword*, 349.

91. Quoted in Stuart A. Cohen, "The Israel Defence Forces: Continuity and Change," in *Armed Forces in the Middle East: Politics and Strategy*, ed. Barry Rubin and Thomas A. Keaney (London: Frank Cass, 2002), 180.

92. Eliot A. Cohen, Michael J. Eisenstadt, and Andrew J. Bacevich, *Knives, Tanks, and Missiles: Israel's Security Revolution* (Washington, DC: Washington Institute for Near East Policy, 1998), 71.

93. Ibid., 73.

94. Concerning IDF helplessness, see Schiff and Ya'ari, 128–167.

7. Comparison

1. Gray offers a discussion of the advantages of master explanations of the type used here. See Colin S. Gray, "The American Way of War," in *Rethinking the Principles of War*, ed. Antony D. McIvor (Annapolis, MD: U.S. Naval Institute Press, 2005), 21.

2. See in Chapter 2 the section titled "The Role of Organizational Culture."

3. Edgar H. Schein, *Organizational Culture and Leadership* (San Francisco: Jossey-Bass, 2004), 30.

4. Mira Sucharov, "Security Ethics and the Modern Military: The Case of the IDF," *Armed Forces and Society* 31:2 (Winter 2005), 169–199.

8. Adopting and Adapting Mission Command

1. Department of the Army, Field Manual 100-5, *Operations* (Washington, DC: Department of the Army, 1982), 2-1, 2-3, 2-7.

2. Shimon Naveh, *In Pursuit of Military Excellence: The Evolution of Operational Theory* (London: Frank Cass, 1997), 292.

3. Richard Lock-Pullan, "How to Rethink War: Conceptual Innovation and Air-Land Battle Doctrine," *Journal of Strategic Studies* 28:4 (August 2005), 680.

4. Ibid., 681.

5. Conrad C. Crane, *Avoiding Vietnam: The U.S. Army's Response to Defeat in Southeast Asia* (Carlisle, PA: Strategic Studies Institute, 2002).

6. Creighton W. Abrams, "Army, 1974: Emphasis Is on Readiness," *Army* 24:10 (October 1974), 9; Suzanne Christine Nielsen, *Preparing for War: The Dynamics of Peacetime Military Reform* (PhD diss., Harvard University, 2003), 182.

7. Quoted in Lewis Sorely, *Thunderbolt: General Creighton Abrams and the Army of His Time* (New York: Simon and Schuster, 2002), 346. Emphasis in original.

8. Naveh, 253.

9. Saul Bronfeld, "Fighting Outnumbered: The Impact of the Yom Kippur War on the U. S. Army," *Journal of Military History* 71:2 (April 2007), 471.

10. Bronfeld, 472; Naveh, 254; Nielsen, 250.

11. Nielsen, 281.

12. Department of the Army, Field Manual 100-5, *Operations* (Washington, DC: Department of the Army, 1976), 5-2.

13. Ibid.

14. Ibid., 3-11, 5-7.

15. Ibid., 5-13–5-14.

16. Ibid., 1-1–1-2.

17. Bronfeld, 483.

18. John L. Romjue, *From Active Defense to AirLand Battle: The Development* of *Army Doctrine, 1973–1982* (Fort Monroe, VA: U.S. Army Training and Doctrine Command, 1984), 13.

19. Nielsen, 284–285.

20. Huba Wass de Czege, *From Vietnam to the 1991 Gulf War: The Struggle to Get the Doctrine Right Enough* (Unpublished monograph, 2006). A version of this monograph was published as Huba Wass de Czege, *Lessons from the Past: Making the Army's Doctrine "Right Enough" Today* (Arlington, VA: Institute of Land Warfare, 2006).

21. Czege, *From Vietnam*, 3.

22. William S. Lind, "Some Doctrinal Questions to the United States Army," *Military Review* 57:3 (March 1977), 58.

23. William S. Lind, *Maneuver Warfare Handbook* (Boulder, CO: Westview, 1985), 6.

24. William S. Lind, "The Theory and Practice of Maneuver Warfare," in *Maneuver Warfare: An Anthology,* ed. Richard D. Hooker Jr. (Novato, CA: Presidio, 1993), 3.

25. Ibid., 3.

26. Lind, *Handbook*, 7.

27. Ibid., 73.

28. Ibid., 76.

29. Ibid., 91.

30. Lind, "Theory," 11–12.

31. Ibid.

32. Richard Lock-Pullan, "The Modern Sources of Maneuver Warfare Doctrine," *British Army Review* 137 (Summer 2005), 12.

33. Lind, *Handbook*, 58–66.

34. Ibid., 62.

35. Edward N. Luttwak, *Strategy: The Logic of War and Peace* (Cambridge, MA: Harvard University Press, 2001), 112, 286–287.

36. Concerning the adoption of maneuver warfare by the Marines, see Terry Terriff, "Innovate or Die: Organizational Culture and the Origins of Maneuver Warfare

in the United States Marines Corps," *Journal of Strategic Studies* 29:3 (June 2006), 475–503.

37. Robert A. Doughty, "The Evolution of U.S. Army Tactical Doctrine, 1946–1976," *Leavenworth Papers* 1 (Fort Leavenworth, KS: Combat Studies Institute, 1979), 43.

38. Naveh, 287–304.

39. Crane, 4.

40. Naveh, 11.

41. Ibid., 251.

42. Huba Wass de Czega and L. D. Holder, "The New FM 100-5," *Military Review* 62:7 (July 1982), 53.

43. Bronfeld, 28,

44. Ibid., 31.

45. Generaloberst Herman Balck (1897–1982) served in the Wehrmacht. In his final wartime post, he served as commander of Army Group G. Generalmajor Friedrich Wilhelm von Mellethin (1904–1997) served as the operation's officer of the *Afrikakorps* and later as chief of staff of Army Group G.

46. William DePuy, *Generals Balck and von Mellenthin on Tactics: Implications for NATO Military Doctrine* (Munich: Bundeswehr University, 2004), 3.

47. Ibid., 14.

48. Ibid.

49. Ibid., 19.

50. Lock-Pullan, "Modern," 14.

51. Ibid.

52. FM 100-5, *Operations* 1982, 2-1.

53. Ibid., 2-2.

54. Department of the Army, Field Manual 100-5, *Operations* (Washington, DC: Department of the Army, 1986), 10.

55. Ibid., 2-6.

56. Lock-Pullan, "Modern," 6.

57. Naveh, 308.

58. Lock-Pullan, "Rethink War," 691.

59. FM 100-5, *Operations* 1986, 17.

60. Naveh, 310.

61. Robert Leonhard, *The Art of Maneuver: Maneuver Warfare Theory and Air-Land Battle* (Novato, CA: Presidio, 1991), 186. See also his detailed analysis in chapters 5–7.

62. For instance, see Robert M. Citino, *The German Way of War: From the Thirty Years' War to the Third Reich* (Lawrence: University Press of Kansas, 2005), 307–311.

63. Concerning German military excellence, see Trevor N. Dupuy, *A Genius for War: The German Army and General Staff, 1807–1945* (Englewood Cliffs, NJ: Prentice-Hall, 1977), 268, 307; Martin van Creveld, *Fighting Power: German and U.S. Army Performance, 1939–1945* (London: Arms and Armour, 1983), 164–166.

64. Roger A. Beaumont, "On the *Wehrmacht* Mystique," *Military Review* 66:7 (July 1986), 48.

65. Daniel Hughes, "Abuses of German Military History," *Military Review* 66:12 (December 1986), 66–76, details the arguments against emulating the German army.

66. Martin van Creveld, "On Learning from the *Wehrmacht* and Other Things," *Military Review* 68:1 (January 1988), 62–71.

67. For example, see Bevin Alexander, *How Hitler Could Have Won World War II: The Fatal Errors That Led to Nazi Defeat* (New York: Three Rivers, 2000); Heinz Magenheimer, *Hitler's War: Germany's Key Strategic Decisions, 1940–1945*, trans. Helmut Bolger (London: Cassell, 1998).

68. Naveh, 117.

69. Daniel P. Bolger, "Maneuver Warfare Reconsidered," in *Maneuver Warfare: An Anthology*, 19.

70. For example, see the debate concerning the concept of intent: David A. Fastabend, "The Application of the Commander's Intent," *Military Review* 67:8 (August 1987), 60–68; Edward J. Filiberti, "Command, Control and Commander's Intent," *Military Review* 67:8 (August 1987), 54–59; Russell W. Glenn, "The Commander's Intent: Keep It Short," *Military Review* 67:8 (August 1987), 49–53. Concerning the center of gravity, see Dale C. Eikemier, "Centre of Gravity Analysis," *Military Review* 84:4 (July–August 2004), 2–5; Milan Vego, "Centre of Gravity," *Military Review* 80:2 (March–April 2000), 23–29.

71. Dov Glazer, *War Is the Province of Uncertainty: The Unique German Approach to Battle, Theory and Doctrine* (Master's thesis, Bar Ilan University, 2006), 73–74 [Heb.].

72. Francis Fukuyama and Abram N. Shulsky, *The Virtual Corporation and Army Organization* (California: RAND, 1997), 42–43.

73. Citino, 310.

74. Department of the Army, Field Manual 3-0, *Operations* (Washington, DC: Department of the Army, 2001), chap. 5, paragraphs 4–9, 61–63, 71–72; chap. 6, paragraphs 37–39.

75. Department of the Army, Field Manual 6-0, *Mission Command: Command and Control of Army Forces* (Washington, DC: Department of the Army, 2003).

76. Comments made by the author of the field manual: William M. Connor, "Emerging Army Doctrine: Command & Control," *Military Review* 82:2 (March–April 2002), 80.

77. Millennium Challenge 2002 (MC02) was a major war game conducted by the Americans during the summer of 2002. Lasting three weeks and costing an estimated $250 million, it involved both live exercises and computer simulations. Riper succeeded in sinking the "blue" naval armada using unconventional methods leading to a suspension of the exercise. When it resumed, both sides were ordered to follow predetermined scripts. Riper resigned soon after. On Riper's approach, see Malcolm Gladwell, *Blink: The Power of Thinking Without Thinking* (New York: Little, Brown, 2005), 99–110, 145–146.

78. Paul van Riper, *Planning for and Applying Military Force: An Examination of Terms* (Carlisle, PA: Strategic Studies Institute, 2006), 13.

79. Daniel Hughes, "Auftragstaktik," in *International Military Defence Encyclopedia*, vol. 1A–B, ed. Trevor N. Dupuy (London: Macmillan, 1993), 332.

80. Hughes, "Abuses," 67.

81. Hughes, "Auftragstaktik."

82. Antulio J. Echevarria, "Auftragstaktik: In Its Proper Perspective," *Military Review* 66:10 (October 1986), 50–56.

83. Creveld, "Learning," 70.

84. David M. Keithly and Stephen P. Ferris, "*Auftragstaktik* or Directive Control in Joint and Combined Operations," *Parameters* 89:3 (Autumn 1999), 118–133; Joseph S. McLamb, "The Future of Mission Orders," *Military Review* 77:5 (September–October 1997), 71–74.

85. Francis Fukuyama and Abram N. Shusky, "Military Organization in the Information Age: Lessons from the World of Business," in *Strategic Appraisal: The Changing Role of Information in Warfare*, ed. Zalmay Khalilzad, John P. White, and Andrew W. Marshall (Santa Monica, CA: RAND, 1999), 329, 340.

86. Robert R. Leonhard, *Fighting By Minutes: Time and the Art of War* (Westport, CT: Praeger, 1994) , 117.

87. John Kiszely, "The British Army and Approaches to Warfare Since 1945," in *Military Power: Land Warfare in Theory and Practice*, ed. Brian Holden Reid (London: Frank Cass, 1997), 198.

88. Colin McInnes, *Hot War, Cold War: The British Army's Way in Warfare, 1945–95* (London: Brassey's, 1996), 56.

89. Ibid., 62.

90. Sangho Lee, *Deterrence and the Defence of Central Europe: The British Role from the Early 1980s to the End of the Gulf War* (PhD diss. King's College London, 1994), 297–298.

91. Ibid., 17.

92. John Waters, "The Influence of Field Marshal Nigel Bagnall," *British Army Review* 130 (Autumn 2002), 38.

93. Kiszely, 199.

94. McInnes, 71.

95. Kiszely, 199.

96. Colonel David Benest, Director of Security Studies and Resilience, Defence Academy. Served with 2 PARA during the Falklands War. Interview with author, 13 December 2005, London.

97. Richard Simpkin, "Maneuver Warfare Theory and the Small Army," *British Army Review* 78 (December 1984), 5–13. The American reformist Starry's opening notes in Simpkin's treaties on maneuver warfare demonstrates reciprocity of ideas: Donn A. Starry, "Forward," in: Richard Simpkin, *Race to the Swift: Thoughts on Twenty-First Century Warfare* (London: Brassey's, 1985), 13–19.

98. Simpkin, *Race to the Swift*, 281–282.

99. Simpkin, "Maneuver," 10, 12.

100. Simpkin, *Race to the Swift*, 284.

101. Benest, interview; Lieutenant Colonel Dr. Jim Storr, General Staff Northern Ireland Study Team, Principal Author of Land Operations Doctrine. Interview with author, 31 March 2006, London; Brigadier General Stephen White, Military Assistant to Chief of the General Staff Sir Nigel Bagnall (1988–1989), Lieutenant Colonel SO1 Doctrine in Army Staff College (1990–1993). Interview with author, 17 January 2006, London.

102. Benest, interview; Storr, interview; White, interview.

103. Ibid., 222–224.

104. Waters, 38.

105. Lee, 266.

106. Benest, interview.

107. Lee, 33–34.

108. Ibid., 36.

109. Ibid., 217–221.

110. John L. Romjue, "The Evolution of the AirLand Battle Concept," *Air University Review* (May–June 1984), available at http://www.airpower.maxwell.af.mil/airchronicles/aureview/1984/may-jun/romjue.html (accessed 28 May 2007).

111. Lee, 84.

112. Ibid., 180.

113. Simpkin, *Race to the Swift*, chap. 3. Mikhail Nikolayevich Tukachevsky (1893–1937) was an original theoretician and chief of the Red Army.

114. Lee, 84.

115. Ibid., 20.

116. Ibid., 159.

117. Benest, interview; Brigadier General Mungo Melvin, Director, MOD Operational Capabilities, Director of Land Warfare British Army. Interview with author, 12 May 2006, London; Storr, interview.

118. Lee, 243–247.

119. Waters, 39. *Design for Military Operations: The British Military Doctrine,* Army Code 71451 (1989).

120. Lee, 224–225.

121. J. G. Williams, "Operational Art and the Higher Command and Staff Course," *British Army Review* 93 (December 1989), 4–7.

122. Michael E. Howard, "Leadership in the British Army in the Second World War: Some Personal Observation," in *Leadership and Command: The Anglo-American Experience Since 1861,* ed. G. D. Sheffield (London: Brassey's, 2002), 124.

123. Lee, 297–298. See also J. J. G. Mackenzie and Brian Holden-Reid, eds., *The British Army and the Operational Art* (London: Tri-Service Press, 1989). This volume offers selected essays penned by High Command Course students.

124. Army Doctrine Publication (ADP) *Command,* vol. 2, Army Code 71564 (1995), 2-4.

125. Brigadier General Stephen White, Military Assistant to Chief of the General Staff Sir Nigel Bagnall (1988–1989), Lieutenant Colonel SO1 Doctrine in Army Staff College (1990–1993). E-mail communication to author, 27 January 2006.

126. Ibid.

127. Ibid., 25 January 2006.

128. Ibid.

129. Ibid.

130. Richard Iron, "What Clausewitz (Really) Meant by Centre of Gravity," *Defence Studies* 1:3 (Autumn 2001), 109–112.

131. ADP, *Command,* 2-4.

132. Ibid., 2-2.

133. ADP, *Land Operations,* Army Code 71819 (2005), 116, 118; Storr, interview.

134. For example, see Ed Blanche, "Is the Myth Fading for the Israeli Army? Part 1," *Jane's Intelligence Review* 8:12 (December 1996), 547–550.

135. Cultural and structural problems were discussed by scholars such as Uri Milstein and Martin van Creveld or retired officers-turned-academics such as Immanuel Wald, Hanan Shai, and Shimon Naveh.

136. On IDF readiness for another round of fighting, see Amos Harel and Avi Isacharoff, *The Seventh War: Why We Won and Why We Lost in the War with the Palestinians* (Tel Aviv: Miscal-Chemed, 2004), 62–65, 74–75 [Heb.].

137. Mission command was officially incorporated in the field manual *Battle Doctrine and General Staff Procedures* (1993). Lieutenant Colonel Dori Pinkas, Head of High Headquarters department in the Doctrine Branch. Interview with author, 13 February 2005, Tel Aviv.

138. This study examined behavioral patterns from 1992 through 1995. Dori Pinkas, *Barriers to Mission Command in the IDF* (Final paper, Staff and Command Course, 1996), 13–14 [Heb.].

139. Ibid., 18–20.

140. Colonel Dani Davidi, Commander of the Tactical Command College. Interview with author, 20 February 2005, Hertzelia, Israel.

141. Lieutenant Colonel David Kanizo, Head of Doctrine Department, Ground Forces Command (MAZI). Interview with author, 10 February 2005, Tel Aviv; Pinkas, interview.

142. Hanan (Schwartz) Shai, "*PUM Barak*, How the Program Was Conceived," in *50 Years Jubilee to the IDF Staff and Command College*, ed. Moshe Shamir and Hila Sagie (Tel Aviv: Ma'arachot, 2004), 22 [Heb.].

143. The Agranat Committee was a national commission of inquiry charged with investigating the events leading to the war through the abortive counterattack of 8 October 1973.

144. Hanan (Schwartz) Shai, *Training Generals* (PhD diss., Hebrew University, Jerusalem, 1996) [Heb.].

145. Colonel (Ret.) Hanan (Schwartz) Shai, Founder and Director, Staff and Command College (1989–1994). Interview with author, 23 February 2005, Hertzelia, Israel.

146. Ibid.

147. Pinkas, interview.

148. Shai, interview.

149. Hanan (Schwartz) Shai, *The Command and Control Method in the Modern Military Organization: An Examination of Its Essence and Validity* (Master's thesis, University of Haifa, 1993), 225 [Heb.].

150. Ibid., 247.

151. Ibid., 252.

152. Regarding *bitsuism* in the IDF today, see Sergio Catignani and Eitan Shamir, "Mission Command and *Bitsuism* in the Israeli Defence Forces: Complementary or Contradictory in Today's Counter-Insurgency Campaign?" in *Dimensions of Military Leadership*, ed. Alistair MacIntyre and Karen Davis (Ontario: Canadian Defence Academy, 2007), 185–214.

153. Shai, "*PUM*," 23.

154. On the selection and training of Israeli junior officers, see Reuven Gal, *A Portrait of the Israeli Soldier* (New York: Greenwood, 1986), 116–126.

155. See statistics in Martin van Creveld, *Training of Officers* (New York: Free Press, 1990), 118.

156. Shai, interview.

157. Martin van Creveld, *The Sword and the Olive: A Critical History of the Israeli Defense Force* (New York: Public Affairs, 1998), 168–169.

158. Shai, interview.

159. Shai, "*PUM*," 24.

160. Shai, interview.

161. Hareal and Isacharoff, 58.

162. Kobi Michael, "The Military Knowledge as a Basis for Arranging of the Dialogue Sphere and the Weakness of Civilian Control in a LIC Reality—The Israeli Case" (unpublished manuscript) [Heb.].

163. Interview with Ya'alon cited in ibid., 10.

164. On the influence of the OTRI on Ya'alon, see Ofer Shelach and Raviv Droker, *Boomerang: The Failure of the Israeli Leadership in the Second Intifada* (Jerusalem: Keter, 2005), 79 [Heb.]. On Naveh's theory of the operational art, see Naveh, *In Pursuit*. The ideas explored in this book served as a basis for the OTRI and the Advanced Operational Command and Staff Course (1996–2002) for division commanders it established. See http://home.no.net/tacops/Taktikk/Kadettarbeid/naveh.htm (accessed 29 December 2005).

165. Michael, 11.

166. Brigadier General (Ret.) Dr. Shimon Naveh, Head of the Operational Theory Research Institute. Interview with author, 14 February 2005, Hertzelia, Israel.

167. Ibid.

168. Ibid.

169. "U.S.-Israeli Seminar on Military Innovation and Experimentation," March 1999, available at http://www.belisarius.com/modern_business_strategy/moore/mie_1 .htm (accessed 20 January 2006). See also John F. Schmitt, *A Systemic Concept for Operational Design*, available at http://www.mcwl.usmc.mil/concepts/home.cfm (accessed 20 June 2007). A Marine, Schmitt was heavily influenced by Naveh.

170. Naveh, interview.

171. Ibid. The Second Lebanon War began a year after this interview was held. Gal Hirsch, one of Naveh's followers, commanded the division that carried the brunt of the fighting. Among other things, Hirsch was criticized for failing to communicate his intent clearly to his brigade commanders. Some of the brilliant tactical commanders Naveh referred to, such as Cochavi and Tamir, did not participate in the campaign. One can only guess whether their participation would have made any difference.

172. Ibid.

173. Moshe Zonder, *Sayeret Matkal: The Elite Unit of Israel* (Jerusalem: Keter, 2000), 230–231 [Heb.].

174. For example, see Amos Gilboa, "IDF Hot Air," *Ma'ariv*, 27 June 2005 [Heb.]; Amir Oren, "Terror Will Always Be," *Ha'aretz*, 29 December 2004 [Heb.].

175. For example, see Yehuda Vagman, "LIC: The Failure," in *Low Intensity Conflict*, ed. Haggai Golan and Shaul Shay (Tel Aviv: Ma'arachot, 2004), 251–298 [Heb.]. See also Shai, interview.

176. Michael, 15.

177. Ibid., 16.

178. Emanuel Wald, *The Wald Report: The Decline of Israeli National Security Since 1967* (Boulder: Westview, 1992), 127.

179. U.S. and British interviewees often describe Naveh as impressive and inspiring. Paul van Riper even partially attributed his success in the Millennium 2002 exercise to the application of Naveh's principles.

180. This was indicated to the author by several officers who chose to remain anonymous. Others praised the introduction of a new theory.

181. Matt M. Matthews, "We Were Caught Unprepared: The 2006 Hezbollah-Israeli War," *Long War Series Occasional Publication 26* (Fort Leavenworth, KS: Combat Studies Institute, 2008); Ron Tira, "The Limitations of Standoff Firepower-Based Operations: On Standoff Warfare, Maneuver, and Decision," *Memorandum 89* (Tel Aviv: Institute for National Strategic Studies, 2007).

9. Testing: Mission Command in Operations

1. "Recent operations" include post–Cold War operations involving large ground elements.

2. Though a nonstate player, Hezbollah possessed conventional characteristics, such as a well-defined command and control structure, technology, highly trained specialized units, and a sophisticated defense system. See Avi Kober, "The Israel Defence Forces in the Second Lebanon War: Why the Poor Performance?" *Journal of Strategic Studies* 31:1 (February 2008), 16, 20.

3. Operation "Iraqi Freedom" includes both the invasion and the subsequent occupation phases.

4. Richard A. Gabriel, *Military Incompetence: Why the American Military Doesn't Win* (New York: Farrar, Straus, and Giroux, 1985), 106, 107; Edward N. Luttwak, *Strategy: The Logic of War and Peace* (Cambridge, MA: Harvard University Press, 2001), 6.

5. Gabriel, 115–116.

6. Ibid., 176.

7. Ibid., 5.

8. Ibid., 15, 195.

9. Stephen Badsey, "Coalition Command in the Gulf War," in *Leadership and Command: The Anglo-American Experience Since 1861,* ed. G. D. Sheffield (London: Brassey's, 2002), 198; Department of Defense, *Conduct of the Persian Gulf War: Final Report to Congress* (Washington, DC: Department of Defense, 1992), 329.

10. Shimon Naveh, *In Pursuit of Military Excellence: The Evolution of Operational Theory* (London: Frank Cass, 1997), 329.

11. Ibid., 326.

12. See, for instance, General Franks's testimony in Tom Clancy and Fred Franks, *On the Ground in Iraq: Into the Storm, a Study in Command* (New York: Berkley, 2004), 465.

13. Jonathan M. House, *Combined Arms Warfare in The Twentieth Century* (Lawrence: University Press of Kansas, 2001), 273.

14. Martin van Creveld, Professor of Military History, Hebrew University. Interview with author, 15 February 2005, Jerusalem.

15. Badsey, 199.

16. Stephen Biddle, "Victory Misunderstood: What the Gulf War Tells Us About the Future of Conflict," *International Security* 2:2 (Autumn 1996), 139–140, 161–165.

17. William S. Lind, "The Theory and Practice of Maneuver Warfare," in *Maneuver Warfare: An Anthology,* ed. Richard D. Hooker Jr. (Novato, CA: Presidio Press, 1993), 15.

18. Richard J. Dunn III, "From Gettysburg to the Gulf and Beyond: Coping with Revolutionary Technological Change in Land Warfare," in *McNair Paper,* vol. 13 (Washington, DC: Institute for National Strategic Studies, 1991), 85.

19. Gray distinguished among three strategic behaviors: attrition, annihilation through maneuver, and paralysis through control. Colin S. Gray, *Modern Strategy* (Oxford: Oxford University Press, 1999), 162.

20. Robert Leonhard, *The Art of Maneuver: Maneuver Warfare Theory and Air-Land Battle* (Novato, CA: Presidio Press, 1991), 269.

21. For further details of the Soviet practice, see ibid., 52–58; Richard Simpkin, *Race to the Swift: Thoughts on Twenty-First Century Warfare* (London: Brassey's, 1985), 288–292.

22. Leonhard, 270.

23. Martin van Creveld, Kenneth S. Brower, and Steven L. Canby, *Air Power and Maneuver Warfare* (Montgomery, Alabama: Air University Press, 1994), 214.

24. Ibid., 219.

25. Robert M. Citino, *The German Way of War: From the Thirty Years' War to the Third Reich* (Lawrence: University Press of Kansas, 2005), 310.

26. Douglas A. Macgregor, *Transformation Under Fire: Revolutionizing How America Fights* (Westport, CT: Praeger, 2003), 99–101.

27. General (Ret.) Sir Rupert Smith, Commander of First British Armoured Division (First Gulf War), GOC Northern Ireland (1996–1999), Deputy Supreme NATO Allied Commander. Interview with author, 1 September 2006, Brussels.

28. Ibid.

29. Rupert Smith, *The Utility of Force: The Art of War in the Modern World* (New York: Penguin, 2006), 93–94.

30. Adam Grissom, *To Digitize an Army: The U.S. Army Force XXI Initiative and the Digital Divide, 1993–2003* (PhD diss., King's College London, 2008), 7.

31. Smith, 94.

32. Badsey, 208.

33. Donald Vandergriff, *The Path to Victory: America's Army and the Revolution of Human Affairs* (Novato, CA: Presidio Press, 2002), 150–153.

34. Ibid., 150–151.

35. Michael R. Gordon and Bernard E. Trainor, *The Generals' War: The Inside Story of the Conflict in the Gulf* (New York: Little, Brown, 1995), 375.

36. Ibid., 371, 376–377.

37. Gordon and Trainor, *The Generals' War*, 380; Barry D. Watts, *Clausewitzian Friction and Future War* (Washington, DC: Institute for National Strategic Studies, 1996), 47–48.

38. H. Norman Schwarzkopf and Peter Petre, *It Doesn't Take a Hero* (London: Transworld, 1993), 528–529, 536.

39. Gordon and Trainor, *The Generals' War*, 380–381; Richard M. Swain, *Lucky War: Third Army in Desert Storm* (Fort Leavenworth, KS: Army Command and General Staff Press, 1994), 238, 247; Schwarzkopf and Petre, 429.

40. Watts, 49–50, and specifically note 39; Schwarzkopf and Petre, 546.

41. Robert H. Scales Jr., *Certain Victory: The U.S. Army in the Gulf War* (London: Brassey's, 1994), 254.

42. Vandergriff, 153.

43. Colin S. Gray, *Another Bloody Century: Future Warfare* (London: Windenfeld & Nicolson, 2005), 94; Watts, 51.

44. Van Creveld, Brower, and Canby, 213–219.

45. Thomas E. Ricks, *Fiasco: The American Military Adventure in Iraq* (New York: Penguin, 2006), 74.

46. John Keegan, *The Iraq War* (London: Hutchinson, 2004), 5–6.

47. Dr. Bruce R. Nardulli, RAND, Senior Analyst, Expert on Operations. Interview with author, 7 September 2006, Washington, DC.

48. Mark Bowden, "Forward," in David Zucchino, *Thunder Run: Three Days in the Battle for Baghdad* (New York: Grove, 2004), xi.

49. Ricks, 125.

50. Nardulli, interview.

51. Michael R. Gordon and Bernard E. Trainor, *Cobra II: The Inside Story of the Invasion and Occupation of Iraq* (London: Atlantic, 2006), 430–431; Ricks, 126.

52. Zucchino.

53. Greg Jaffe, "Rumsfeld's Vindication Promises a Change in Tactics, Deployment," *Wall Street Journal*, 10 April 2003.

54. Lieutenant Colonel Dr. Isaiah (Ike) Wilson III, Director of American Politics, Policy & Strategy, West Point, Former Staff Officer with 101st in Iraq. Interview with author, 13 September 2006, West Point, NY; Gordon and Trainor, *Cobra II*, 119–121, 175; Ricks, 79, 101–104.

55. Ricks, 75–76.

56. Ibid., 81–82.

57. Lieutenant General (Ret.) Paul van Riper, Commanding General, Marine Corps Combat Development Command, Quantico, VA. Telephone interview with author, 8 September 2006.

58. Tommy Franks, *American Soldier* (New York: HarperCollins, 2004), 368.

59. Wilson, interview.

60. Dr. Adam Grissom, RAND, Expert on Army Digitization. Interview with author, 5 September 2006, Washington, DC.

61. Douglas A. Macgregor, "The Failure of Military Leadership in Iraq, Fire the Generals!" in *Counterpunch!* 26 May 2006, available at http://www.counterpunch.org/macgregor05262006.html (accessed April 2007).

62. Ibid.

63. Ibid.

64. Ricardo Sanchez, *Wiser in Battle: A Soldier's Story* (New York: HarperCollins, 2008), 361.

65. For a discussion of the system and the significance and meaning of its name, see Chapter 7.

66. Grissom, 12.

67. Ibid., 2.

68. Gordon and Trainor, *Cobra II*, 162; Wilson, interview.

69. Donald P. Wright, Timothy R. Reese, and the Contemporary Operations Study Team, *On Point II: Transition to the New Campaign: The United States Army in Operation Iraqi Freedom, May 2003–January 2005* (Fort Leavenworth, KS: Combat Studies Institute Press, 2008), 77–80, 160–161.

70. Ricks, 182, 185, 272.

71. Wilson, interview.

72. Nigel Aylwin-Foster, "Changing the Army for Counterinsurgency Operations," *Military Review* 84:6 (November–December 2005), 7.

73. This is somewhat analogous to the Israeli *bitsuism* culture. See Chapter 4.

74. Aylwin-Foster, 7.

75. Kevin C. M. Benson, "OIF Phase IV: A Planner's Replay to Brigadier Aylwin-Foster," *Military Review* 86:2 (March–April 2006), 61.

76. Ibid., 63–65.

77. Ibid., 65.

78. William S. Wallace, "TRADOC Commander, TRADOC Commander's Replay to Brigadier Aylwin-Foster," *Military Review* 86:2 (March–April, 2006), 117.

79. Ibid., 118.

80. Susan Craig, "Aylwin-Foster's Critique," *Military Review* 86:2 (March–April, 2006), 118.

81. Roundtable discussion at the RAND Arroyo Centre, Army Research Division. Discussion included a group of RAND senior analysts, 5 September 2006, Washington, DC.

82. Peter J. Boyer, "Downfall: How Donald Rumsfeld Reformed the Army and Lost Iraq," *New Yorker*, 20 November 2006.

83. Ibid. Concerning the general's revolt, see "Anatomy of a Revolt," *Newsweek*, 24 April 2006, 24–29; *Guardian*, 14–17 April 2006; *International Herald Tribune*, 17 April 2006, 24 April 2006; Fred Kaplan, "The Revolt Against Rumsfeld: The Officer Corps Is Getting Restless," *Slate*, 12 April 2006, available at http://www.slate.com/id/2139777/ (accessed February 2006).

84. Greg Newbold, "Why Iraq Was a Mistake," *Time*, 17 April 2006.

85. Ibid.

86. Macgregor, "The Failure."

87. Colin McInnes, *Hot War, Cold War: The British Army's Way in Warfare, 1945–95* (London: Brassey's, 1996), 101.

88. Colin McInnes, "The Gulf War 1990–1991," in *Big Wars and Small Wars*, ed. Hew Strachan (Oxford: Routledge, 2006), 175–176.

89. McInnes, *Hot War*, 109.

90. Smith, interview.

91. Sangho Lee, *Deterrence and the Defence of Central Europe: The British Role from the Early 1980s to the End of the Gulf War* (PhD diss. King's College London, 1994), 353.

92. McInnes, "The Gulf War," 165.

93. Lee, 346.

94. Ibid., 339–341.

95. McInnes, *Hot War*, 92.

96. Smith, interview.

97. In that sense, they were similar to U.S. Marine Corps doctrine.

98. Clancy and Franks, 264.

99. McInnes, *Hot War*, 111.

100. Lee, 383–384; McInnes, *Hot War*, 112.

101. Jim Storr, *The Nature of Military Thought* (PhD diss. Cranfield University, Wiltshire, 2001), 46.

102. Ibid.

103. John Keegan, *The Iraq War* (London: Hutchinson, 2004), 166–169, 179–181.

104. Colonel David Benest, Director of Security Studies and Resilience, Defence Academy. Served with 2 PARA during the Falklands War. Interview with author, 13 December 2005, London; Lieutenant Colonel Dr. Jim Storr, General Staff Northern Ireland Study Team, Principal Author of Land Operations Doctrine. Interview with author, 31 March 2006, London.

105. For an updated version of the report, see Jim Storr, "The Command of British Land Forces in Iraq, March to May 2003," Proceedings of the 9th International C2 Research and Technology Symposium, Copenhagen, September 2004. The report is based on extensive research, including hundreds of documents, memos, radio logs, interviews, and personal diaries. See ibid., 2.

106. Ibid., 3–7.

107. United Kingdom Ministry of Defence, "Operations in Iraq: An Analysis from the Land Perspective," Army Code 71816, 4-12.

108. Ibid., 4-6.

109. Jim Storr, "Size Matters," *British Military Review* 144 (April 2008), 72–73.

110. United Kingdom Ministry of Defence, "Operations in Iraq," 4-5, 4-6.

111. Ibid., 4-9.

112. Ibid., 4-10.

113. Concerning the importance of concise orders, see Chapter 3.

114. Storr, "The Command," 11.

115. United Kingdom Ministry of Defence, "Operations in Iraq," 4-11.

116. Ibid., 4-12.

117. According to Storr, this was acknowledged in an early draft of the ADP *Land Operations* (2002), the publication of which was held in order to incorporate the lessons of Telic. The manual was finally issued in 2005. Storr, interview.

118. Storr, "The Command," 15.

119. Ibid., 3.

120. Alex Fishman, "Battle of Egos," *Yedioth Ahronoth*, 12 November 2004 [Heb.].

121. After the massacre, Sharon called Israelis "to fight to protect our homes." Cited in Amos Harel and Avi Isacharoff, *The Seventh War: Why We Won and Why We Lost in the War with the Palestinians* (Tel Aviv: Miscal-Chemed, 2004), 255 [Heb.].

122. Gal Hirsh, "From 'Solid Lid' to 'Other Way': Campaign Development in Central Command, 2000–2003," in *Low Intensity Conflict,* ed. Haggai Golan and Shaul Shay (Tel Aviv: Ma'arachot, 2004), 242–246 [Heb.].

123. See "Eyewitness: Netanya Bombing," *BBC Online News*, 28 March 2002, available at http://news.bbc.co.uk/1/hi/world/middle_east/1897940.stm (accessed 28 March 2002).

124. Ari Shavit, "The Enemy Within," *Ha'aretz*, 29 August 2002 [Heb.].

125. Rami Hazut, "The Palestinians Are an Existential Threat: Iraq Is Not," *Yedioth Ahronoth*, 23 August 2002, available at http://israelvisit.co.il/cgi-bin/friendly .pl?url=Aug-23-02!IDF (accessed 14 March 2003) [Heb.].

126. For a discussion of the OTRI, see Chapter 8, 124–129.

127. Quoted in Harel and Isacharoff, 113. On the indoctrination of Central Command staff, see Kobi Michael, "The Military Knowledge as a Basis for Arranging of the Dialogue Sphere and the Weakness of Civilian Control in a LIC Reality—The Israeli Case" (forthcoming paper), 12 [Heb.].

128. Alex Fishman, "Hold Us Arik," *Yedioth Aharonot,* 21 January 2005 [Heb.]. Concerning Sharon's legacy, see Chapter 4.

129. Ofer Shelach and Raviv Droker, *Boomerang: The Failure of the Israeli Leadership in the Second Intifada* (Jerusalem: Keter, 2005), 195, 220, 318 [Heb.].

130. Amos Harel, "Test of Their Lives," *Ha'aretz*, 25 June 2005 [Heb.].

131. Harel and Isacharoff, 58, 224–227, 251–260; Shelach and Droker, 195–197, 218–220.

132. Giora Segal, "Mission Oriented Command in LIC," paper presented at MAZI 1st International Conference on LIC Warfare, 22 March 2004 [Heb.].

133. For a personal account, see Ofek Bochris, "Command and Leadership in Defensive Shield Operation," *Ma'arachot* 388 (July 2003), 32–37 [Heb.].

134. Gal Hirsh, "On Dinosaurs and Hornets: A Critical View on Operational Moulds in Asymmetric Conflicts," *RUSI Journal* 148 (August 2003), 60–63; Chris McGreal, "Send in the Bulldozers: What Israel Told Marines About Urban Battles," *Guardian*, 2 April 2005.

135. Lieutenant Colonel Dori Pinkas, Head of High Headquarters department in the Doctrine Branch. Interview with author, 13 February 2005, Tel Aviv.

136. Brigadier General (Ret.) Dr. Shimon Naveh, Head of the Operational Theory Research Institute. Interview with author, 14 February 2005, Hertzelia, Israel.

137. Shelach and Droker, 216, 220.

138. Sergio Catignani, "The Strategic Impasse in Low Intensity Conflicts: The Gap Between Israeli Counter-Insurgency Strategy and Tactics During the Al-Aqsa Intifada," *Journal of Strategic Studies* 28:1 (February 2005), 57–75.

139. Malka M. Rozin, "Low Intensity—High Impact: IDF Involvement in Policy Making During Low Intensity Conflicts," paper presented at IUS Armed Forces and Society Conference, Chicago, 22 October 2005.

140. Keren Helerman, "What Is Special About Special Forces?" *Beyn Haziroot* 3 (July 2004), 27 [Heb.].

141. Vered Winocur-Chair and Yotam Amitai, "The War of the Junior Command in the Prolonged Confrontation in the Gaza Strip," *Ma'arachot* 389 (May 2003), 34 [Heb.].

142. Shelach and Droker, 195–197.

143. Shelach and Droker (318) provide examples of two raids conducted by conventional forces, in which twenty-three Palestinian were killed, half of whom were women and children.

144. David Eshel, "The Battle of Jenin," *Jane's Intelligence Review* 14:7 (July 2002), 20–23; *UNRWA Gaza Field Assessment of IDF Operation Days of Penitence*, available at http://www.un.org/unrwa/news/incursion_oct04.pdf (accessed 20 October 2004); "Israel 'Pauses' Rafah Operation," *BBC News*, available at http://news.bbc.co.uk/2/hi/middle_east/3744533.stm (accessed 25 May 2004).

145. Yehuda Vagman, "What in Fact Was the Mission?" *Ma'arachot* 403–404 (December 2005), 69 [Heb.].

146. Schelach and Droker, 220.

147. Quoted in "Israel Needs Ya'alon," *Foreign Report*, 6 November 2003, available at http://frp.janes.com (accessed 23 June 2004).

148. Michael, 15.

149. Winocur-Chair and Amitai, 34.

150. Harel and Isacharoff, 291–292.

151. The war lasted from 12 July to 14 August. Concerning the Israeli perception of the war, see Alex Fishman, "Why We Didn't Win," *Yedioth Ahronot*, 18 August 2006 [Heb.].

152. Vinograd National Inquiry Commission into the Second Lebanon War, Part A (April 2007), 65 [Heb.]; available at: http://www.vaadatwino.co.il, Ofer Shelach and Yoav Limor, *Captives in Lebanon: The Truth About the Lebanon War* (Tel Aviv: Yedioth Ahronoth, 2007), 56–58, 66–76 [Heb.].

153. Vinograd Commission, 48–50. For a critical analysis of EBO doctrine, see Ron Tira, "The Limitations of Standoff Firepower-Based Operations: On Standoff Warfare, Maneuver, and Decision," in *Memorandum,* vol. 89 (Tel Aviv: Institute for National Strategic Studies, 2007), 43–44. As IAF commander, Dan Halutz stated in 2001 that "decision is a question of consciousness, the Air Force has a critical impact on the enemy consciousnesses." Alex Fishman, "Infected by a Virus," *Yedioth Ahronot*, 15 December 2006 [Heb.].

154. Shelach and Limor, 63.

155. Shlomo Brom, "Political and Military Objectives Against Guerrilla Organization," in *The Second Lebanon War, Strategic Dimensions,* ed. Meir Eliran and Shlomo Brom (Tel Aviv: Yedioth Ahronoth, 2007), 21 [Heb.].

156. Vinograd Commission, 51.

157. Giora Rom, "The Test of the Strategies of the Rivals—as if Two Ships Pass Each Other in the Night," in *The Second Lebanon War, Strategic Dimensions,* 51 [Heb.].

158. Shelach and Limor, 325–344.

159. On the use of ambiguous and unprofessional jargon, see ibid., 195–200. Regarding the lack of forward command, see an internal IDF report published in Yossi Yehoshua, "The Decline of Values," *Yedioth Ahronot*, 13 July 2007 [Heb.].

160. Shelach and Limor, 194–197.

161. Fishman, "Why We Didn't Win."

162. On the importance accorded to the reserves in previous wars, see Chapter 6.

163. For a prewar discussion of this aspect, see Alex Fishman, "Reserve in Reserve," *Yedioth Ahronot*, 10 March 2006 [Heb.].

164. For example, only four of the fourteen members of the general staff who participated regularly in the situation assessment were graduates of the Staff and Command Course. Fishman, "Why We Didn't Win." See also "Report of the Israeli Parliament Committee for Security and Foreign Affairs Chaired by Brigadier (Ret.) Efi Eytam" [Heb.].

165. Yehuda Vagman, "Anti-War: Has the IDF Really Lost Its Ability to Win Wars?" *Strategic Assessment* 9:4 (March 2007), 75.

166. Concerning the degradation of command in the IDF, see Gabriel Siboni, "Command in the IDF," *Strategic Assessment* 9:4 (March 2007), 72.

167. Alex Fishman, "Ready to Absorb," *Yedioth Ahronot*, 13 October 2006 [Heb.].

168. Concerning *Pum Barak*, see Chapter 10, 182–185.

169. Giora Segal and Gabi Siboni ed., *The Second Lebanon War* (Tel Aviv: Ministry of Defence, January 2009). Internal papers by IDF commanders on the 2006 Lebanon war.

170. Ibid.

171. Ibid.

172. Vinograd Commission, 412.

173. Internal IDF study on command and control at HQ level during the second Lebanon War conducted by former Chief of Staff Dan Shomron and Col. Res. Hanan Shai. Excerpts from the report were leaked to the press. See Fishman, "Infected by a Virus."

174. Vinograd Commission, 401, 409–412.

175. Ibid., 412.

176. Alex Fishman, "We Didn't Let Our Junior Commanders Win," *Yedioth Ahronoth*, 12 October 2007 [Heb.].

177. Notes from the IDF Ground Forces Psychology Conference, 24 October 2007.

178. Basic Doctrinal Publication *Command and Control* (Israel Defense Forces, 2006), advocating mission command, was issued shortly before the war.

179. Interview with Haertzi Levi, Paratroop Commander, *Yedioth Ahoronot*, 23 January, 2009.

180. This is according to a 2009 internal briefing by a 2006 IDF Second Lebanon War division commander.

181. Abe F. Marrero, "The Tactics of Operation Cast Lead," in Matt M. Matthews, *Back to Basics: A Study of the Second Lebanon War and Operation Cast Lead* (Fort Leavenworth, KS: Combat Studies Institute Press, US Army Combined Arms Center, 2009), 90.

182. Ibid.

183. Matthews, *Back to Basics*, 31.

184. Sergio Catignani, "Variation on a Theme: Israel's Operation Cast Lead and the Gaza Strip Missile Conundrum," *RUSI Journal* 154:4 (August 2009), 69–70.

185. Amir Shoan and Amira Lam, "Commander in Chief," *Yediot Ahronot*, 23 January 2009.

10. The Praxis Gap

1. Charles C. Moskos, John Allen Williams, and David R. Segal, eds., *The Post Modern Military: Armed Forces After the Cold War* (New York: Oxford University Press, 2000), 1. The events of September 11th have nullified some of their observations but not the major trends they identified.

2. Ibid., 2.

3. Rupert Smith, *Utility of Force: The Art of War in the Modern World* (London: Allen Lane, 2006), 3.

4. Rupert Smith, first lecture in an RSA series on the changing nature of war, "Utility of Force," October 2006. www.theRSA.org.

5. Richard A. Gabriel and Paul L. Savage, *Crisis in Command: Mismanagement in the Army* (New York: Hill and Wang, 1978), 42–50, 181–184.

6. Tom Clancy and Fred Franks, *On the Ground in Iraq: Into the Storm, a Study in Command* (New York: Berkley, 2004), 105–106.

7. John Hillen, "Must US Military Culture Reform," *Parameters* 29:3 (Autumn 1999), 20. See also "American Military Culture in Twenty First Century," a report of the CSIS International Security Program, Centre for Strategic & International Studies (CSIS), February 2000.

8. Douglas A. Macgregor, *Transformation Under Fire: Revolutionizing How America Fights* (Westport, CT: Praeger, 2003), 192.

9. Edward N. Luttwak, "Toward Post Heroic Warfare," *Foreign Affairs* 74:3 (May–June 1995), 109–122.

10. Ibid., 115.

11. Concerning the widening gap between civilian and military cultures, see Hillen, 10, 21.

12. Macgregor, *Transformation*, 200.

13. Colonel (Ret.) Dr. David E. Johnson, RAND, Group Manager, Security Policy, Expert on Army Culture and Operations. Interview with author, 7 September 2006, Washington, DC; Colonel Dr. Douglas A. Macgregor, Military Analyst, Center of Technology and National Security, National Defense University. Interview with author, 8 September 2006, Washington, DC.

14. Macgregor, *Transformation*, 205.

15. Peter D. Feaver and Christopher Gelpi, *Choosing Your Battles: American Civil-Military Relations and Use of Force* (Princeton, NJ: Princeton University Press, 2005), esp. chapters 4 and 5.

16. Charles C. Krulak, "The Strategic Corporal: Leadership in the Three Block War," *Marines Corps Gazette* 83:1 (January 1999), 18–22.

17. Department of the Army, FM 3-24/MCWP 3-33.5, *Counterinsurgency* (Washington, DC: Department of the Army, 2006), 1-26, 7-4.

18. See: Eitan Shamir, "Peace Support Operations and the Strategic Corporal: Implications for Military Organization and Culture," in *The Transformation of the World of Warfare and Peace Support Operations,* ed. Kobi Michael, Eyal Ben-Ari, and David Kellen (Westport, CT: Praeger, 2009), 53–65.

19. Smith, RSA lecture.

20. The incident received wide media coverage: Edward Wong and Jason Horowitz, "Italian Hostage Returns Home After 2nd Brush with Death," *New York Times*, 5 March 2005, available at http://www.nytimes.com/2005/03/05/international/middleeast/05italy.html?ex=1401595200&en=935183cee9a4bd49&ei=5007&partner=USERLAND (accessed 16 October 2007).

21. "Bush Apologizes to Italy Again for Shooting of Agent," *NY1 News*, 4 May 2004, available at http://208.198.20.182/ny1/content/index.jsp?stid=3&aid=50591 (accessed 16 October 2007); "Mario Lozano," *Wikipedia*, available at http://en.wikipedia.org/wiki/Mario_Lozano (accessed 16 October 2007).

22. For the strategic implication, see Ricardo S. Sanchez, *Wiser in Battle: A Soldier's Story* (New York: HarperCollins, 2008), 375–434.

23. Ibid., 278, 378.

24. Seymour M. Hersh, "Torture at Abu Ghraib: American Soldiers Brutalize Iraqis, How Far up Does the Responsibility Go?" *New Yorker*, 10 May 2004, available at http://www.newyorker.com/archive/2004/05/10/040510fa_fact (accessed 16 October 2007).

25. Lieutenant Colonel Dr. Isaiah (Ike) Wilson III, Director of American Politics, Policy & Strategy, West Point, Former Staff Officer with 101st in Iraq. Interview with author, 13 September 2006, West Point, NY.

26. Suzanne Christine Nielsen, *Preparing for War: The Dynamics of Peacetime Military Reform* (PhD diss., Harvard University, 2003), 142–150.

27. Westmoreland quoted in Ibid., 145.

28. Ibid., 145–150.

29. Richard Lock-Pullan, "How to Rethink War: Conceptual Innovation and Air-Land Battle Doctrine," *Journal of Strategic Studies* 28:4 (August 2005), 693–694.

30. Donald Vandergriff, *The Path to Victory: America's Army and the Revolution of Human Affairs* (Novato, CA: Presidio Press, 2002), 308.

31. Ibid., 118.

32. Ibid., 123–126.

33. On the development of the AirLand battle doctrine, see Chapter 5.

34. Robert H. Scales Jr., *Certain Victory: The U.S. Army in the Gulf War* (London: Brassey's, 1994), 27–28; Robin P. Swan, "A Defence of SAMS by the School Director," *Armor* 109:1 (January–February 2000), 3.

35. John D. Johnson, *Mission Orders in the United States Army: Is the Doctrine Effective?* (Fort Leavenworth, KS: Army Command and General Staff College, 1990).

36. Vandergriff, 139–140.

37. Ibid., 138.

38. Ibid., 142–143.

39. Macgregor, interview.

40. Macgregor, *Transformation*, 207.

41. Ibid., 205.

42. Concerning this extraordinary exercise, see Malcolm Gladwell, *Blink: The Power of Thinking Without Thinking* (New York: Little, Brown, 2005), 99–111.

43. Lieutenant General (Ret.) Paul van Riper, Commanding General, Marine Corps Combat Development Command, Quantico, VA. Telephone interview with author, 8 September 2006.

44. Vandergriff, 143.

45. Macgregor, *Transformation*, 207.

46. Ibid., 196–197.

47. Ibid., 199.

48. Ibid.

49. David E. Johnson, *Preparing Potential Senior Army Leaders for the Future: An Assessment of Leader Development Efforts in the Post-Cold War Era* (Santa Monica, CA: RAND, 2002), 27.

50. Macgregor, *Transformation*, 190.

51. Macgregor, *Transformation*, 203; Vandergriff, 161, 181.

52. The author participated in a joint RAND-IDF discussion devoted to these issues at the IDF Dado Center for Interdisciplinary Military Studies, Israel, February 2008.

53. Thierry Gongora, "The Revolution in Military Affairs: What Should the CF Do About It?" *Defence Association National Network, National Network New* 5:2 (Summer 1998). For a critique of RMA theory, see Elliot Cohen, "A Revolution in Warfare," *Foreign Affairs* 75:2 (March–April, 1996), available at http://www.foreignaffairs .org/19960301faessay4186/eliot-a-cohen/a-revolution-in-warfare.html (accessed 8 December 2006); John A. Gentry, "Doomed to Fail: America's Blind Faith in Technology," *Parameters* 32:4 (Winter 2002–2003), 88–104.

54. James R. Blaker, *Understanding the Revolution in Military Affairs: A Guide to America's 21st Century Defense* (Washington, DC: Progressive Policy Institute, 1997); Elinor C. Sloan, *The Revolution in Military Affairs* (Montreal: McGill University Press, 2002), 3.

55. Herbert R. MacMaster, *Crack in the Foundation: Defense Transformation and the Underlying Assumption of Dominant Knowledge in Future War Center for Strategic Leadership* (Center for Startegic Leadership, U.S. Army War College, Carlisle Baracks, PA , Student Issue Paper, S03-03, 2003), 16; Herbert R. MacMaster, "On War: Lessons to Be Learned," *Survival* 50:1 (2008), 26.

56. These technologies can be roughly divided into two groups: precision-guided munitions (PGMs) and information technologies.

57. Bill Owens, *Lifting the Fog of War* (New York: Farrar, Straus & Giroux, 2000), 15. On the dominance of this approach in U.S. military thinking, see MacMaster, *Crack in the Foundation*, 3–34.

58. Gary Chapman, "An Introduction to the Revolution in Military Affairs," presented at the 15th Amaldi Conference on Problems in Global Security, Helsinki, September 2003, available at http://www.lincei.it/rapporti/amaldi/papers/XV-Chapman .pdf (accessed 1 June 2005).

59. Ibid., 5.

60. Peter Spiegel, "We Now Have the Armaments to Accomplish in 24 or 36 Hours What Took Seven Days in 1991," *Financial Times: Military Technology*, 20 March 2003.

61. John W. Charlton, "Digital Battle Command Baptism by Fire," *Armor* 112:6 (November–December 2003), 26–30.

62. Robert R. Leonhard, *Fighting by Minutes: Time and the Art of War* (Westport, CT: Praeger, 1994), 111–122; Robert R. Leonhard, *The Principles of War for the Information Age* (Novato, CA: Presidio Press, 1998), 179–180.

63. Robert L. Bateman, "Force XXI and the Death of Auftragstaktik," *Armor* 105:1 (January–February 1996), 16–20; Robert L. Bateman, "Pandora's Box," in *Digital War: The 21st Century Battlefield*, ed. Robert L. Bateman (New York: ibooks, 1999), 12–22.

64. Chris C. Demchak, "Complexity and a Midrange Theory of Networked Militaries," in *The Sources of Military Change: Culture, Politics, and Technology*, ed. Theo Farrell and Terry Terriff (Boulder, CO: Lynne Rienner, 2002), 221–263. A 1999 report concluded

that the system had increased battle effectiveness in a significant measure. Daniel Verton, "GAO Report: Benefits of Army Digitization Program Uncertain," available at http://www.fcw.com/aricles/1999/FCW_080299_822.asp (accessed 2 February 2004).

65. Jim Dunivan, "Surrendering the Initiative? C2 on the Digitized Battlefield," *Military Review* 73:5 (September–October 2003), 2; David M. Keithly and Stephen P. Ferris, "*Auftragstaktik* or Directive Control in Joint and Combined Operations," *Parameters* 89:3 (Autumn 1999), 118–133.

66. Martin van Creveld, *Command in War* (Cambridge, MA: Harvard University Press, 1985), 274–275.

67. Joseph S. McLamb, "The Future of Mission Orders," *Military Review* 77:5 (September–October 1997), 71–74.

68. Jack Kammerer, "Preserving Mission-Focused Command and Control," available at http://www.cgsc.army.mil/milrev (accessed 29 September 2003).

69. Chapman, 10.

70. Macgregor, *Transformation*, 99.

71. Concerning American reliance on technology, see Gentry. Concerning corporate culture, see Macgregor, *Transformation*, 216.

72. Adam Grissom, *To Digitize an Army: The US Army Force XXI Initiative and the Digital Divide, 1993–2003* (PhD diss., King's College London, 2008), 2.

73. Ibid., 18–19.

74. For a similar example, see James Corum, "A Clash of Military Cultures: German and French Approaches to Technology Between the World Wars," paper presented at a USAF Academy Symposium, September 1994. Concerning the "theory of use," see Chapter 2.

75. Martin Edmonds, "The British Army 2000: External Influences on Force Design," *Strategic and Combat Studies Institute Occasional Papers* 21 (1996), 10–12; Colin McInnes, *Hot War, Cold War: The British Army's Way in Warfare, 1945–95* (London: Brassey's, 1996), 22–24.

76. Max Hastings, "Britain's Armed Forces Under Threat: A Journalist's Lament," *RUSI* 150:5 (October 2005), 32–36.

77. Edmonds, "The British Army," 55–56.

78. Michael Edmonds, *Armed Services and Society* (Boulder, CO: Westview, 1991), 24–25, 95–98.

79. Ibid.

80. Edmonds, "The British Army," 57.

81. Christopher Coker, "The Unhappy Warrior," *RUSI* 150:4 (December 2005), 13–16.

82. Colonel David Benest, Director of Security Studies and Resilience, Defence Academy. Served with 2 PARA during the Falklands War. Interview with author, 13 December 2005, London; Brigadier General Mungo Melvin, Director, MOD Operational

Capabilities, Director of Land Warfare, British Army. Interview with author, 12 May 2006, London; Colonel Mike Ralph, Expert on Current Operations and Campaigning, Defence College, Shrivenham. Telephone interview with author, 30 May 2006; Lieutenant Colonel Dr. Jim Storr, General Staff, Northern Ireland Study Team, Principal Author of Land Operations Doctrine. Interview with author, 31 March 2006, London. All of the interviewees mentioned above reflected on the direct causality between the two.

83. "UK Soldiers Face War Crimes Trial," available at http://news.bbc.co.uk/2/hi/uk_news/4698251.stm (accessed 15 February 2007); Michael Evans, "War Crimes Colonel May Be Promoted, Staff College Beckons for Colonel Jorge Mendonca, Despite Looming Court Martial," available at http://www.timesonline.co.uk/tol/news/uk/article775122.ece (accessed 21 December 2007). Allison Martin, "I Quit Army: Cleared Hero Goes in Despair at New Probe of Iraq Abuse," *Mirror News,* available at http://www.mirror.co.uk/news/top-stories/2007/06/01/mendonca-i-quit-army-115875-19229373/ (accessed 1 June 2007).

84. Melvin, interview; Ralph, interview.

85. D. C. Eccles, "Risk Aversion and the Zero Defect Culture: A Checklist for British Armed Forces," *British Army Review* 122 (Autumn 1999), 94–96.

86. Colin Cape, "The Myth of Mission Command: The Impact of Risk Aversion and Cultural Dissonance on Current and Future Operational Effectiveness," (Master's thesis, Staff and Command College, Shrivenham, 2005), 20.

87. Ibid., 36–39.

88. R. A. M. S. Melvin, "Mission Command," *British Army Review* 130 (Autumn 2002), 4.

89. Patrick Mileham, "Fifty Years of British Army Officership, 1960–2010, Part I: Retrospective," *Defence & Security Analysis* 20:1 (March 2004), 83.

90. Storr, interview. First an officer in Northern Ireland, Storr later joined the British Army Northern Ireland study group, which examined the lessons of that campaign. See also McInnes, *Hot War,* 182.

91. Robert M. Cassidy, "The British Army and Counterinsurgency: The Salience of Military Culture," US Army Professional Writing Collection, available at http://usacac.leavenworth.army.mil/CAC/milreview/download/English/MayJun05/cassidy.pdf (accessed 10 July 2007). See discussion in Chapter 4.

92. John A. Nagl, *Learning to Eat Soup with a Knife: Counterinsurgency Lessons from Malaya and Vietnam* (Chicago: University of Chicago Press, 2002), 42–43.

93. Johnson, interview; Colonel (Ret.) Hanan (Schwartz) Shai, Founder and Director, Staff and Command College (1989–1994). Interview with author, 11 February 2005, Hertzelia, Israel; General (Ret.) Sir Rupert Smith, Commander of First British Armoured Division (First Gulf War), GOC Northern Ireland (1996–1999), Deputy Supreme NATO Allied Commander. Interview with author, 1 September 2006, Brussels.

94. A. S. Duncan, "Israel's Defence Forces: Some Lessons That We Might Teach Each Other," *British Army Review* 69 (December 1981), 14.

95. Storr, interview.

96. Chobham is the armor of the British Challenger tank, reputedly the best in the world.

97. Spartacus, "The British Army and the Failure of Mission Command," *British Army Review* 118 (April 1998), 87–88.

98. Ibid.

99. Lieutenant Colonel Avi Peled, Commander of the elite infantry Egoz unit. Interview with author, 23 June 2004, Shrivenham, UK.

100. Benest, interview.

101. Spartacus.

102. P. A. Sturtivant, "Escaping from the Prison of History: On the Eve of the Millennium Overcoming Obstacles to Implementing Mission Command in the British Army," *British Army Review* 122 (Autumn 1999), 26.

103. Colonel Richard M. Iron, Assistant Director, Land Warfare Doctrine. Interview with author, 8 June 2005, Upavon, UK. See also Duncan, 14.

104. Sturtivant, "Escaping," 32.

105. Storr, interview.

106. Spartacus, 87.

107. Dr. Aryeh Nusbacher, Senior Lecturer, Sandhurst Military Academy, Military Historian. E-mail communication to author, 7 July 2006.

108. Cape, 49.

109. P. J. Macy, "Mission Command—All Talk No Action," *British Army Review* 118 (April 1998), 88–90.

110. Sturtivant, "Escaping," 26.

111. Ibid.

112. Eccles.

113. Cape, 39–41.

114. Eccles.

115. Regarding the laissez-faire tradition, see Chapter 5.

116. Sturtivant, "Escaping," 27.

117. Ibid., 29.

118. Quoted by Nusbacher, e-mail communication.

119. Sturtivant, "Escaping," 30.

120. Ibid., 26.

121. Benest, interview.

122. Iron, interview. This view was also reflected in Benest, interview; Melvin, interview; Commander Dr. David Slavin, Commander in the Royal Navy, Veteran of the

Falklands War, 1981–2002. Interview with author, 16 January 2006, London; Smith, interview.

123. This may represent perception rather than reality, as both have adopted practices from one another. For example, see Paul Cornish, "Myth and Reality: US and UK Approaches to Casualty Aversion and Force Protection," *Defence Studies* 3:2 (Summer 2003), 121–128.

124. David Betz and Anthony Cormack, "Iraq Afghanistan and British Strategy," *Orbis* (Spring 2009), 321.

125. Thomas Donnelly, "The Cousins' Counter-Insurgency," *RUSI Journal* 154:3 (June 2009), 8.

126. Melvin, interview.

127. Theo Farrell, "The Dynamics of British Military Transformation," *International Affairs* 84:4 (2008), 777–778.

128. Ministry of Defence, *Delivering Security in a Changing World: Defence White Paper* (Norwich: Her Majesty's Stationary Office, 2003), 11.

129. Farrell, 788–789.

130. Gordon Adams et al., *European C4ISR Capabilities and Transatlantic Interoperability* (Washington, DC: George Washington University, 2004), 24.

131. David Potts and Jake Thackray, "No Revolutions Please, We're British," in *The Big Issue: Command and Combat in the Information Age,* ed. David Potts (Washington, DC: Command and Control Research Program, 2003), 29.

132. Bernard Jenkin, "Blair's Ambition for an Army on the Cheap," *Financial Times*, 29 April 2003.

133. Andy McNab, "USA Has the Gear but We've Had the Patience," *Mirror*, 26 March 2003. A former SAS trooper, McNab fought in 1991 and went on to become a renowned author.

134. Adams et al., 25.

135. Potts and Thackray, 37.

136. Jim Storr, "A Command Philosophy for the Information Age: The Continuing Relevance of Mission Command," in *The Big Issue: Command and Combat in the Information Age,* 92–93.

137. C. S. Grant, "The 2015 Battlefield," *British Army Review* 128 (Winter 2001–2002), 11.

138. R. A. M. S. Melvin, "Continuity and Change: How British Army Doctrine Is Evolving to Match the Balanced Force," *RUSI* 147:4 (August 2002), 41; Melvin, "Mission Command," 8.

139. Farrell, 788.

140. Major S. Cattermull, "Digitization: Its Effects on the British Way of Warfighting," *British Army Review* 127 (Summer 2002), 25.

141. Farrell, 790.

142. Ibid., 806.

143. Reuven Gal, *A Portrait of the Israeli Soldier* (Westport, CT: Greenwood, 1986), 58–76, 115–121.

144. Ahron Shenhar and Amos Yarkoni, "Summery of the Forum for Strategic Thinking in Economics: Culture and Israeli Management Style," in *Israeli Management Culture*, ed. Ahron Shenhar and Amos Yarkoni (Tel Aviv: Z'erkiover, 1993), 384 [Heb.].

145. Marlin Levin and David Halev, "Israel," in *Fighting Armies: Antagonists of the Middle East—A Combat Assessment*, ed. Richard A. Gabriel (Westport, CT: Greenwood, 1983), 7.

146. Gal, *Portrait*, 104.

147. Yagil Levy, *The Other Army of Israel: Materialist Militarism in Israel* (Tel Aviv: Yedioth Ahronoth, 2003), 236–243 [Heb.].

148. Ibid., 234–235.

149. Donna Rosenthal, *The Israelis: Ordinary People in an Extraordinary Land* (New York: Free Press 2003), 75–97.

150. Quoted in ibid., 77.

151. Nir Barkat, "Army and High-Tech," *Ma'ariv*, 18 September 2000 [Heb.].

152. Aryeh J. S. Nusbacher, *Sweet Irony: The German Origins of Israel Defence Forces' Maneuver Warfare Doctrine with Particular Reference to Israeli Land Operations on the Golan Heights 1973* (Master's thesis, Royal Military College of Canada, Ontario, 1996), 53–60.

153. Edward Luttwak, and Dan Horowitz, *The Israeli Army* (London: Allen Lane, 1975), 173.

154. Notes from a lecture delivered by Prof. Alon Kadish on special forces during a Ground Forces Psychology Conference, 15 February 2006.

155. Creveld, *Command*, 199.

156. Shenhar and Yarkoni, 384.

157. Peled, interview.

158. Demchak, 110.

159. Sergio Catignani, *Dilemmas of a Conventional Army: The Israel Defence Forces During the Two Intifadas* (PhD diss. King's College London, 2006), chap. 5.

160. Martin van Creveld, Professor of Military History, Hebrew University. Interview with author, 15 February 2005, Jerusalem.

161. Ibid.

162. Yossi Yehoshua, "November 04, Motivation Is Up," *Yedioth Ahronoth*, 25 November 2004 [Heb.]. According to this report, 91 percent of all recruits asked to be assigned to a combat unit. See also Levy, 418.

163. Lieutenant Colonel Shlomo Cohen, Deputy Commander of the Tactical Training Center. Interview with author, 9 February 2005, Ts'eelim Training Center, Israel; Lieutenant Colonel David Kanizo, Head of Doctrine Branch, Ground Forces Command (MAZI). Interview with author, 10 February 2005, Tel Aviv; Brigadier General (Ret.) Dr. Shimon Naveh, Head of the Operational Theory Research Institute. Interview with author, 14 February 2005, Hertzelia, Israel; Lieutenant Colonel Dori Pinkas, Head of High Headquarters department in the Doctrine Branch. Interview with author, 13 February 2005, Tel Aviv; Colonel (Ret.) Hanan (Schwartz) Shai, Founder and Director, Staff and Command College (1989–1994). Interview with author, 11 February 2005, Hertzelia, Israel.

164. Ofer Shelach and Yoav Limor, *Captives in Lebanon: The Truth About the Lebanon War* (Tel Aviv: Yedioth Ahronoth, 2007), 398–405 [Heb.].

165. Brigadier General Friedman, "Commander of NCO Course, an Interview," *BaMachane* 27 (August 2004), 11 [Heb.].

166. Giora Segal, "Mission Oriented Command in LIC," paper presented at MAZI 1st International Conference on LIC Warfare, 22 March 2004 [Heb.].

167. Moshe (Chicko) Tamir, *Undeclared War* (Tel Aviv: Ma'arachot, 2006), 275–276 [Heb.].

168. Pinkas, interview.

169. Kanizo, interview.

170. Stuart A. Cohen, "The Israel Defence Forces: Continuity and Change," in *Armed Forces in the Middle East Politics and Strategy*, ed. Barry Rubin and Thomas A. Keaney (London: Frank Cass, 2002), 164–179.

171. Oz Almog, *The Sabra: A Profile* (Tel Aviv: Am Oved, 1997) [Heb.]; Anita Shapira, *Land and Power* (Tel Aviv: Am Oved, 1992) [Heb.]; Yehuda Vagman, "Service in the IDF, National Service or a Profession?" *Ma'arachot* 362 (January 1999), 8–15 [Heb.].

172. Stuart A. Cohen, "Towards Too Much Subordination of the IDF: Changing Civil Military Relations in the IDF," *Ma'arachot* 403–404 (December 2005), 18 [Heb.].

173. Sergio Catignani and Eitan Shamir, "Mission Command and *Bitsuism* in the Israeli Defence Forces: Complementary or Contradictory in Today's Counter-Insurgency Campaign?" in *Dimensions of Military Leadership*, ed. Alistair MacIntyre and Karen Davis (Ontario: Canadian Defence Academy, 2007), 185–214.

174. Lieutenant Colonel Eado Keren, Head of Basic Doctrine Branch in the Doctrine Branch. Interview with author, 13 February 2005, Tel Aviv.

175. Kanizo, interview.

176. Cohen, interview.

177. Alex Fishman, "Reserve in Reserve," *Yedioth Ahronoth*, 10 March 2006; Kanizo, interview; Shai, interview.

178. Cohen, interview.

179. Kanizo, interview.

180. Yossi Yehoshua, "Colonel at 36: The End of the Era of Young IDF Commanders," *Yedioth Ahronoth*, 15 December 2005 [Heb.].

181. Ya'akov Amidror, "The Essence of the Profession of Military Command," *Ma'arachot* 369 (February 2000), 26–31 [Heb.]; Ya'akov Amidror, "What Is Professional Military Knowledge?" *Ma'arachot* 372 (August 2000), 26–31 [Heb.]; Ya'akov Amidror, "Why the Lack of Military Knowledge?" *Ma'arachot* 378–379 (September 2001), 20–24 [Heb.].

182. Amidror, "Why the Lack?"

183. Tamir, 275.

184. Amidror, "Why the Lack?"

185. Hanan (Schwartz) Shai, "PUM Barak, How the Program Was Conceived," in *50 Years Jubilee to the IDF Staff and Command College*, ed. Moshe Shamir and Hila Sagie (Tel Aviv: Ma'arachot, 2004), 24 [Heb.]. The program was named for the Barak armored brigade destroyed on the Golan Heights in the 1973 war.

186. Moshe Shamir and Hila Sagie, (eds.), *50 Years Jubilee to the IDF Staff and Command College* (Tel Aviv: Ma'arachot, 2004), 15–16 [Heb.].

187. Hours dedicated to the study of doctrine were increased from seven to seventy. Shai, interview.

188. Shai, "PUM," 25.

189. Shai, interview.

190. For a personal account of the program's impact on self-development, see the memoirs of Brigadier General Chicko Tamir: Tamir, 43. The program's impact was a recurring theme in many interviews: Brigadier General Zvika Gendelman, IDF Defence Attaché, London, Division Commander (1999–2001). Interview with author, 20 October 2004, London; Brigadier General Yitzhak Gershon, Commander of Thirty-fifth Paratroopers Brigade, Division Commander. Interview with author, 30 June 2006, London.

191. Shai, "PUM," 28.

192. Reuven Gal, "Examining the Current Model of the Israeli Officer," *Ma'arachot* 346 (February 1996), 25 [Heb.].

193. Colonel Dani Davidi, Commander of the Tactical Command College. Interview with author, 20 February 2005, Hertzelia, Israel; Lieutenant Colonel Gideon Sharav, Deputy Commander of the Tactical Command College. Interview with author, 20 February 2005, Hertzelia, Israel.

194. Itay Asher, "The Art of War and Couples Theory," *Ma'ariv*, 11 July 2003 [Heb.].

195. Gideon Sharav, "The Tactical Command Academy," in *50 Years Jubilee to the IDF Staff and Command College*, 54 [Heb.].

196. Colonel (Ret.) Moshe Shamir, Research Fellow at the IDF Tactical Environment Research Institute. Interview with author, 14 February 2005, Hertzelia, Israel.

197. Shamir and Sagie, 18.

198. Ya'akov Zigdon and Amira Raviv, "Military Academy: The Feature That Identifies Professional Militaries," *Ma'arachot* 390 (July 2003), 48–53 [Heb.]; Shamir, interview.

199. Shai, interview.

200. Sa'ar Raveh and Maya Peker-Rinat, "To Win and Remain Human: The Challenges of Leadership in LIC," *Ma'arachot* 385 (July 2002), 20–25 [Heb.]. These military psychologists proposed to educate officers to frame problems in terms of "systems" using system theory to deal with the complexities of strategic environment faced by the strategic corporal.

201. Cohen, interview.

202. Concerning the IDF operational concept, see Chapter 5.

203. Colonel Abraham Boaz, Commander of Brigade HQ Training Center (Ma'amat-Z'eelim). Interview with author, 14 February 2005, Ts'eelim Training Center, Israel.

204. Report of the Israeli Parliament Committee for Security and Foreign Affairs, Chaired by Brigadier (Ret.) Efi Eytam [Heb.].

205. However, the program was reinstituted in 2006 following the war, after the Dado Center was established in the OTRI's place. Named after the former October 1973 war chief of staff, the institute serves as both a school for advanced military learning and a research center.

206. This is in contrast to the existing situation wherein higher military education is conducted under the auspices of a civilian Israeli university.

207. Meir Pinkel, "Worshiping Technology in the IDF: Recovering the Balance for Ground Forces Development," *Ma'arachot* 407 (June 2006), 40–45 [Heb.].

208. "The Israeli High Tech Sector," *The Jewish Virtual Library*, available at http://www.jewishvirtuallibrary.org/jsource/Economy/eco4.html (accessed 17 March 2006).

209. "High-Tech Miracle in the Desert," *Forbes*, available at http://www.forbes.com/2000/08/07/feat2_print.html (accessed 17 March 2006).

210. "The Israeli High Tech Sector."

211. Demchak, 101–102.

212. Sharon Sadeh, "Israel's Defence Industry in the 21st Century: Challenges and Opportunities," *Strategic Assessment* 7:3 (December 2004), available at http://www.tau.ac.il/jcss/sa/v7n3p5Sad.html (accessed 21 March 2006).

213. Eliot A. Cohen, Michael J. Eisenstadt, and Andrew J. Bacevich, *Knives, Tanks, and Missiles: Israel's Security Revolution* (Washington, DC: Washington Institute for Near East Policy, 1998), 118–119.

214. Shabtai Shai, "Towards a Fourth Revolution in IDF Military Thinking," *Ma'arachot* 392 (January 2002), 9–12 [Heb.].

215. Alex Fishman, "Reserves in Reserve," *Yedioth Ahronoth*, 10 March 2006 [Heb.].

216. Amonon Barzilai, "IDF Digitization," *Ha'aretz*, 15 December 2004 [Heb.].

217. Lieutenant Colonel Rami Malchi, Head of Army Digitization Project. Interview with author, 9 February 2005, Tel Aviv.

218. Brigadier General (Ret.) Moni Horev, Senior Advisor for Land Forces Digitization. Interview with author, 15 February 2005, Hertzelia, Israel.

219. Aric Bendar, "We Have No Solution to the *Kasam* Rockets on Sderot," *Yedioth Ahronoth*, 3 January 2006 [Heb.].

220. Damchek, 110.

221. Davidi, interview.

222. Shelach and Limor, 320–322.

223. Davidi, interview.

224. Pinkel, 43.

225. James N. Mattis, *Memorandum for U.S. Joint Forces Command* (Norfolk, VA: Department of Defense, U.S. Joint Forces Command, 2008). There is a debate whether this was a concise application of EBO; regardless, the obvious preference of Halutz and his general staff was to rely on stand-off fire and the air force alone.

11. Summary Remarks and Wider Implications

1. For a discussion of the American culture of war, see Chapter 4. See also Colin Gray, "The American Way of War," in *Rethinking the Principles of War,* ed. Antony D. McIvor (Annapolis, MD: Naval Institute Press, 2005), 13–40.

2. Martin Samuels, *Command or Control: Command, Training and Tactics in the British and German Armies, 1988–1918* (London: Frank Cass, 1995), 49–60.

3. Spencer Fitz-Gibbon, *Not Mentioned in Despatches: The History and Mythology of the Battle of Goose Green* (Cambridge: Lutterworth, 1995), 182–184.

4. General (Ret.) Sir Rupert Smith, Commander of First British Armoured Division (First Gulf War), GOC Northern Ireland (1996–1999), Deputy Supreme NATO Allied Commander. Interview with author, 1 September 2006, Brussels.

5. Interestingly, during its "mobile" phase (1948–1973), the IDF relied little on U.S. hardware or doctrine.

6. Richard Simpkin, *Race to the Swift: Thoughts on Twenty-First Century Warfare* (London: Brassey's, 1985), chap. 14.

7. Lieutenant Colonel Dr. Jim Storr, General Staff, Northern Ireland Study Team, Principal Author of Land Operations Doctrine. Interview with author, 31 March 2006, London.

8. Regarding the British approach, see Robert Egnell, "Explaining U.S. and British Performance in Complex Expeditionary Operations: The Civil Military Dimension," *Journal of Strategic Studies* 29:6 (December 2006), 1041–1075.

9. Army Doctrine Publication, *Land Operations,* Army Code 71819 (2005), 115.

10. Giora Eiland, "The IDF: Addressing the Failures of the Second Lebanon War," in *The Middle East Strategic Balance, 2007–2008,* ed. Mark A. Heller (Tel Aviv: Institute for National Strategic Studies, 2008), 34.

11. Ibid., 37.

12. Ibid., 36. Concerning this culture of open debate, see Chapter 4.

13. For a comprehensive review of the literature concerning military change and innovation, see Adam Grissom, "The Future of Military Innovation Studies," *Journal of Strategic Studies* 29:5 (October 2006), 905–934.

14. One exception is Emily Goldman and Leslie Eliason, ed., *The Diffusion of Military Technology and Ideas* (Palo Alto, CA: Stanford University Press, 2003).

15. Robert C. Camp, *Benchmarking: The Search for Industry Best Practices That Lead to Superior Performance* (Portland: Productivity, 2006).

16. Alan L. Wilkins, *Developing Corporate Character: How to Successfully Change an Organization Without Destroying It* (San Francisco: Jossey-Bass, 1989), 7–19.

17. Ibid., 17.

18. Ibid., 52.

12. Final Verdict

1. For a discussion of the British experience with LIC, see pp. 170–171. Regarding the new US doctrine for counterinsurgency see Field Manual 3-24/ MCWP 3-33.5 *Counterinsurgency* (Washington, DC: Department of the Army, 2006).

2. Robert M. Citino, *The German Way of War: From the Thirty Years' War to the Third Reich* (Lawrence: University Press of Kansas, 2005), 310.

3. For a discussion of RMA- and military transformation-related doctrines, see Chapter 5. James N. Mattis, "Memorandum for U.S. Joint Forces Command" (Norfolk, VA: Department of Defense, U.S. Joint Forces Command, 14 August 2008), 3, 6.

4. Ibid., 5.

5. *The Army Capstone Concept: Operational Adaptability,* 21 December 2009, available at: http://www.tradoc.army.mil/pao/2009armycapstoneconcept.pdf.

INDEX